POPE PIUS XII LIBRARY, ST. JOSEPH COL.
3 2528 11057 4870

D1447134

ANGOLA

This book is dedicated to the memory of Christine Messiant

Patrick Chabal & Nuno Vidal
editors

Angola

The Weight of History

Columbia University Press
New York

Columbia University Press
Publishers Since 1893
New York, Chichester, West Sussex

Library of Congress Cataloging-in-Publication Data

Angola : the weight of history / Patrick Chabal & Nuno Vidal, editors.
p. cm.
Includes bibliographical references and index.
ISBN 978-0-231-70015-3 (cloth : alk. paper)
1. Angola—Politics and government. 2. Angola—History. 3. Angola—Economic conditions. I. Chabal, Patrick, 1951– II. Vidal, Nuno. III. Title.

DT1348.A54 2007
967.3—dc22

2007018737

♾
Columbia University Press books are printed on permanent and durable acid-free paper.
This book is printed on paper with recycled content.
Printed in India

c 10 9 8 7 6 5 4 3 2 1

CONTENTS

Preface *page* vii
The Contributors ix

1. *E Pluribus Unum:* Transitions in Angola 1
Patrick Chabal

2. Angola in Historical Context 19
Malyn Newitt

3. The Mutation of Hegemonic Domination 93
Christine Messiant

4. The Angolan Regime and the Move to Multiparty Politics 124
Nuno Vidal

5. The Economic Foundations of the Patrimonial State 175
Tony Hodges

6. Social Neglect and the Emergence of Civil Society 200
Nuno Vidal

Index 237

PREFACE

This volume stems from the conviction that an analysis of contemporary Angola is best achieved by a multi-authored and multidisciplinary enterprise. Indeed, so intricate is the trajectory of that former Portuguese colony that there is yet to appear a comprehensive account of its history. Nor is there today a wholly convincing study of its post-colonial evolution. Competing explanations offer diverging views about the nature of the regime and the consequences of the civil war. Of course, there is no denying that Angola's case is complex, touching as it does on an unusually wide range of issues—from its ethnic and racial complexion to its oil-based economy. Nevertheless, it is now time to attempt a more systematic examination of this important country—if only because it is likely to become an increasingly dominant player in the region.

The study of Angola has often been constrained by an approach that stresses its uniqueness: *inter alia*, the alleged importance of its 'organic' link with Portugal, the long history of armed hostility between the MPLA government and its UNITA challenger, or the country's immense mineral wealth. Although there is no denying that these factors have been critical, their significance has often been overplayed. Furthermore, surveys of Angola have tended to fall into two very different camps: either Lusophone specialists of Angola's history, society, culture and economy or experts from international institutions with special interest in the country's current development. There has been very little dialogue between the two. It is time to look at Angola from a different analytical angle.

The editors have brought together scholars with special knowledge of Angola and Africa generally, who were all convinced of the need to study the country from a comparative and multi-strand perspective. The contributors to this volume are all Lusophone specialists but they work within different disciplines and approach the study of Angola from varied standpoints. Our colleague Christine Messiant, who died before she could make final revisions to her chapter, is recognised as the foremost expert on the history of the anti-colonial movement and of postcolonial Angola. Malyn Newitt is one of a handful of scholars with a comprehensive knowledge of the history of Portugal in Africa. Tony Hodges is an economist, whose knowledge of Angola's post-independence political economy is probably unrivalled. Finally, Nuno Vidal's special expertise in the social complexion of Angola provides the basis for a convincing account of the nature of the country's political regime to date.

The aim of this book is not to seek to provide a 'definitive' interpretation of present day Angola, even less to forecast its future evolution. Rather, it is to provide a multi-faceted examination of its political, economic and social realities in their appropriate historical and cultural context. The hope is that a cumulative and multi-layered analysis will contribute to a more subtle and enlightening explanation of Angola's contemporary condition. Although the contributors approached their task from their individual perspectives, they have also made every effort to weave together the many diverse strands of the country's history. Indeed, it is the very recognition of the weight of that history which links the readings offered by the various contributors.

London, July 2006 P.C.

THE CONTRIBUTORS

Patrick Chabal is professor of Lusophone African Studies at King's College London. He is the author of a large number of articles on the history, politics and cultures of African countries. His book publications include: *Culture Troubles: Politics and the Interpretation of Meaning* [with J. P. Daloz] (2006); *A History of Postcolonial Lusophone Africa* [with others] (2002); *The Postcolonial Literature of Lusophone Africa* [with others] (1996); *Amilcar Cabral: Revolutionary Leadership and People's War* (1983 reissued 2002).

Tony Hodges has been studying and writing on Angola since he first visited the country as a journalist during the transition to independence in 1975. For 16 years (1978-94) he wrote the quarterly country reports on Angola published by the Economist Intelligence Unit (EIU), where he was also Africa Editor in 1983-87. He subsequently worked in Angola for United Nations agencies for much of the period between 1994 and 2002. His major study of Angola's political economy is *Angola: Anatomy of an Oil State* (2004). He is currently in China as head of the Social Policy Section of the United Nations Children's Fund (UNICEF).

Christine Messiant, who died while this book was being completed, was by all accounts the foremost analyst of contemporary Angola. A sociologist by training, she worked at the Ecole des Hautes Etudes en Sciences Sociales (Paris). She was the author of a vast number of publications on Angola (listed after her chapter). Her main books include *Les chemins de la guerre et de la paix, Fins de conflicts en Afrique orientale et australe* [with Roland Marchal] (1997); *Angola 1961. Histoire et société, les prémisses du mouvement nationaliste* (2006);

L'Angola post-colonial. Sociologie politique d'une oléocratie (2006) and *Angola. Sociedade e economia politica do poder* (forthcoming).

Malyn Newitt has devoted his entire career to the study of the Portuguese overseas expansion in Africa. He was Deputy Vice Chancellor of Exeter University and held the Charles Boxer Chair of History at King's College London until his retirement in 2005. His books include *Portuguese Settlement in the Zambesi* (1973), *Portugal in Africa* (1981), *São Tomé and Príncipe* [with Tony Hodges] (1988), *A History of Mozambique* (1995) and *A History of Portuguese Overseas Expansion* (2005).

Nuno Vidal is an Angolan researcher with over a dozen years of experience conducting research projects on Angola, often involving long and intensive field research periods throughout the country and in regular collaboration with international research teams. He lectures in the Faculty of Economics at the University of Coimbra in Portugal. His main publications are, as editor, a volume on Angola's transition to a multiparty system and, as author, *Angola: Preconditions for Elections* (2005).

1

INTRODUCTION

E Pluribus Unum: Transitions in Angola

Patrick Chabal

Since the end of the war against UNITA in 2002 there has been renewed hope that a nation so rich in natural resources would finally evolve a more democratic political system, ensuring sustained development and greater well being for all its people. Angola, it is argued, could be on the cusp of a giant leap forward, laying down the basis for the economic prosperity of the country and making possible a form of development that would benefit all its citizens. But is this a realistic scenario?

The question that concerns us most here is that of the nature and impact of Angola's transition to multiparty politics. Some chapters in this volume discuss the details of the current political situation within the dynamics of a troubled historical trajectory. They touch on the consequences of the civil war and the importance of the 1992 electoral experience. Other contributors discuss the potential for political change in a country that has suffered authoritarian single party rule since independence and where civil society is both shallow and weak. Here, I want to focus attention on the more general significance of such transitions as have occurred since 2002 for future political, economic and social change.

My aim is to consider current trends in Angolan politics within the broader framework of the socio-economic and political evolution of postcolonial African countries, with special emphasis on those that are oil rich. One of my arguments is that the analysis of Angola has been marred by an excessive Lusophone perspective—that is, the view that the understanding of that country is best advanced by a study of the specificities of what appears on the surface to be a very singular case in Africa. I try to show instead that it is more fruitful to consider the fate of Angola within the overall African context, even if we must pay proper attention to those aspects of its history that differ markedly from other countries on the continent. Indeed, I would maintain that this is the only approach that makes possible an assessment of the likely effects of the present transition in Angola.

This chapter is in two parts. The first re-examines the historical circumstances that have conditioned the genesis of present Angola. The second discusses the relevance of a comparative African analysis to the assessment of the likely impact of the current transitions.

I

Those who seek to explain Angola's contemporary predicament stress three sets of factors. One has to do with the pre-colonial and colonial configuration of power that derived from the special status of what has come to be known as the Luanda Creole community *and* the impact of Portuguese rule on the relationships between the principal ethnic and regional social groupings. The other concerns the consequences for the country's evolution of the particular dynamics of anti-colonial and nationalist competition before and after independence, which resulted in a civil war lasting 27 years. The last touches on the effects of oil wealth upon the socio-economic, but particularly political, development of the country since 1975.

All three are critical but the key question is how they have interacted over time and what degree of causal significance might be ascribed to any one of them. I do not intend here to summarise the extensive scholarship devoted to these various issues, or to enter the debate about the relative relevance of external and domestic factors for the current state of affairs in the country. Rather, I should like to revisit some of the key arguments within an African, rather than strictly Lusophone, perspective. Before I do this, however, I reflect briefly on the dominant themes of Angolan historiography as presented by scholars of Portuguese-speaking Africa.

The most salient pre-colonial historical consideration has rightly been the very special place occupied by the Luanda Creole community. There has been much debate about the changes that took place from the mid-nineteenth century onwards, and especially during the colonial period. Clearly, one cannot simply speak of a 'single' community. Yet, there is little doubt that, whatever the complexion of this grouping, it has presided over the destiny of Luanda, its hinterland, and large swathes of what eventually became Angola from the pre-colonial period to the present. Such socio-economic and political supremacy, though not entirely unique in Africa, is certainly a significant aspect of the colony's history. It remains a central feature of the country's make up and it forms a historical legacy that will continue to impinge on Angola's future whatever the modalities of present transitions.

Another important feature is the impact of colonial rule on Portuguese Angola. Here, emphasis is placed on three attributes commonly perceived to be singularly Lusophone. The first is that Angola became a colony of settlement but that, unlike its British Eastern African counterparts, it introduced into the territory poor and poorly qualified Portuguese, many of peasant origin. This skewed the economic development of the country and resulted in certain forms of racial discrimination, which added further complexity to the ethnic and regional rivalries that had already been exacerbated by the nature of the colonial economy. The second is that colonial rule brought Angola a backward and singularly rigid form of bureaucracy that cast a large shadow over the postcolonial administration, since it rapidly dovetailed with the 'socialist' (and some would say 'Stalinist') party-state being put in place by the MPLA. The last is that the authoritarian and unrepresentative nature of the Portuguese regime required excessive repression and ultimately led to a colonial war that entrenched violent forms of political expression.

Yet another consideration that has surfaced regularly is that Angola was in some sense a special colony—as it were, the 'jewel in the crown' of the Portuguese African Empire, on which the mother country lavished exceptional attention. Although this may appear a secondary issue, it has in fact coloured perceptions in many different ways. Angola has often been seen to be more 'Portuguese' than, say Guinea Bissau or Mozambique—whatever that may mean, it has conveyed the idea of a different form of politics, not least because the Luanda Creole community (or some parts of it) have historic ties with Portugal and Portuguese is their mother tongue. Many in Portugal have thus been loath to accept that the country's postcolonial trajectory may well be similar to that of the rest of Africa: however culturally 'Portuguese' many of the Angolan elite appear to be, their politics is primarily conditioned by local factors.

One final issue has come to assume great importance in the standard explanation of the contemporary situation in Angola: foreign actor involvement, particularly during the period of the Cold War. There is of course no denying the impact of outside interference in the country since 1975 but, as much scholarship has shown, such intrusion fuelled rather than caused internal divisions, violence and civil war. Furthermore, it is equally significant that the internal actors themselves sought to maintain an international dimension to domestic politics so as better to serve their own purpose. The foreign aspect is important but it is by no means unique to Angola.

I now resume discussion of the three sets of factors mentioned above. Of those, the first (the role of the Luanda Creole community) is undoubtedly both singular to Angola and of protracted significance. Yet, the manner in which it continues (and will continue) to condition Angolan politics is not straightforward. As is mentioned in some of the chapters that follow, since the colonial period this community has grown and diversified. It now includes a large number of different groupings, distinguished by socio-economic, class, racial, political and other attributes, and many individuals have mingled with those coming from different horizons. As a result of the civil war, Luanda and its environs have become multi-ethnic and multi-regional settings. This is important and will likely weigh heavily on the future of the capital and the country as a whole.

Of course, there is a political elite, centred on the President, which has deep roots in the historic Luanda Creole community. However, ascriptive attributes are no longer as determinant as they are sometimes assumed to be. The present configuration of power turns around a form of neo-patrimonialism that relies on shrewd cooptation and modulated authoritarianism in ways that transcend what is often perceived as Creole domination. The changes that have taken place under dos Santos' stewardship are better explained by the nature of the regime over which he presides than by the fact that he continues to favour Creoles. The MPLA has always been construed, and used, as the crucible for a national, supra-ethnic, political 'machine'. Multiparty political competition requires that this pan-Angolan claim be kept firmly in the foreground.

Undoubtedly, there is in Luanda a significant grouping, closely tied to the centre of power, which harks back to specific Creole roots and considers itself primarily a Portuguese-speaking community. At the same time, the dynamics of postcolonial politics, which the present transition is bound to reinforce, have brought about a system in which the President has had to extend the concentric circles of his clientelistic power well beyond this historical Creole group. Furthermore, the criteria that guide his hands are primarily of an instrumental nature, rather than being based on identity. He shuffles the political cards so as to assert and maintain the dominance of the President's 'party', the tentacles of which reach to all corners of society. For this reason, we must beware of simplistic interpretations of the current configuration of power.

Paradoxically, therefore, it may well be that the significance of Creole political domination lies less in the reality of the accusation than in the widespread perception outside the Luanda region that this charge is indeed accurate. Whatever the present complexion of the party, it is to be expected that UNITA and other political competitors will seek to portray the MPLA regime as the instrument of Creole (that is, in their eyes, 'non-African') supremacy. In many ways, then, the issue has become a myth—like all myths at once real and imaginary, at once significant and irrelevant. It colours the perceptions of the country's history and has yet to be played out in full.

The second set of factors turns around the consequences of nationalist competition for today's Angola. Here also we need to be analytically cautious. Although it may appear that there was continuity between the anti-colonial groups' rivalry and the civil war that lasted until 2002, there were in fact quite clear and dramatic changes in the nature of the conflict. Competition for the control of an independent Angola was over by 1976—even if it took massive foreign (Soviet and Cuban) involvement for the MPLA to defeat its rivals. Thereafter, there was a straightforward struggle for power that had less to do than is commonly assumed with the vagaries of nationalist antagonism as they had emerged before independence. Neither party could claim uncontested legitimacy. Neither could assert military dominance. Moreover, that struggle went through distinct phases, which changed the nature of political competition over time.

The first was the period of the Cold War, which was marked by two distinct phases: until the mid-eighties it had a strong international dimension; after the Namibian settlement and the departure of the Cubans from Angola, it became much more focused on a search for territorial and resource advantage. Following the end of the Cold War, there was clearly an attempt by the international community to engineer peace. Here, the turning point was the decision by the United States to recognise the MPLA regime in 1993 and to distance itself from UNITA. From then until 1998, the two parties fought a war of attrition, made possible by the use of vast mineral resources on both sides. After 1998, however, the MPLA regime was in a position to seek military victory, a policy the West now unofficially condoned.

The point here is that the political implications of the civil war differed during those distinct periods, with domestic and international advantage accruing to either side on the basis of a number of factors, most of which had little to do with the two parties' 'nationalist' heritage. Although the MPLA clearly benefited from its association with the victorious Lusophone anti-colonial movements that had formed the CONCP, its nationalist credentials quickly dissipated after 1977, when the attempted Nito Alves coup gave rise to massive repression and acute authoritarianism. UNITA, for its part, evolved from a political organisation with a legitimate claim to speak for those who did not feel represented by the MPLA into a war machine serving Jonas Savimbi's insatiable ambitions. Whilst UNITA managed eventually to gain control of a majority of Angola's provinces, the megalomaniac behaviour of its leader conspired to alienate those who might have voted him and his party into power in 1992.

The MPLA benefits today from the considerable advantages of having held power continuously since independence, rather than from any legitimacy attached to its success in having defeated its anti-colonial rivals. The legacy of nationalism no longer means much—even less than in Mozambique, where FRELIMO enjoyed uncontested nationalist credentials at independence—and in this way the situation in Angola is much as it is in most other African countries. The political contest today is not about 'historical legitimacy' but about who is in power. Despite the important differences between the colonial and postcolonial histories of the two southern African Lusophone countries, Angola is politically in a situation similar to that of Mozambique in 1994: the party in power since 1975 is facing the challenge of its erstwhile military foe. The difference, and we have yet to assess how crucial it is, is that the MPLA defeated its enemy by military means.

The third set of factors relates to the impact of the mineral resource (particularly oil) dividend on the country. This is of course decisive, but the question is whether its effects are unique or whether what has happened in Angola bears resemblance with other similar cases. There is no space here to discuss the extensive literature on the so-called 'oil curse' or the effects of what is often dubbed 'the Dutch disease'—much of which is entirely relevant to Angola. What I want to stress is that Angola's political future is likely to be conditioned by the fact that the country is mineral rich in ways that are both distinct from and similar to other African nations. The difficulty for analysis is to understand how. Here I focus on Angola's specificities; in the second section I shall discuss more general processes.

The important aspects of the Angolan case are three. The first is that the oil is offshore and is thus confined to a safe enclave that can easily be protected—as was evident during the war. The second is that the oil revenues are entirely in the hands of Sonangol, which is controlled by the President and thus very largely outside the purview of government and administrative supervision. Finally, the government has authorised oil-collateralised loans that are not properly accounted for in the state budget, and clearly mortgage the future of the country in financial deals that are linked to the regime rather than the state. In short, despite all manner of outside pressure, the oil revenues are very largely at the disposal of the president.

Of course, such a situation is not dissimilar to that which prevails in other African oil producing countries, but the combination of these three factors has provided the Angolan regime with a mightily powerful economic instrument. It has bestowed upon it an extraordinary degree of power, which has been further boosted by the fact that the Western countries whose companies are extracting Angolan oil have been exceedingly accommodating of such practices. Given the United States' wish to increase imports of oil from Africa (so as to lessen dependence on the Middle East) and an aggressive Chinese (and soon Indian) quest for more oil, it is not unreasonable to expect that the Angolan regime will continue to hold a decisive trump card in its dealings with the international community.

This means, clearly, that the matter of who holds power in Angola is critical. With tenure of office comes control of the oil revenue, the amount and destination of which remain opaque. Again, such a situation is not uncommon in Africa, but both the size of the dividend and the degree of patrimonial command are greater than in most other cases. The stakes are accordingly higher, which means that the competition for power is likely to be all the more intense. Since the President has now been in office for over twenty-five years, his grip on Angola's major resource is very firm indeed. It would take a political earthquake to force him (or his designated successors) to relinquish it. This hard fact will colour all aspects of present and future political transitions.

II

I now return to a comparative analysis of present political transitions within the African context. On the face of it, the situation in Angola is clear enough. The war is over, UNITA has completed its transition into a consolidated political party and all sides agree that the future lies in multiparty electoral politics. Equally, the international community is strongly supportive of the transition towards democracy, which it has long advocated. Outside business interests are keen to invest in a country with promising economic potential. Furthermore, given the importance of Angola, there is little doubt that the UN and other international organisations will be able to assist the preparation for, and the organisation of, present and even future elections.

Before I discuss the prospect that multiparty elections may usher in 'democracy' in Angola, I would like to touch briefly on some of the most common assumptions about political transitions in Africa—assumptions that specialists on Angola, or Lusophone Africa, seldom discuss. Ever since the early nineties, when the end of the Cold War and the instigation of political conditionalities for aid conjoined, African countries have been compelled to move away from one-party state systems. This has been justified on two grounds: first, single party governance failed to bring about development; second, development is more likely to derive from the political, but mostly economic, potential of (civil) society—unleashing the potential of the market that had been shackled by authoritarianism. It is also part of a belief that there is a worldwide wave of democratisation, which signals the long overdue recognition of the ultimate superiority of liberal democracy and capitalism.

These assumptions led to relentless outside pressure on African governments to open up their political systems and allow multiparty competition. Both multilateral and bilateral aid became conditional on such 'democratisation'. For reasons that have to do with the precarious economic situation of the continent and its acute need for foreign transfers, African governments had no choice but to acquiesce to these demands. Angola, however, belongs to a very select group of countries with sufficient internal resources and export revenues to hold out against the conditions imposed on Africa by the IMF and the World Bank. Even when the financial situation of the country has deteriorated markedly over the recent past, Angola's 'oil clout' and trade income have allowed the regime to implement economic and political reform at its own leisurely pace—and frequently to renege on previously agreed policies such as greater disclosure of oil revenues or serious liberalisation of the political system.

Since international constraints have made it impossible for the President to refuse political reform, it is useful to view the scope and pace of the present transition as those which are most congenial to the regime under existing circumstances. The fact that elections were delayed so long after the end of the war is a clear indication that the regime sought to position itself favourably before the beginning of the move to multiparty politics. Since UNITA did relatively well in the 1992 polls and many in the opposition today are convinced that the MPLA will eventually lose—if not now then later—why should the regime have agreed to hold the elections at all? The common answer is that they could postpone them no longer. True as this may be, it is not a sufficiently convincing argument. We need to look more carefully into the assumptions presently made by those who believe the opposition will ultimately prevail. We must also seek to understand what the regime's strategy is.

The supposition that the MPLA will eventually lose its electoral majority is derived from two strands of thinking, which are not necessarily compatible. The first is that with the end of the war and greater political freedom, Angolans will in due course muster the courage to punish a party that has done little for the immense majority of the population. In other words, it is believed that most people want regime change. The second is that there is now a credible opposition able to take over the government. But both of these assumptions are debatable. Although it is true that it is always difficult to predict the outcome of multiparty elections, especially where public opinion is so hard to gauge, there are grounds for thinking that the present regime is confident of winning competitive polls, and this for reasons that are only partly connected to the specificities of the Angolan case.

This is why I now offer a comparative interpretation of the present political transition. My argument is in three parts. One has to do with the nature of the Angolan regime. The other turns on an analysis of the political implications of the Angolan oil economy. The last is linked with an assessment of the complexion of political transitions in Africa since the early nineties.

(i) The Angolan regime is both similar to and distinct from other comparable ones in Africa. It is distinct in that it combines a number of historical, social and economic attributes that are not often found on the continent. It is in the hands of an all-powerful President who gathers support from a coalition of (political and military) supporters drawn largely from a relatively homogeneous social and cultural elite. That elite—broadly the Luanda Creole community, its allies and clients—has a long history of social, economic and political domination. It also has an experience of political mobilisation and domination associated with the nationalist campaign and the tightening of political control that followed the attempted Nito Alves coup in 1977. Finally, it has now been in power for over 30 years and has ensured thereby almost total political and economic hegemony. Generation after generation of politicians has risen to the top at the behest of the President, who is still relatively young.

It is similar, however, in that the current political dispensation is far from uncommon in Africa. The present system is essentially a variant of presidential neo-patrimonialism, the details of which are discussed at length in the present volume. This means that the President conspires to stay in power by means of a careful balance of cooptation and repression. Since he has absolute control of the country's exchequer, he can use patrimonial largesse to command support. Equally, he is in charge of the armed forces and police, so that he can demand compliance and avert the dangers of any significant challenge to his rule. I will discuss the political significance of the country's wealth below. Let me here explain why the history of Angola since independence provides the President with a degree of power that equals, or surpasses, that of the most 'successful' authoritarian leaders in Africa.

The strength of the regime derives from two main sources. There is first the party, the MPLA, which has benefited from a long experience of tough political battles both internally and externally going back to its origins in the late fifties and early sixties. It has become over time a formidable political instrument. It is true that the presidential system as it was consolidated by dos Santos after Neto's death does not depend on the party since it is in the hands of a single man. All the same, the party is organised and disciplined enough to be used as an effective tool when called upon to do so. Since there is no meaningful distinction between party and state, the MPLA can never be short of resources to mount whatever campaign (electoral or otherwise) is required by the leader.

The second, and by no means negligible, pillar of the regime is the army. Here also, the long experience of real battle has fashioned an organisation that is both militarily effective and politically compliant. Since the army too is integrated into the neo-patrimonial system in place, it fits in well within the political edifice over which dos Santos presides. In the long run, the absence of an internal armed enemy, the politicisation of the armed forces and the circulation of its commanders for political reasons may undermine the effectiveness of the Angolan army. As of now, however, it remains the dominant military machine in the region—as it has demonstrated time and again in its foreign forays. Now that the threat of internal war has dissipated, the army will no doubt become increasingly politicised and fractured. But this is in the future. For now it is indeed a powerful actor in any political transition.

(ii) The political implications of the oil economy are many and, again, there are similarities here with other countries, such as Nigeria or Gabon. The main feature shared by all these regimes is their ability to dispose of the export rent virtually at will. This gives them an extraordinary degree of power since they can exercise unparalleled, almost unlimited, domestic patronage. At the same time, because oil is such an essential commodity, the supply of which is diminishing worldwide, such regimes are able to extract concessions from the outside world, one of which is to ignore political abuses. Despite current pressures on all these governments to democratise and promote development, it is simply fanciful to suppose that there is any will within the international community as a whole to boycott their precious export. Oil is king and those rulers who control it are mighty.

The consequences for governance of the petroleum bonanza are complex but some key lessons can be learnt from the experience of African oil producing countries since independence. The oil industry does not benefit the local population since there is little employment of local labour and all income accrues to the government. Oil revenues are notoriously opaque and thus easy to conceal from domestic and international scrutiny; they are ideally 'liquid', to be hoarded or transferred inconspicuously. The oil dividend is rarely invested in productive activities but is used primarily for unproductive patrimonial purposes and personal enrichment. The size of export revenues is such as to enable governments to buy in political support or buy their way out of most political problems. Finally, the control of these resources is so vital that it pushes very high the stakes of political competition: the winner does take all. And the winner does not relinquish power easily.

For this reason, the recent attempts by the international community to force the Angolan regime to agree to a greater degree of transparency and financial accountability with respect to oil revenues have largely failed. Nor is it clear that Western governments will manage to compel their own oil companies into the disclosures that would make it possible to account for their dealings with the Angolan oil company, Sonangol. Consequently, the political cost for the Angolan regime of failing to comply with these outside *desiderata* is low, if not negligible. At the same time, the political cost of losing control of the oil rent is extraordinarily high, as it would strike at the heart of patrimonial power. Whatever happens in the near future, the process of political transition is unlikely to change the nature of the country's political economy. Dos Santos's challengers may bemoan the secrecy that surrounds the oil rent but they would no doubt prize it if they came to power.

But perhaps the most significant political attribute of an oil economy in Africa is the degree to which it is suited to the continent's type of power relation: that is, neo-patrimonialism. Whereas other forms of economic activity, such as the export of agricultural or manufactured products, involve a significant number of actors, the oil industry operates away from prying eyes and requires few, if any, domestic intermediaries between foreign businesses and local rulers. Additionally, there are limited financial steps involved between granting a license for exploration and collecting revenue from the company extracting the oil. This facilitates smooth income flows that can easily be controlled by a handful of politically secure 'accountants'. The net result is that rulers are in the ideal position of being able to dispense patronage from a revenue fund about which the population at large knows practically nothing.

(iii) The last part of the discussion has to do with an assessment of the nature of political transitions in Africa since the early nineties. To date most African countries have instituted multiparty regimes and most have held several successive multiparty polls. We are therefore in a position to assess how these elections took place, whether they were 'free and fair' and what political change they have brought about. Admittedly, Angola's postcolonial trajectory has been different from that of most other African countries and it is important to take these factors into consideration. Nevertheless, as the recent history of Mozambique has shown, a post-conflict transition to multiparty politics ultimately favours a return to the type of politics that is common elsewhere on the continent. Indeed, comparing the two countries suggests that neither the specificities of the Lusophone experience nor the effects of protracted civil war result in a 'model' of political transition that is significantly at variance from the rest of Africa. However, what happened in Mozambique is relevant to an appreciation of what is likely to take place in Angola.

The lessons of the Mozambican transition are relatively clear. There was in the first instance great support, both inside and outside the country, for a move towards multiparty politics, which was seen by all as a means of instituting a peaceful form of political competition. However, despite surprisingly strong support for Renamo, the ruling party was able to exploit the advantages of office to ensure electoral victory. The holding of elections revived the legitimacy of the regime, gave a new lease of life to the government and made it possible for it to reject calls for a coalition government of reconciliation. The party in power conceded to the opposition as little as it had to and worked steadily to erode the opponent's political support both at the national and local level. Decentralisation reforms were postponed or neutralised. Over time, single party dominance was further consolidated. Once the electorate came to realise that the opposition had little chance of taking office, participation decreased drastically (as was obvious in the last elections). Therefore, Mozambique is today politically similar to most other African countries—that is, effectively, a single party government sanctioned by multiparty elections. The factors that will determine whether Frelimo remains in power are those that impinge on all other African regimes.

The situation in Angola is not entirely similar to that in Mozambique and the differences are not likely to be conducive to greater political liberalisation. In Angola, the regime won the civil war; it did not have to compromise politically in order to achieve peace. Nor did it have to accept outside modalities and a timetable for the transition to multiparty politics. It is able to organise, prepare and carry out elections largely on its own terms—which means that it can control the degree of political openness, the ease with which the opposition is able to express itself politically, the complexion of the Electoral Commission, the process of voter registration and the organisation of the elections—all with only minimal interference from the international community. Finally, it has access to virtually unlimited financial means with which to campaign and 'convince' voters that they are better off sticking with the incumbent. Of course, there is no absolute guarantee that such factors will always ensure electoral victory, but they represent huge and likely decisive advantages for the MPLA—advantages that Frelimo did not have.

In this respect, the situation in Angola is more similar to that of countries where the single party was long entrenched and the regime commanded huge resources, which it was able to deploy to secure its dominance. The experience of such cases makes it possible to draw a number of inferences about the impact of multiparty elections on political change. On the positive side, international pressure and monitoring undoubtedly made possible greater freedom of expression and the flowering of much freer means of communication (press, radio, public meetings, etc.). It also enabled the opposition to engage in a systematic critique of incumbent regimes and force governments to debate important policy issues. Finally, it exposed the mechanisms of nepotism, clientelism and corruption. Equally, a large number of so-called civil society organisations were formed, many with a view to voicing the concerns of the marginalised sections of the population and pressuring governments to take issues of development and equity more seriously. These achievements are considerable and there is every chance that many will be long-lasting.

Nevertheless, the balance sheet of over fifteen years of multiparty politics in Africa is not overly positive. Here, it is important to distinguish two separate aspects of the political transitions that have taken place: one has to do with the entrenchment of multiparty elections over time; the other concerns the extent of systemic change. On the first, there has been a trend towards the continuation of multiparty polls, if only because it is now a *sine qua non* of foreign aid. Some of these elections have resulted in regime change but, on the whole, it is clear that African governments have now become adept at finding the means of being re-elected. The net effect has not been, as was initially envisaged in the West, that such electoral contests would result in 'poor' governments being swept from office. Whether they are removed or not has tended to hinge on factors that have less to do with their performance and more to do with the ability to control the electoral process or to 'buy' support. Looking at the history of electoral results in Africa over this period, it is difficult to establish any strong correlation between accomplishment in office (particularly in respect of promoting development or reducing poverty) and electoral victory or defeat.

The reasons for this are complex but they seem to derive from two sets of factors. The first is that incumbent regimes habitually win elections if the opposition is divided, which is often the case. Where the opposition is united, competition is fiercer but sitting governments are not reluctant to manipulate the elections if they fear defeat, which gives them a significant advantage. Despite intermittent international disapproval, they usually get away with it. Where regimes lose, they often regain control at subsequent elections, for the simple reason that the new government is rarely able to do better and often does not command the resources accumulated by those who had been in power for so long. Finally, the newly elected regimes rarely behave differently in government from those they have unseated.

This brings us to the final consideration, which is the fact that regime change in Africa has hitherto not brought about systemic political reform. Indeed, the overwhelming conclusion to be drawn from fifteen years of multiparty elections is that it has not resulted in notable improvement in governance. Neither the regimes that have managed to stay in power nor those that have replaced them have introduced markedly more accountable governments and more development-oriented policies. With few exceptions, there has been a continuation of neo-patrimonial politics, a form of governance that is (at least in the long run) quite simply incompatible with economic and social development.

Furthermore, multiparty elections have not been cost free. In many cases, the increasingly fierce competition they have generated has heightened social, regional or ethnic tension—leading in some instances to outbreak of violence or even civil war. Where single party rule relied on a combination of cooptation and authoritarianism, multiparty contests force rival politicians to employ antagonistic means to prevail over their opponents. So, the record forces us to question whether such multiparty contests are inherently favourable to the democratisation of society.

There is of course no way of predicting the future evolution of Angola. However, a study of the history of the country and an analysis of the genesis and nature of the regime as well as an assessment of the experience of multiparty elections in Africa, can provide a useful framework for envisaging the possible course of present political transitions. The fate of Angola rests in the hands of its people but it is not unreasonable to assume that for the foreseeable future the MPLA regime will continue to have the political, coercive and financial means to hold on to the reins of power.

2

ANGOLA IN HISTORICAL CONTEXT

Malyn Newitt

Introduction

Modern Angola is a child of its own history. The political traditions of its leaders, their relation to the population and their attitude to wealth accumulation are all rooted in five hundred years of historical development. Until the twentieth century Angola was a land divided into small kingdoms whose rulers held power with the backing of armed followers who were rewarded with the spoils of war and slaving. The population was traditionally divided between those of slave and those of free descent and the influence of witchcraft and spirit cults dominated everyday life. Angola was also a land of traders and from the time of the discovery of the New World participated in the Atlantic economy, developing strong commercial, social and political links with Europe and America. It was the ethnic group called in this chapter the Afro-Portuguese who most successfully developed their ties with the Atlantic world and, although as a group they suffered a decline in status during the early twentieth century, it was the Afro-Portuguese who seized power in 1975 and subsequently took control of Angola's wealth.

The part of Africa that became Angola was only brought under the effective control of a single government after the First World War. Before that, although the various regions of the country were all linked through long distance trade, they had been sufficiently distinct for them to form different cultural zones—the great Angolan rivers carving the country into geographical blocks with distinct political identities.[1]

Most of the north and north east of Angola is well-watered and agriculture supports a relatively dense population, but it is unsuitable for domestic animals and the accumulation of cattle wealth has therefore been impossible. The region forms part of the drainage basin of the Zaire on which the major tributaries and trade routes all converge. In the north the dominant language is Kikongo, which creates strong cultural ties between the people of northern Angola and those north of the river. The largest of the southern tributaries of the Zaire are the Kwango and the Kasai, which have formed cultural and political frontiers as well as highways for migration and trade. A great variety of language groups are found on the upper reaches of the Kwango and the Kasai and in the two centuries prior to the establishment of colonial rule the region beyond the Kasai was dominated by elites tributary to the Lunda paramount king. In the nineteenth century this region was divided three ways between the colonial powers.

The north-western region bounded by the Kwango, the Zaire and the sea at one time formed the old kingdom of Kongo whose titular king continued to have a symbolic and ritual importance for the people of the region until the end of the colonial period. The region north of the Zaire, where the Cabinda enclave is located, belongs to the equatorial forest zone and became attached to Angola entirely through the accident of history. The coastal region is very dry throughout its length and becomes desert in the south. Agriculture is virtually impossible, except in a few coastal oases, and the area traditionally had a very scanty population. Behind the coast lies a highland plateau from which descend a number of rivers, the most important of which, the Dande, the Bengo and Kwanza, are all navigable on their lower reaches and provide routes for trade and

1 Jill Dias, 'Angola', in Valentim Alexandre and Jill Dias (eds), *O Império Africano 1825-1890,* Nova História da Expansão Portuguesa vol x Lisbon: Estampa, 1998, p. 321.

communication with the interior. This part of the highlands is the homeland of Kimbundu-speaking people whose political and social culture was formed through contacts with the kingdom of Kongo to the north, the Afro-Portuguese of the coast and the Ovimbundu to the south.

The central highland plateau between the valley of the Kwanza and the sea is a region of good agricultural land with a mild climate and regular rainfall. It has always been the most densely populated part of Angola and in the seventeenth century became divided into small kingdoms, which grew up around fortified mountain strongholds and depended on the ability of a ruling elite to distribute the proceeds of slave raids and long distance trade. Although there are parts of the highlands and the main river valleys that are reliably well-watered and able to sustain communities even in periods of drought, the capriciousness of the African climate left many people with a precarious existence on the margins of the more stable and permanent settlements.

The southern part of the highlands, between the Kunene and the sea, forms the Huila plateau, the only part of the south to receive sufficient rain for arable farming to be possible. This region was controlled by small Nyaneka chieftaincies, while to the south and east were the kingdoms of the Herero and Ovambo largely dependent on the accumulation and distribution of cattle wealth.[2] Beyond the Kunene lies the Namibian sand veldt—the lower reaches of the river providing the frontier between Namibia and Angola. In the far south east the rivers drain into the Okavango. The population of this region, where there was little long distance trade and which has been culturally isolated from the rest of Angola, lived along the rivers and

2 Joseph Miller, *Way of Death. Merchant Capitalism and the Angolan Slave Trade 1730-1830*, Madison: University of Wisconsin Press, 1988 pp. 45-6; Carlos Estermann, *The Ethnography of Southwestern Angola, Vol. 1 The Non Bantu Peoples. The Ambo Ethnic Group*, New York and London: Africana Publishing Company, 1976.

is often collectively referred to as Ngangela. There are also groups of San and Khoi hunters.[3]

Long before any outside traders from the Mediterranean, the Atlantic or the Indian Ocean reached the region south of the Zaire, economic specialisation had led to the growth of long distance commerce. The main items of trade were salt, especially from pans near the coast; iron tools and weapons; copper from mines near Kisama and the regions which later became known as the 'copper belt'; *nzimbu* currency shells obtained from Luanda island, bark cloth (a specialised product of the lower Zaire), *cori* beads and slaves.

The trade in slaves, particularly women and children, was important for communities whose strength lay in the productive power of the lineage. In this part of Africa, 'capital was people'.[4] Slaves were added to the lineage to increase its numbers and enhance its wealth and security. The possession of slaves was also vital for the rulers, and the need to obtain them was the principal cause of the endemic warfare in much of this region.[5] Long distance trade was controlled and taxed by chiefs and was essential to the maintenance of their authority. The other source of chiefly legitimacy that the spirit cults were attached to was the land, through which the ancestors spoke to the people, shared their lives and secured their prosperity. With the exception of the Kongo kingdom and that of the Lunda, most states in this region remained very small both in territorial extent and in population.

The Angolan region becomes part of the Atlantic economy

Late in the fifteenth century Portuguese caravels reached the Zaire River. In 1483 Diogo Cão and his men sailed up to the Jellala rapids, carved their names on the rocks and made contact with the Kongo

3 W.G.Clarence-Smith, *Slaves, peasants and capitalists in Southern Angola 1840-1926,* Cambridge University Press, 1979, p. 11.

4 Joseph Miller, *Way of Death,* p. 43.

5 John Thornton, *Africa and Africans in the Making of the Atlantic World, 1400-1800,* Cambridge University Press, 1992, Chapter 4.

kingdom. In 1491 a full scale embassy was sent to Kongo and a permanent Portuguese trading factory was established. The arrival of the Portuguese opened up vast new trading opportunities for the Kongo elites. Exotic foreign imports widened the range of prestige goods that could be distributed, while Portuguese coastal shipping allowed Kongo products to be exported to other markets in Africa. Portuguese ship owners were soon operating as middlemen in a flourishing expansion of regional trade.[6]

The Portuguese Crown wanted to maintain a monopoly of trade. The Portuguese royal factors and the king of Kongo agreed that all trade would be conducted through the port of Mpinda in the Zaire estuary from which a well-trodden road led to the Kongo capital. The Portuguese found that the Kongo king was unexpectedly keen to adopt Christianity. The leading members of the ruling royal lineages were baptised and Christianity was made the official religion of the country, with the capital renamed São Salvador. The kings of Kongo saw in Christianity a powerful spirit cult, which they could control and which would give them important new spiritual sanctions to support their authority. Early in the seventeenth century, for example, the king of Kongo was still able to control the appointment of parish priests throughout his kingdom and through them to exert influence at a provincial level. Moreover, Christian priests and the Portuguese who ran the royal factory constituted a powerful body of supporters to buttress the king's power. [7] They opened the kingdom to the influence of the Afro-Portuguese creole culture that was being formed in the trading ports of the West African coast. The Kongo elites adopted Portuguese names, styles of dress and even habits of daily

6 For Cão's voyage see Eric Axelson, *Congo to Cape. Early Portuguese Explorers* London: Faber and Faber, 1973 and for the 1491 embassy Carmen Radulet, *O Cronista Rui de Pina e a 'relação do Congo'. Mare Liberum,* Lisbon: Comissão Nacional para as Comemorações dos Descobrimentos Portugueses, 1992; Anne Hilton, *The Kingdom of Kongo,* Oxford: Clarendon Press, 1985.

7 David Birmingham, 'Central Africa from Cameroun to the Zambesi', chapter 5, *Cambridge History of Africa,* Volume 4, Cambridge University Press, 1975. pp. 332, 335.

life. Some of them acquired literacy enabling them to correspond with Portugal and Rome. Contacts with the Atlantic world led to the import of American food crops. Maize, cassava and yams greatly increased crop yields and enabled subsistence farmers to occupy more of the marginal land and to support a growing population.[8]

However, just as the Kongo king had to face the opposition of provincial chiefs, the trade monopoly of the king of Portugal was undermined by the private ship owners and traders from São Tomé, who sought their profits outside the formal structures established by Lisbon. Some of these traders based themselves near the important *nzimbu* shell fishery at Luanda island, which had always been treated as part of the Kongo kingdom. Here contact was made with some of the Kimbundu-speaking chiefs who wanted to share in the rapidly expanding external commerce of the Kongo kingdom.[9] The Portuguese Crown wanted to prevent this southern trade from undermining the royal monopoly and itself opened formal negotiations with the Ngola, the king of Ndongo, to see if a basis for long term commercial relations could be established.[10]

The rise of the Afro-Portuguese

Ethnicity in Africa is very fluid. Although some political groupings and spirit cults are ancient and can survive even major changes in the political landscape, new political loyalties and ethnic affiliations can arise quite suddenly and can grow as the founding group attracts clients, slaves and new kinship alliances. As Joseph Miller has said, 'successful entrepreneurs in the end turned their material 'profits' back into people: dependent kin, clients and slaves'.[11] The arrival of Portuguese traders and missionaries at the end of the fifteenth cen-

8 Joseph Miller, *Way of Death*, p. 20.

9 For São Tomé see Robert Garfield, *A History of São Tomé Island 1470-1655*, San Fransisco: Mellen Research University Press, 1992.

10 David Birmingham, *Trade and Conflict in Angola*, Oxford: Clarendon Press, 1966), Chapter 2.

11 Joseph Miller, *Way of Death*, p. 46.

tury led to the emergence of a new and increasingly powerful Afro-Portuguese ethnic group in the region south of the Zaire river.

Of the Portuguese who reached the Kongo kingdom, some came directly from Portugal, including the officials who headed the embassies and ran the royal trading factory, the missionary priests, the artisans and seamen. Others arrived from São Tomé. The latter were subject to the jurisdiction of the captain of the island and included convicts, Jewish exiles and the mulatto children of African mothers. Their knowledge of, and loyalty to, metropolitan Portugal was at best doubtful. Most of the Portuguese took African wives and their children, while retaining their Portuguese identity, were brought up in the country and after two generations were indistinguishable from the local populations. Some of these Afro-Portuguese were employed by the king of Kongo as secretaries, priests, commercial officials or soldiers. Others lived a more autonomous existence in the interior as traders. Early in the seventeenth century one estimate suggested that there were a thousand 'Portuguese' trading in the interior of Kongo.[12] The Afro-Portuguese built up their numbers in the same way as other African ethnic groups, through local marriages and by acquiring slaves and clients.

At first the Afro-Portuguese were only interested in trade, but developments in the middle of the sixteenth century led to their establishing themselves as a separate ethnic group independent of the Kongo or any other king. In the 1560s the Portuguese Crown, which was planning a major conquest of the gold mines in eastern Africa, was presented with reports on the highland regions of Angola. Persuaded partly by the Jesuits, who wanted a quasi-independent African domain comparable to their jurisdictions in Brazil and Japan, and partly by the siren voices that told the Portuguese there must be silver mines in Africa comparable to those being discovered in Spanish America, the Crown decided to attempt the conquest and settlement of the highlands to the south of the Kongo kingdom. The

12 David Birmingham, 'Central Africa from Cameroun to the Zambesi', Chapter 5, *Cambridge History of Africa,* Volume 4, p. 336.

plan was to divide the area into a royal governorship and an autonomous captaincy. Paulo Dias, who had already spent years in Africa, was nominated as both governor and *capitão-donatário*. Dias died in 1589 having failed to make any conquests in the Angolan highlands. However, he had founded the city of Luanda and had taken control of the lower Kwanza valley, making the chiefs of that area tributary to Portugal.[13] With the founding of the city of Luanda and the control of the Kwanza valley the Afro-Portuguese had their own sovereign territory. Although the king of Portugal was nominally the sovereign, in practice the new settlement was dominated by powerful Afro-Portuguese families.

The initial weakness of the Luanda-based Portuguese was that they had no strong African allies. Paulo Dias had alienated the Mbundu chiefs and a series of inconclusive and debilitating wars continued for thirty years after his death. These wars hindered peaceful commerce and the trade in salt and copper, to which the Portuguese had attached such importance, never developed. The silver mines turned out, after the expenditure of much effort and many soldiers' lives, to be non-existent. In the first half of the seventeenth century, however, the growth of the slave trade caused the balance of commercial advantage to tilt increasingly towards Luanda. With the opening of the sugar plantations in Brazil towards the end of the sixteenth century, the need for slaves rose rapidly. The kingdom of Kongo was not able to meet this demand and early in the seventeenth century virtually ceased to export slaves.[14] The Afro-Portuguese then found new sources of supply from the African kingdoms of the highlands. By 1617 the trade was growing so rapidly that some of the Afro-Portuguese opened a second port at Benguela, three hundred miles south of Luanda, from where access to the southern part of the highlands was much easier. The rapid growth of the slave trade, and the huge

13 David Birmingham, 'Central Africa from Cameroun to the Zambesi', Chapter 5, *Cambridge History of Africa*, Volume 4, p. 334.

14 John Thornton, *Africa and Africans in the Making of the Atlantic world*, p. 110.

wealth it generated, had the effect of reconciling the highland chiefs to the Afro-Portuguese who now found willing allies along the trade routes to the interior and at the inland fairs. The Afro-Portuguese and the Luanda authorities also realised that they were able to recruit black soldiers (usually known generically as Jaga).[15]

The second factor that enabled the Afro-Portuguese of Luanda to supplant São Salvador were the links they cultivated with the wider Atlantic world. Commerce with Brazil was now so important that Brazilians crossed to Angola to secure their trade, to find outlets for their goods and to take part, when necessary, in the wars that frequently occurred in the interior. The most striking example of this was provided when the Dutch seized control of Luanda in 1641. The Angolan Portuguese refused to collaborate and in 1648 an expedition sent from Brazil defeated the Dutch and restored Luanda to Portuguese control.

The kings of Kongo were never able to develop these wider contacts, though they tried to establish direct links with Rome to circumvent the control the Portuguese exerted over the Christian cult. Between 1622 and 1665 a series of wars erupted between Angola and the Kongo and after the defeat and death of the Kongo king at the battle of Ambuila in 1665, the power of the monarchy rapidly declined. Provincial rulers now dealt directly with Luanda or with other Europeans north of the Zaire. As the profits of trade drained away, the king of Kongo lost the practical means to exert his authority over his provincial nobles.[16] Rival clans competed to control the titular kingship and Kongo became a virtual state whose king, while venerated as ritual head of the kingdom, wielded less and less real power. São Salvador, which had boasted a cathedral and monastic buildings, became once again a small African town.

15 David Birmingham, 'Central Africa from Cameroun to the Zambesi', Chapter 5, *Cambridge History of Africa,* Volume 4, p. 336.

16 David Birmingham, 'Central Africa from Cameroun to the Zambersi', Chapter 5, *Cambridge History of Africa* Volume 4, p. 337.

Meanwhile, Luanda and its satellite port of Benguela flourished. The Portuguese Crown endowed it with a *Senado da Câmara* and a *Misericórdia,* which institutionalised the power of the Afro-Portuguese not only locally but within the wider Portuguese world. It was through Luanda that imports of cloth, metalware and Brazilian tobacco flooded the interior. The Afro-Portuguese had become a powerful ethnic group whose state was comparable in size and influence to the most important of the African kingdoms of the interior.

The Slave Trade

By 1600 about 4,500 slaves were being sent every year from the area south of the Zaire. This number rose to 8,000 by 1650 and 11,000 by 1700. In all about two million slaves were exported from the ports of Angola in the two and a half centuries after 1600—an average of about 8,000 a year. Although numbers might fluctuate from year to year, the trade remained highly profitable and came to dominate the commercial economy of central Africa.

It has sometimes been claimed that, because it was the Afro-Portuguese who acted as middlemen, the Angolan slave trade differed from that of Guinea where African traders predominated. However, by the seventeenth century the Afro-Portuguese had become an African ethnic group which, like the Vili of the Loango coast, specialised in long distance trade. They were the principal organisers of trading caravans that took Brazilian and Portuguese trade goods to the interior slave markets, the most important of which were in the kingdoms of Matamba and Kasanje. The close commercial relations led to a certain mutual dependency between the ruling elites of the coastal ports and the inland states as both relied on the profits of the trade to maintain their authority.[17]

Slaves were obtained from the whole of the territory that later became Angola (except the thinly populated south and south-east) as well as from north of the Zaire—a region which may have had a

17 Jill Dias, 'Angola', Valentim Alexandre and Jill Dias eds, *O Império Africano 1825-1890,* p. 335.

total population in the eighteenth century of around twelve million.[18] By the middle of the century Afro-Portuguese traders from the west coast had penetrated to the Lunda states of Kazembe and Mwata Yamvo, which provided at least a third of all slaves exported in the final phase of the Atlantic trade.[19] The Lunda trade also gave rise to the idea of the *contra costa*, the opening of a trade route across the continent. In 1795 an expedition was actually organised in Mozambique to cross Africa and early in the nineteenth century two Afro-Portuguese from Angola did complete the journey to Mozambique.

The Ovimbundu kingdoms originally developed in response to slave raids from the Imbangala but their rulers were not slow to see the profits to be made from slaving and they attracted Afro-Portuguese traders to their capitals. As had happened further north, the trade in slaves overshadowed most other forms of commerce and by the eighteenth century as many slaves were being sent from Benguela as were leaving Luanda. In the ninety years after 1740, 400,000 slaves were exported from Benguela to Brazil.[20] Benguela became, in effect, a second Afro-Portuguese coastal state, which gradually exerted its control over the whole lowland region as far as the escarpment.

Joseph Miller has pointed out that, contrary to the view that the slave trade led to chaos and disorder, there was great political stability in the interior of Angola throughout the eighteenth century. 'The continued high volume of slaves sent to the Americas provided the glue which held the entire system together.'[21] It was only in the nineteenth century, when control of the trade by the African kings and the Afro-Portuguese was undermined by new entrepreneurs, and

18 Joseph Miller, *Way of Death*, p. 8.

19 Jill Dias, 'Angola', Valentim Alexandre and Jill Dias eds, *O Império Africano 1825-1890,* p. 335.

20 Linda Heywood, *Contested Power in Angola, 1840s to the present,* Rocherster NY: University of Rochester Press, 2000, p.12

21 Joseph Miller, 'Slaves, slavers and social change in nineteenth century Kasanje', F-W Heimer ed., *Social Change in Angola,* Munich: Weltforum Verlag, 1973, p. 12.

when the Atlantic trade was finally brought to an end, that political conditions in the interior became unstable.

A considerable slave trade was also carried on from the north of the Zaire where Dutch, French, Brazilian as well as Portuguese traders had establishments on the Loango coast. The Portuguese had always been reluctant to trade firearms but their European rivals found that selling muskets was the surest way to gain a foothold in the commerce of this region. However, the middlemen who operated out of Cabinda and neighbouring Loango, were the Vili and not the Afro-Portuguese.[22]

The end of the slave trade

The slave trade expanded rapidly in its last days up to 1840 when the Septembrist regime in Portugal ended the legal participation of the metropolitan Portuguese. An illicit trade then continued until first France, then Brazil and finally the United States ended the import of slaves. By 1865 the sea-borne trade from West Africa was limited to the shipping of slaves to the Portuguese plantations in São Tomé.

However, this by no means ended the African slave trade, which had always existed as much to supply internal as external markets. The two trades were complementary. While the market overseas required mostly male slaves, the internal market set a premium on females, who were acquired to increase the size of lineages and boost the agricultural labour force.[23] Slaves continued to be captured in raids and bought in slave markets by the Kongo chiefs and the kings of the highlands. Indeed the decline of the external market had the effect of increasing the internal trade and the reliance of the elites on their slave populations. Moreover, the slave trade directed to the Indian Ocean markets continued undiminished and east coast slav-

22 Phyllis Martin, *The External Trade of the Loango Coast,* Oxford Univeristy Press, 1972.

23 Jill Dias, 'Angola', Valentim Alexandre and Jill Dias eds, *O Império Africano 1825-1890,* p. 324.

ers now regularly sought supplies among the peoples of the upper Zambesi and Zaire.

Nor did the closing of the Atlantic slave trade end the participation of Angolans in the Atlantic economy. The demand for palm oil, ivory and, later in the century, rubber replaced the demand for slaves, thus diversifying the economy and stimulating long distance trade. Large caravans, numbering sometimes as many as a thousand people, continued to bring goods from the coast to inland fairs, penetrating beyond the Kasai into the area of the Lunda kingdom. The caravans bought ivory, wax, honey, gum and skins as well, of course, as slaves for whom there was still a market within Africa, and who were anyway required to provide porters to carry the goods to the coast.

At first most of these caravans were organised, as the slave ones had been, by Afro-Portuguese merchants who had longstanding agreements with the kings of the highlands and the Kongo. The payments made by these caravans to 'open the roads' formed a substantial part of the income of the rulers of the plateau kingdoms and helped them to maintain their authority. The missionary Frederick Arnot mentions a Portuguese trader having to pay the king of Bihe 'three four gallon kegs of rum, a case of gin, six hundred yards of cloth, fifty pounds of powder, and one or two guns' and he adds 'Senhor [Silva] Porto never returns from the coast without bringing as tribute far more than this'.[24] However, as the nineteenth century progressed, the profits to be derived from trade brought new entrepreneurs onto the scene. Some of these were commoners from the highland kingdoms who had invested their wealth in the caravan trade; others were new participants like the Chokwe from the upper Kwanza who increasingly dominated the interior trade routes in the second half of the century. The Afro-Portuguese lost their pre-eminence and the highland kings, who had been their partners in the slave trade, found their position weakened as new wealthy and powerful social groups emerged and, by acquiring slaves, were able

24 Fred. S. Arnot, *Garenganze; or Seven Years' Pioneer Mission Work in Central Africa,* London: James E.Hawkins 1889, p. 137.

to establish lineage networks that were effectively independent of the traditional chiefs. [25]

Faced with a threat to their commercial supremacy in the interior, the Afro-Portuguese began to rely increasingly on the wealth to be derived from direct control of land and population. The inhabitants of those areas directly under the influence of Luanda and Benguela, like those subject to the kingdoms of the plateau, were now subjected to a more exacting regime of tribute payment and labour service, which frequently caused opposition and resistance. This was met by armed punitive raids, which gradually extended the area ruled directly from the two Afro-Portuguese states. Precisely similar action was taken by the plateau kings to stem the erosion of their income and authority.[26]

Production of crops to supply the overseas market was clearly another option, but this required a reliable supply of labour. Security was also an issue, as fixed capital in the form of crops, warehouses or machinery was vulnerable to warfare or raiding. Nevertheless, in the 1840s African and Afro-Portuguese landowners began to grow coffee in the interior of Kazengo and Kasange, while others concentrated, as they had always done, on growing food to supply the urban settlements and trade caravans.[27] Frederick Arnot, travelling through the highlands in 1884 with the Portuguese trader Silva Porto, was astonished that food should be so cheap and plentiful—'a piece of calico, about the size of a handkerchief, will buy about twenty pounds of meal or a calabash of honey.'[28]

The expansion of international commerce in the nineteenth century resulted in the development of new ports. British, French, Dutch and Portuguese traders began to build warehouses and jetties at dif-

25 Jill Dias, 'Angola', Valentim Alexandre and Jill Dias eds, *O Império Africano 1825-1890*, pp. 332-4.

26 Linda Heywood, *Contested Power in Angola, 1840s to the present*, p. 18.

27 David Birmingham, 'The Coffee Barons of Cazengo', David Birmingham ed., London: St Martin's Press, *Portugal and Africa*, 1999.

28 Fred. S. Arnot, *Garenganze; or seven years' pioneer mission work in Central Africa*, p. 100.

ferent places in the Zaire estuary where there was no effective Afro-Portuguese presence and where the authority of the king of Kongo was no longer recognised. They negotiated directly with local rulers for concessions in a waterway teeming with traffic but where there was no overall authority. South of the Zaire, coastal harbours like Ambriz gradually expanded, first as autonomous ports conducting an illegal traffic in slaves but eventually acknowledging the government in Luanda. Other ports such as Catumbela and Novo Redondo also emerged to handle the illicit trade.[29]

However, it was the new port at Moçamedes that was to have the greatest long term importance.[30] Like other areas of Angola, the southern coast had been visited from time to time by Afro-Portuguese traders, although no slave trade had ever grown up there. In 1840 the authorities in Lisbon decided to try to plant a colony and emigrants from Brazil and fishermen from southern Portugal were given land and encouraged to settle. For the first forty years the small town struggled to survive. However, gradually Moçamedes attracted a permanent population of Afro-Portuguese traders with their slaves, who were collectively known as Mbali and spoke a dialect of the Kimbundu of Luanda. Moçamedes also provided a port for the communities in the Huila highlands where cattle owning Nyaneka had for long been largely excluded from Atlantic commerce.[31]

The heyday of the Afro-Portuguese

Although the decline of the Atlantic slave trade had threatened the livelihood of the Afro-Portuguese, the nineteenth century can be seen in retrospect as the heyday of the power and prestige of this particular ethnic group. The Afro-Portuguese families had no doubts about

29 Jill Dias, 'Angola', Valentim Alexandre and Jill Dias eds, *O Império Africano 1825-1890,* p. 371.

30 For the founding of Moçamedes see W.G. Clarence-Smith, *Slaves, peasants and capitalists in southern Angola 1840-1926.*

31 W.G. Clarence-Smith, *Slaves, Peasants and Capitalists in Southern Angola 1840-1926,* pp. 8, 15, 42-3.

their Portuguese identity but most of them spoke Kimbundu, which was the language of the coastal towns, rather than Portuguese. The heartland of the Afro-Portuguese states were the Atlantic ports of Luanda and Benguela, sometimes referred to as '*reinos*' (kingdoms). There the wealthiest Afro-Portuguese families had their residences and warehouses and it was there that they did business with ship-owners and merchant houses from Brazil and Portugal. Some had interests in São Tomé and Brazil, where their children were often sent for education. Indeed, so close were their links with Brazil that some even contemplated joining that country in its bid for independence from Portugal in the 1820s.[32]

The leading Afro-Portuguese families, generically referred to by the Portuguese as *moradores,* controlled the town councils and the local militia, commanding the garrisons of black troops in the nine *presídios* in the interior.[33] They also staffed the rudimentary Portuguese administration. They came technically under the control of the Portuguese governor but outside Luanda the governor's influence was limited and the Afro-Portuguese families were largely autonomous. Deeply rooted in the interior, they owned landed estates on the lower reaches of the rivers near Luanda and Benguela. However, the best known of their settlements in the interior was Ambaca, and in much of the nineteenth century literature they were referred to as Ambaquistas. Pungo Ndongo was another of their centres which was also used by the Portuguese authorities as a convict settlement.

On their estates in the interior the Afro-Portuguese had large followings of clients and slaves—three quarters of all slaves officially registered in Angola in the early nineteenth century being located around Ambaca. They maintained commercial relations with Portuguese as well as non-Portuguese trading houses. They led caravans themselves or accompanied the caravans of others as interpreters or

32 Jill Dias, 'Angola', in Valentim Alexandre and Jill Dias eds, *O Império Africano 1825-1890*, p. 369.

33 Jill Dias, 'Angola', in Valentim Alexandre and Jill Dias eds, *O Império Africano 1825-1890,* p. 357.

commercial agents.[34] Many settled at the courts of the highland kings with semi-official positions as resident 'representatives' of Luanda or Benguela.[35] The Afro-Portuguese, coming from the coast or from Ambaca, were especially numerous in the kingdom of Bihe, making this one of the most important nodes of the slave trade in the later eighteenth and early nineteenth centuries.[36]

The leading Afro-Portuguese, like the ruling elites of the highlands, reinforced their position by marrying amongst themselves or forming unions with the ruling families of the other African states. As with the Afro-Portuguese communities in Guiné and the islands, a prominent position was occupied by women who often became the wives or concubines of the transient Portuguese traders, soldiers and officials and who inherited their property when they died in Angola.[37] Jill Dias has commented that 'a defining characteristic of those belonging to this creole elite was the substitution of individual property for the collective ownership of lands and moveable goods.'[38]

In addition to the slaves the Afro-Portuguese owned, they had authority over the vassal chiefs, or *sobas*. In 1825 the population subject to Luanda and Benguela was estimated to be between 250,000 and 300,000, which would have made these two '*reinos*' approximately the same size as the larger of the highland kingdoms. The Africans subject to the *sobas* could be drafted for carrier service. The right to conscript the labour of subject peoples, it has been argued, was

34 Beatrix Heintze, 'Between Two Worlds: the Bezerras, a Luso-African family in nineteenth century Western Central Africa', in Philip J. Havik and Malyn Newitt eds, *Creole Societies in the Portuguese Colonial Empire,* Bristol University (2007).

35 Jill Dias, 'Angola', in Valentim Alexandre and Jill Dias eds, *O Império Africano 1825-1890,* pp. 350-2, 360-2.

36 Jill Dias, 'Angola', in Valentim Alexandre and Jill Dias eds, *O Império Africano 1825-1890,* pp. 364-5.

37 Jill Dias, 'Angola', in Valentim Alexandre and Jill Dias eds, *O Império Africano 1825-1890,* p. 350.

38 Jill Dias, 'Uma questão de identidade: Respostas intelectuais às transformações económicas no seio da elite crioula da Angola portuguesa entre 1870 e 1930', *Revista Internacional de Estudos Africanos,* 1, 1984, p. 64.

crucial to the status and power of the elites of this part of Africa and constituted a kind of 'credit account' on which the rich and powerful could draw when necessary.[39]

Spiritual sanctions were an essential adjunct to political power in this part of Africa and chiefs invariably either controlled spirit cults or themselves claimed to have supernatural powers. The Afro-Portuguese also had their own cult; they carried with them sacred objects to provide protection and to give spiritual power, which Arnot referred to contemptuously as 'a few Christian relics added to the heap of native charms'.[40] The prestige of the Christian cult, however, remained strong in various parts of Angola, notably in the Kongo region and in the latter part of the nineteenth century spread into the central highlands.

By the early nineteenth century, the Afro-Portuguese coastal states had acquired a distinct identity, which was deeply rooted in the history of the people of the coast and at the same time shared in the creole cultures of the Atlantic world. The late nineteenth century was to see the attempt by the peoples of the coast to conquer and colonise the interior. The civil wars, which occurred after the withdrawal of the Portuguese in 1975 also assumed the character of a conflict between the old Afro-Portuguese coastal states and the inland peoples.

The influence of the Afro-Portuguese was most pronounced in the region inland from Luanda, as far as Kasanje. The people who inhabited this part of the country were of various origins: slaves of the Afro-Portuguese, the free subjects of vassal *sobas* and other fragments of African population. Beyond the effective control of the Portuguese were chieftaincies, notably those of Kasanje and Matamba where the main slaving fairs were located. All the peoples of this central swathe of Angola were welded into an ethnic identity by the predominant Kimbundu language and in the twentieth century were referred to as

39 Joseph Miller, *Way of Death,* p. 47.

40 Fred. S. Arnot, *Garenganze; or Seven Years' Pioneer Mission Work in Central Africa,* p. 119.

Mbundu. It was the Mbundu who formed the natural constituency of the Afro-Portuguese political leaders during the period of the Republic and when they formed the MPLA in the late 1950s.[41]

International intervention in Africa

Although Angola had always been closely integrated into the Atlantic economy, it was not until the second half of the nineteenth century that there was any international interest in its inland regions. If increased trade stimulated curiosity about conditions in the interior, the end of the railway building boom in India and the United States aroused the interest of speculative investors in the 'dark continent'. Steam navigation, the laying of the Atlantic cables and the opening of the Suez Canal in 1869 all brought tropical Africa closer to Europe and the Americas; it made the prospect of investing in Africa seem realistic. Moreover, the downturn of the European economy after 1873 gradually persuaded all the major industrialised economies to introduce measures to protect their trade and industry and gave rise to fears that the freedom to trade with Africa, however unimportant this might be in relative terms, would soon be curtailed.

In the late 1870s there was a stream of Europeans travelling into the interior of the continent. Scientists and explorers, many of them Portuguese or German, were matched by missionaries from a variety of Protestant sects and from the new Catholic missionary orders like the Holy Ghost Fathers and the White Fathers. These outsiders established direct links between the inland peoples and the wider world. They brought not only increased trade but new ideas and new opportunities, which challenged the traditional social customs and the dominance of the traditional ruling elites.

The accounts of conditions in the interior that were published by travellers like Cameron had given the Afro-Portuguese a bad press. Cameron claimed that, although the Atlantic slave trade had been abolished twenty years earlier, slave trading in the African interior

41 Fernando Pacheco, 'Agricultura e Sociedade Rural na Angola dos Anos 60-0 Caso de Malanje', unpublished paper, 1991, pp. 7-9.

remained as active as ever. The fact that the Afro-Portuguese participated in this commerce and themselves held slaves enabled Cameron to portray Portugal itself as being deeply implicated. 'I have no hesitation in asserting', he wrote, 'that the worst of the Arabs are... angels of light in comparison with the Portuguese and those who travel with them.'[42] In this way a new 'black legend' began to be formed which was to burden Portuguese colonial rule until it came to an end in 1975.[43]

The Portuguese government felt increasingly threatened by these developments. In 1875 the Lisbon Geographical Society had been founded to promote a more active policy in Africa and in 1879 negotiations with Britain began over the building of a railway from Delagoa Bay to the Transvaal and over the future of Zambesi navigation. The purpose of these negotiations, which in 1881 were extended to western Africa, was to try to secure recognition of Portugal's privileged position in the region of the Zaire and Zambesi valleys. Two treaties were signed (though never ratified), the second of which secured Portugal's position in the region south of the Zaire in return for guarantees about free trade and open access for missionaries.[44] Both France and Germany refused to accept this bilateral agreement and a Conference was called in Berlin to resolve the international status of the Zaire basin and the Niger.

After four months of negotiations it was decided that the lower Zaire basin should be divided between a French occupation of the region north of the river and Portuguese sovereignty recognised over the south bank extending fifty miles from the sea, with the rest of the Zaire basin divided between France and the newly created Congo Free State under Leopold of the Belgians. The Portuguese were also

42 V.L. Cameron, *Across Africa,* 2 vols, London: Dalby Isbister, 1877 Vol 2, p. 106.

43 For the creation of the 'black legend' in the nineteenth century, see M. Newitt, 'British Travellers' Accounts of Portuguese Africa in the Nineteenth Century', *Revista de Estudos Anglo-Portugueses,* 11 (2002) pp. 103-129.

44 For these lengthy negotiations see Roger Anstey, *Britain and the Congo in the Nineteenth Century,* Oxford: Clarendon Press, 1962.

allocated the enclave of Cabinda, where they had maintained an active trading post since the eighteenth century. The old kingdom of Kongo was divided in two by a line running from Boma on the Zaire to the Kwango river. The economic effect of this partition was intended to be minimal as the whole basin of the Zaire was to be subject to an internationally monitored customs regime—which incidentally showed how important was the fear of commercial protectionism. Nevertheless, the southern tributaries of the Zaire had now been divided between Leopold and the Portuguese, the new border slicing across the old trade routes and allocating the peoples of the interior to two different European overlords.

Leaving to one side the issue of whether Europeans had any right to partition Africa at all, the outcome of the Conference was grossly unfair to Portugal. The Berlin treaty declared that effective occupation was necessary to substantiate any claims to African territory, but in 1885 the only European country with any presence in the interior at all was Portugal. At this time, Britain, France and Germany had no settlements of any description away from the coast.

A flurry of diplomatic activity followed the Berlin treaty, accompanied by more or less brutal and perfunctory flag raising expeditions on the ground. Germany, the South African Republic, Britain and King Leopold were all felt by the Portuguese to be threatening the traditional hinterland of the old port-colonies of Benguela and Luanda. In the area of the kingdom of Kongo the papacy had authorised the activity of French missionaries. German explorers were busy in the Lunda region, while in 1884 Bismarck had declared a German protectorate over the Namibian coast as far as the Kunene river. In 1881 a number of Boer trekkers crossed the Kalahari and entered the Huila highlands, raising the very real possibility that a new Boer Republic would be established in the hinterland of Moçamedes.

Portugal responded to these threats with surprising vigour. The Lisbon Geographical Society organized exploratory expeditions; Portuguese missionaries returned to São Salvador and the Portuguese government embarked on a diplomatic offensive. In 1886 and

1887 treaties were signed with Germany and France drawing the southern frontier between Angola and German South West Africa and marking out spheres of influence in Guiné. To these treaties the Portuguese appended the so-called Rose Coloured Map, staking out claims to an unbroken band of territory extending across central Africa from coast to coast.[45] The Rose Coloured Map precipitated a crisis with Britain, which led inexorably to the Ultimatum of January 1890 and the boundary treaty forced on Portugal in 1891 that separated Angola from Mozambique by a swathe of British territory and ended once and for all the dream of the *contra costa.*

Although the extent of African territory which came under Portuguese rule was larger than Portugal could easily control or administer, the Portuguese continued to feel that they had been cheated not only by their old ally Britain but by a conspiracy of the great European powers in league with international capital. Evidence for this was soon provided when Portugal heard of the terms of a secret agreement reached between Germany and Britain in 1898 to take over Portugal's colonies if Portugal's parlous financial position should force it to give them up. The suspicion and insecurity created by the Ultimatum and the 1898 treaty were to reverberate throughout the colonial period both in the Republic's anxiety to join the winning side in the First World War and in Salazar's suspicion of foreign capital as well as his wish to insulate the Portuguese colonies from outside interference. Echoes of these attitudes can perhaps be heard today in the hostility of the MPLA government in Angola towards the interference of the World Bank and IMF.

The modern world reaches the Angolan interior

Before the Berlin Conference had even met, the effects of the world market had begun to change the traditional political and social structures of the highland communities. The ruling elites struggled to maintain their authority as their hold over economic life was

45 C.E. Nowell, *The Rose-Coloured Map,* Lisbon: Junta de Investigações Científicas do Ultramar, 1982.

loosened. People from the non-elite groups made money through trading or selling their goods to passing caravans. Outsiders in the form of missionaries and Afro-Portuguese commercial agents entered the highlands in growing numbers. Hoping that an alliance with the coastal cities would strengthen their position, many of the traditional rulers turned for help to the Portuguese from the coast, allowing Residents to be appointed in their capitals and permitting the Portuguese to build forts and establish garrisons.

It has often been said that Portugal never tried to operate a system of indirect rule in alliance with traditional authorities. However, in the years immediately following the Berlin Conference the Portuguese found that working with the chiefs was the quickest and most cost effective way of carrying out their international obligations to establish effective occupation, suppress the slave trade and control the trade in drink and arms.

Initially, few attempts were made to establish direct administration and the *postos militares* manned by black soldiers were little more than centres from which influence could be exerted over local affairs. However, the arrival of Portuguese political agents and their escorts of colonial troops helped to precipitate change and gave the Luanda government fresh opportunities to intervene in African politics. An example of this occurred in 1890 when Portuguese forces occupied Bihe, one of the most important of the highland kingdoms, and established a form of indirect rule through a compliant king.[46] The presence of Portuguese forces opened the way for still more traders and adventurers to reach the plateau and a dangerous vacuum was created with the kings powerless to exert any real control and the Portuguese lacking any direct form of administration.

In 1902 war broke out in Bailundu and spread to the neighbouring kingdoms. The leaders of the revolt wanted to expel the outsiders and return to the slave-based rule of the old chiefly families. Altogether elements from eight of the kingdoms took part in the war but the traditional rivalries and outlooks of the leaders prevented their

46 Linda Heywood, *Contested Power in Angola, 1840s to the Present*, p. 26.

mounting an effective military campaign. Moreover, many Ovimbundu aided the Portuguese from the outset or went over to their side in the course of the war. The victory of the Portuguese forces was a victory for the changing order and marked the end of a political and economic system that had lasted since the earliest days of the slave trade. By effectively ending the existence of the semi-autonomous kingdoms, the war also opened the way for the emergence of a new identity, which relied less on historic allegiances and more on a perceived common Ovimbundu cultural heritage.[47]

Events in the Kongo region followed a similar course. The expansion of trade in rubber and palm oil to the ports on the Zaire and the northern coast had undermined the control which the traditional chiefly families had exerted in the days of the slave trade. Successful new traders organised their own caravans and sought to deal directly with European merchant houses. Political power became increasingly fragmented. Some chiefs tried to exercise regional authority and to tax the caravan trade, their power resting on the slaves they were still able to acquire. Among these the kings of Kongo clung to vestiges of their old prestige. As regional chiefs residing in the old capital of São Salvador they were of local importance; they also exerted some control over the native Kongolese church and the secret societies that had their origin in the Christian past. However, their real authority scarcely extended fifty miles from their capital.

It was in these circumstances that Portugal tried to revive the Catholic mission. The Portuguese resented the attempt by Rome to send French priests to the region but matters became more complicated when British Baptists, backed financially by businessmen from the north of England, established a mission in 1878. The arrival of both Baptist and Catholic missions was welcomed by the Kongo king and by some other chiefs for much the same reasons as the original mission had been received in 1491. The outsiders were seen as useful allies in the struggle to reinforce a steadily weakening authority. The

47 Linda Heywood, *Contested Power in Angola, 1840s to the Present,* pp. 29-30.

chiefly families allowed their children and even their wives to attend church services and the mission schools.[48]

Although the partition agreement of 1885 had divided the southern watershed of the Zaire between Portugal and the Congo Free State, neither at first imposed any form of administration and the Portuguese contented themselves with sending Residents to co-operate with the local chiefs. True to the spirit and practice of indirect rule, the Portuguese used the chiefs to enlist carriers and supply other forms of labour. The chiefs at first did not resist and the missionaries raised few protests. Meanwhile the rubber boom continued with large numbers of Bakongo involved in its collection, carriage and sale, and increasing numbers of people drawn out of the subsistence economy into the world of commercial markets. The rubber trade collapsed in 1912 and when finally war broke out in the Kongo region in 1913, it was against a background of commercial crisis exacerbated by a disputed succession to the titular kingship of Kongo.

Up to that time Portuguese Residents had influenced the succession without too much friction, but in 1913 the king was challenged by a coalition of the rival factions. The war was very much a Kongolese civil war and its suppression opened the way for the Portuguese administration to replace the old chiefs.[49]

It was only in the last days of the Monarchy, twenty years after the Berlin Conference, that a serious attempt was made to establish direct Portuguese rule throughout Angola—or, to use the parlance current at the time, to 'pacify' the country. The secret partition treaty signed by Britain and Germany in 1898 gave Lisbon a strong incentive to press ahead with the formal occupation of the colony. The 1902 Bailundo war made possible the complete occupation of the Central Highlands, but it was only after 1905 that military posts were

48 J.A.Vos, 'The Kingdom of Kongo and its Borderlands, 1880-1915' unpublished PhD thesis, University of London, 2005; R.H. Carson, Graham, *Under Seven Congo Kings,* London: Carey Press, 1930.

49 J.A.Vos, 'The Kingdom of Kongo and its Borderlands, 1880-1915'.

established beyond the Kwango and in Lunda province. In 1907 the Portuguese finally attempted the military occupation of Dembos.

Henrique de Paiva Couceiro, a militant monarchist who was governor of Angola from 1907 to 1909, was a strong advocate of military occupation, which he justified on the grounds that the surrounding territories were all being pacified and Angola was becoming a refuge for rebels and escaped criminals. He was clear exactly what pacification, which he believed would pay for itself, entailed—that is, 'peace and civilization through work' and 'occupying the country by force and thereafter opening the roads, establishing relations with the people, and by advice, example and agricultural instruction little by little introducing new moral horizons and better ways of life'. The pursuit of formal occupation was to cost Portugal many lives, especially in Dembos and in the south among the Kwanyama, and it was not completed until the end of the First World War.[50]

The occupation of the south was a more complex story. In 1881, 300 Boer trekkers reached the remote Huila highlands. The Boers were cattle farmers but they were also hunters and wagon drivers. The traditional mode of transport in Angola had been by carrier and head portage but the Boer settlers introduced the ox-wagon, a mode of transport, which was expensive and very slow but had the advantage of being able to move heavy loads. Ox-wagons gradually penetrated most of central and southern Angola, linking for the first time regions that had been isolated and separated from one another, thus helping to create the infrastructure for a modern economy. The Boers also provided the Portuguese with a force of white mercenaries for use in the wars to subdue the peoples in the far south.

Shortly after the arrival of the Boers, the Germans declared a protectorate over the South West African coast. The possibility that the Germans might use the presence of the Boers as a reason to extend their protectorate into the Huila highlands appeared to have been

50 Henrique de Paiva Couceiro, *Angola: dois annos de governo junho 1907–junho 1908. História e Commentários,* Lisbon: 1948, pp. 9, 50. For the wars of pacification see René Pélissier, *Les Guerres Grises,* Orgéval, 1977.

prevented by the frontier treaty signed with Germany in 1886 but it did not end Portugal's need to establish effective occupation in the region. In Mozambique, charter companies had been formed so that effective occupation of large parts of the colony could be achieved at no cost to Portugal. In 1894, the Portuguese created a chartered concession for the Moçamedes Company, which covered the far south of Angola. At the same time the Holy Ghost Fathers were granted extensive privileges to set up missions. The government brought in large numbers of Madeiran settlers and planned to build a railway from Moçamedes to overcome the problems of accessing the interior. [51]

The levying of local taxes and the recruitment of labour were signs that Portugal's authority had been recognised and that effective occupation had been achieved. However, by the end of the Monarchy in 1910, there were still many areas of the interior where the influence of the coast was negligible, where traditional authorities remained largely autonomous, where African law continued to be applied in a traditional manner in African courts and where all public and private business was carried on in the local languages.

Gradually the colonial government put in place some major administrative changes, though at first these existed only on paper. In 1906 African taxation had been regulated, and the same year an administrative structure was proposed which divided the colony into provinces, *circunscrições* and *concelhos*. [52] Throughout Angola the economy continued to function with extensive use of unfree labour. Portugal had decreed the formal abolition of slavery in 1875 but the former slaves, renamed *libertos*, were to be forcibly contracted to their former masters. However, although in some areas there were riots and protests from the former slaves hoping that the legislation would

51 W.G. Clarence-Smith, *Slaves, Peasants and Capitalists in Southern Angola 1840-1926*, pp. 17-18

52 Linda Heywood, *Contested Power in Angola, 1840s to the present*, p. 35.

result in genuine freedom, this measure had little or no effect on social relations or on relations of production.[53]

Not only did slave labour survive well into the twentieth century but the ownership of slaves by the elite families of the coast and the interior actually increased. Slaves were also important for the newly emergent entrepreneurs who had profited from long distance trade and wanted to acquire slaves as carriers and labourers or simply to enhance their social status within traditional society. Farmers producing for the expanding market for foodstuffs also needed to employ slaves, and slaves were needed to meet the demands of the administration for labour.

The Portuguese government was signatory to various international treaties regarding the suppression of slavery and the slave trade, so that the continuation of what amounted to slavery in Angola and São Tomé was denounced by foreign missionaries and journalists. For the colonial elites, still closely allied with the old Afro-Portuguese families, the continuation of slavery was at the same time difficult to countenance officially but impossible to dispense with in practice. The solution was to make compulsory labour a universal obligation for all those who could not prove their civilised status. The 1899 labour law, which was intended to be applied throughout the empire, had imposed on all Africans the 'moral obligation' to work either for the state or for private concerns on all Africans. This framework legislation was applied differently in different parts of the colonies and the Portuguese were slow to impose it universally in Angola. In practice, therefore, slavery continued.

There was also a steady demand for labour from the plantation owners on São Tomé and Príncipe. Between 1890 and 1910, 3,000 workers a year were being sent to the islands, most of whom came from Angola. This amounted to a continuation of the slave trade (at about half the rate of the Atlantic trade in the eighteenth century) since the pretence that the labour sent to the islands was free deceived

53 W.G. Clarence-Smith, *Slaves, Peasants and Capitalists in Southern Angola 1840–1926*, p. 40.

no one. In the first decade of the twentieth century international pressure built up against the continuation of this practice, not least because of the sleeping sickness epidemics which at one time caused a mortality rate of 25 per cent per annum on Príncipe. As a result the Luanda authorities were forced to ban the recruitment of contract labourers for São Tomé altogether in 1910.

Taxation was only introduced gradually after 1906 and was seen by the government in Luanda more as a symbolic recognition of Portuguese overlordship than as a serious fiscal device. However, throughout the first twenty-five years of the century tax rates were gradually raised and collection widened—although one estimate suggests that up to 80 per cent of the rural population systematically evaded paying.[54]

The continuation of slavery into the twentieth century was to create lasting division between those of free and unfree status, which was almost as important as the distinction made by the Portuguese between *indígena* and *não indígena* and was to stand in the way of effective nation-building after independence.

The infrastructure of a modern economy

Under pressure from its European rivals to establish effective control in its colonies and to promote 'civilisation' and economic development, all Portuguese governments had as their central objective the creation of a modern state with an economy tuned to the needs of the mother country. However, agreement about how this was to be achieved and the resources to bring it about were usually lacking.

The need to improve infrastructure was the one area of policy that did command almost universal agreement. Railway building had opened up the interior of North America and fuelled the growth of its economy. Angola had been closely linked to the Atlantic world since the sixteenth century and it was only to be expected that the technological change that was transforming the Atlantic economies

54 Linda Heywood, *Contested Power in Angola, 1840s to the present*, p. 38.

would soon change Angola as well. Steam navigation had been introduced on the Kwanza in the 1860s to serve the towns of the Afro-Portuguese coastal state[55] but serious railway investment in southern Africa only began with the discovery of diamonds in 1867. Angola then found itself strategically placed since a railway to its ports would cut the sea journey from the interior of southern Africa to Europe by thousands of miles.

Plans for a transcontinental railway to give effect to the dream of the *contra costa* were drawn up and the grandly named Real Companhia de Caminha de Ferro Através de Africa began construction in 1885 from Luanda.[56] In 1902, in the teeth of opposition from King Leopold, the Germans, the BSA Company and even the British Colonial Office, Robert Williams, one of the founders of Union Minière, obtained a license to build a railway and telegraph from Benguela to Katanga—a concession which included mineral prospecting rights and commercial privileges extending 120 kilometres each side of the line.[57] The concession was granted rapidly and secretly. It was seen by the Portuguese as a demonstration of its independence from both Britain and Germany since this railway, owned by a British company, would run through the part of Angola allocated to Germany in the secret Anglo-German agreement of 1898.[58]

A third railway was planned to link the mines in German South-West Africa to the port at Moçamedes, but the Germans eventually decided to build their own line. However, work began in 1905 on a railway from Moçamedes to the Huila highlands, which it only reached in 1923.

55 D. Wheeler and R. Pélissier, *Angola* London: Pall Mall Press, 1971, p. 68.

56 Henrique Galvão and Carlos Selvagem, *Império Ultramarino Portuguese,* 4 vols. Lisbon: Empresa Nacional de Publicidade, 1952 vol 3, 283; W.G. Clarence-Smith, *The Third Portuguese Empire 1825-1975,* Manchester: Manchester University Press, Manchester, 1985, pp. 98-9.

57 S.E. Katzenellenbogen, *Railways and the Copper mines of Katanga,* Oxford: Clarendon Press, 1973, pp. 39-41.

58 Robert Hutchinson and George Martelli, *Robert's People,* London Chatto and Windus, 1971. pp. 146-7.

The opening of the interior of Angola proceeded slowly. The railway from Luanda only reached Malanje in 1919 and Robert Williams's railway did not arrive in the central highlands until 1911. Nevertheless, as had happened in the United States, the railways brought with them economic change. Whereas access to the highlands had been restricted to traditional caravans of porters or Boer ox carts, it was now possible to bring goods and people in large quantities up the rail from the new port at Lobito. As the line advanced, the colonisation of the interior proceeded apace and the Portuguese began to construct the first major inland city at Huambo (later called Nova Lisboa). From there roads were engineered across the plateau and in the second decade of the century lorries, for the most part owned and operated by Portuguese from the coast, began to replace the carriers who had operated the transport system for centuries.[59]

The economic ideas prevailing in the 1890s were strongly protectionist. The colonies were seen as markets for metropolitan produce—especially textiles and wines—in return for which they would produce tropical raw materials for consumption in Portugal and for re-export to earn foreign exchange. The north of Angola formed part of the basin of the Congo where duties were controlled by international agreement, but in 1892 a general tariff was introduced by the Portuguese government which affected the whole of the rest of the colony. The tariff gave Angolan exporters preference in the Portuguese market for their coffee, sugar and cotton and effectively excluded foreign imports, the most dramatic effects being felt in the textile sector. By the end of the 1890s, 94 per cent of Angola's imports of bleached cottons came from Portugal. Angola was beginning to experience the unifying force of centrally directed policy and law.[60]

59 Linda Heywood, *Contested Power in Angola, 1840s to the present*, 439-40; for an account of the last days of head portage and the early years of the Benguela railway see Malcolm Burr, *A Fossicker in Angola,* London: Figurehead, 1933.

60 W.G. Clarence-Smith, *The Third Portuguese Empire 1825-1975,* 1985, p. 91.

The conflict between the Portuguese administration and the Afro-Portuguese

Prior to the Berlin Conference the elite of the coastal settlements of Luanda, Benguela and Moçamedes had primarily been made up of two groups: a small number of transient Portuguese and Brazilian businessmen or administrators, who seldom settled in Angola for long, and the Afro-Portuguese families, who were overwhelmingly dominant in the church, trade and farming and in the administration and the military at the local level. Douglas Wheeler described the capital as 'creole Luanda—an African town, patrolled by African police, protected by an African army, repaired and waited on by African workmen.'[61]

However, the economic position of the Afro-Portuguese had been steadily undermined since the abolition of the slave trade, and after 1885 there was growing tension between them and the settlers and administrators from Portugal—tension that was exacerbated by the international rivalries of the Scramble for Africa period.[62] The British and Germans made no secret of their contempt for Portugal's colonising efforts, and there was increasing pressure on Portugal to demonstrate that it could emulate its two big neighbours in directly controlling its territory and in promoting 'civilisation in darkest Africa'. It was this that persuaded the Lisbon government to undertake expensive wars of 'pacification' and to pursue a settlement policy, which it was intended would gradually replace the dominant Afro-Portuguese with a European population.

Attracting white settlers, however, proved far from easy. Sending convicts to Angola had the predictable consequence of creating a white criminal class. According to Paiva Couceiro, a quarter of the white population of Luanda in the first decade of the twentieth century were convicts or ex-convicts 'whose penury of various kinds has driven onto the pavements of the public square… a large body of

61 Douglas Wheeler and René Pélissier, *Angola,* p. 70.

62 Jill Dias, 'Uma questão de identidade: Respostas intelectuais às transformações económicas no seio da elite crioula da Angola portuguesa entre 1870 e 1930', *Revista Internacional de Estudos Africanos,* 1, 1984.

people showing the most pitiful moral and material misery.'[63] Meanwhile government-sponsored settlement schemes, such as those that brought 1,500 Madeirans to the Huila highlands in the late 1880s, tended to fail since the immigrants had few skills and no capital.[64] They lived in extreme poverty, left the land to work as petty traders and run stores or joined the shiftless unemployed in the towns. The poor fishermen who tried to make a living off the southern coast only survived because the government prevented the introduction of motorised fishing vessels, which would have driven them out of business.[65] The other identifiable groups of whites in Angola included the missionaries—mostly British or American Baptists and Methodists who were felt to be hostile to the Portuguese—and the Boers of the Huila highlands. Those Europeans who did settle in Angola concentrated in the towns and by the end of the Republic in 1926, it was estimated that two thirds of the total European population of the central highlands (estimated at 5,268) lived in the single city of Huambo.[66]

Although the efforts to build up a white population met with only limited success, the colonisation schemes were accompanied by a marked change in colonial ideology. The Afro-Portuguese who had for so long sustained the economic and political life of the coastal cities, and who had at one time been lauded as the principal defenders of the worldwide Portuguese empire, were now denounced as degenerates. In a paper published in 1902, F.X. da Silva Teles maintained (as summarised by Rosa Williams) that 'secure racial superiority is disrupted by the silent, implicit threat of African women diluting Portuguese blood and the explicit threat of pollution from an Af-

63 Henrique de Paiva Couceiro, *Angola: dois annos de governo junho 1907-junho 1908*, p. 162.

64 W.G. Clarence-Smith, *Slaves, Peasants and Capitalists in Southern Angola 1840-1926*, p. 44-5.

65 W.G. Clarence-Smith, *Slaves, Peasants and Capitalists in Southern Angola 1840-1926*, p. 29; Gerald Bender, *Angola under the Portuguese* London: Heinemann, 1978, Chapters 3 and 4.

66 Linda Heywood, *Contested Power in Angola, 1840s to the present*, p. 47.

rican physical and cultural environment.'[67] They were increasingly excluded from the colonial civil service and from higher positions in the army and local government. Their economic status also deteriorated as the railways, steamers and lorries gradually replaced the old trade caravans. Moreover, Portuguese preferences and tariff policies favoured metropolitan interests at the expense of the local economy (for example, Portuguese wine over locally produce rum). By 1910 the old Afro-Portuguese families were being marginalised and forced to earn their living in more and more menial ways.[68]

This decline in status found full expression in the press where journalists from the leading Afro-Portuguese families gave vent to their resentment against the colonial government. The most famous of these was José de Fontes Pereira who in 1873 began writing for the republican newspaper *O Cruzeiro do Sul*, published in Luanda. Fontes Pereira died in 1891 but ten years later there appeared a collection of articles written by Afro-Portuguese journalists, entitled *Voz d'Angola clamando no deserto,* which voiced trenchant criticism of Portugal's colonial failures.[69] These writings became of great significance and were frequently evoked when the Afro-Portuguese began to organise politically to expel the Portuguese in the 1960s and 1970s.

The position of the Afro-Portuguese was threatened from another direction as the urbanised and educated African population began to grow. Africans educated in the missions now competed for urban employment alongside the poor white immigrants and the Afro-Portuguese. A strict application of a colour bar was not only against

67 Rosa Williams, 'Migration and Miscegenation: maintaining boundaries of whiteness in the narratives of the Angolan colonial state 1875-1912', in Philip J.Havik and Malyn Newitt eds, *Creole Societies in the Portuguese Colonial Empire,* Bristol University (2007).

68 Jill Dias, 'Uma questão de identidade: Respostas intelectuais às transformações económicas no seio da elite crioula da Angola portuguesa entre 1870 e 1930', *Revista Internacional de Estudos Africanos,* 1 1984.

69 Douglas Wheeler, 'Origins of African Nationalism in Angola: Assimilado Protest Writings, 1859-1929', Ronald Chilcote ed., *Protest and Resistance in Angola and Brazil,* London: University of California Press. 1972, pp. 67-87.

Portuguese law and tradition but would have been impractical in the face of the realities of colonial family structures. However, the colonial government introduced a distinction between *indígena* and *não indígena*—native and non-native. The native would live by African custom, would be ruled by traditional chiefs and would be subject to the labour laws of the colony. The *não indígena* would be treated as a civilised Portuguese citizen. The government needed to have a workable system for deciding when an African could be included in this category and, as a result, adopted the French practice of assimilation. To become an *assimilado* a person had to display stipulated levels of education, Portuguese culture and economic independence, criteria that could be raised or lowered to regulate admission into the colonial elite.

The assimilation policy, codified in 1954 before being abolished in 1961, had far reaching consequences for the development of Angola. Virtually all Afro-Portuguese were accorded this status and by 1960 there were also about 50,000 Africans who were classified as *assimilados*. These formed a narrow educated elite, clearly separated by upbringing, legal status and opportunity from the majority of the population. As many commentators have pointed out, the leadership of the nationalist movements came overwhelmingly from this group, so that the colonial social distinctions were perpetuated in the post-colonial social formation of the country.

Republican Angola

Under the Monarchy government policy had lacked coherent central direction and was limited to protective tariffs, the creation of economic infrastructure and the encouragement of white settlement. The Republicans had more ambitious plans for the colonies and with the arrival of José de Norton de Matos as Governor-General in 1912 Angola was to experience a co-ordinated drive for modernisation. Norton de Matos was determined to impose effective central government throughout the country and to deal with the arbitrary implementation of the labour laws.

The labour question had by this time come to dominate discussions on colonial policy. Whereas the white settlers believed that only vigorous coercive measures would bring the African onto the labour market, there was a growing body of opinion in Portugal and abroad that called for the end of forced labour. In 1910 slavery was once again formally abolished and in most areas there was an almost seamless transition to a system of forced contract labour which replaced the slave with the *serviçal*. In 1911 a set of laws was drawn up to regulate the labour regime in Angola. All Africans were obliged either to work as *voluntários* for a private employer or to risk being forcibly contracted by the government. The government also reserved to itself the right to impose penal labour and to recruit unpaid *corvée* labour for public works like road building.

Like his immediate predecessor, Norton de Matos wanted to end the reliance on unfree labour, which had characterised socio-economic relations for centuries. He began to enforce the regulations that prohibited the re-contracting of workers (a practice which amounted to a continuation of slavery) and allowed Africans to seek their own employers. His aim was to move to a completely free, market-driven, labour regime. In typically confident and assertive manner he described this as 'a veritable revolution in the labour regime' and claimed that, with the exception of those that were effectively bankrupt, all plantations now had more labour than before.[70] He also abolished compulsory service in the militia and in 1912 prohibited the importation or possession of firearms. He was to claim that 250,000 trade guns were handed in as a result of this policy.[71]

Traditional African society proved able to adjust to the labour demands of the state. Under the Monarchy and Republic there was no attempt to evict African peasants from their land, the device which was used in Rhodesia and South Africa to force Africans onto the labour market, because the demand for *serviçal* labour was largely

70 Major Norton de Matos, *A situação financeira e economica da Provincia de Angola,* Lisbon: Tipografia da Coop Militar, 1914, p. 26-28.

71 René Pélissier, *Les Guerres Grises*, p. 183.

met from among former slaves or unfree members of lineages—the same groups which had been vulnerable during the days of the Atlantic slave trade. The free members of the lineages were, for the most part, successful in evading labour service. As late as 1924, for example, it was estimated that in the central highlands only 30 per cent of the eligible population were being recruited into the colonial economy.[72] In the south, when slavery gave way to wage labour on the plantations and fisheries, it was again the former slave population (numbering in 1913 some 10,000) which provided the bulk of the contracted labour.[73] On the supply side, there was no shortage of unfree labour as the effects of droughts in 1913-16 and 1924-5 drove many to the last resort of enslaving themselves.[74]

Norton de Matos also pressed for greater autonomy for the colonial government. The Republicans wanted to reverse the centralising tendencies of the Monarchy and planned to grant each colony a *Carta Constitucional*, which in the case of Angola was published in 1913 but not implemented until after the War. The Charter specified that Angola was to be governed by a High Commissioner, who would control the colonial budgets and would be able to pass local laws governing such issues as native policy, white immigration, land and labour. He was also permitted to raise loans and implement development plans. However, little was done to set up representative institutions and in practice the High Commissioners became pocket dictators who remained deeply suspicious of the white settlers and *assimilados* who might have been their natural allies.

The first High Commissioner was Norton de Matos, who returned to Angola in 1921 determined to push ahead with rapid modernisation and economic expansion. This was to take the form of increased white immigration, a speeded up policy of infrastructure development and the encouragement of the plantation sector, all to

72 Linda Heywood, *Contested Power in Angola, 1840s to the present*, p. 46.

73 W.G. Clarence-Smith, *Slaves, peasants and capitalists in southern Angola 1840-1926*, p. 33.

74 Linda Heywood, *Contested Power in Angola, 1840s to the present*, p. 44.

be paid for by loans and deficit spending. Unknown to him a large part of the private investment reaching Angola came through the bank founded by Alves Reis on the back of his massive forgery of Portuguese banknotes! In 1921 the High Commissioner granted a monopoly over diamond prospecting and extraction to Diamang, a company with Belgian, South African and French capital that had been mining diamonds in the East of Angola since 1916. In return for allowing the Angolan government 40 per cent of the profits, Diamang effectively became a chartered company controlling the policing, administration and provision of services in the Lunda province. In 1924 it took over the prospecting rights of the Moçamedes Company in the south as well.[75]

Postwar Portugal suffered from hyper-inflation and from severe financing problems stemming from budget deficits. Norton de Matos's profligate policies launched Angola into a giddy downward spiral of debt and inflation, which threatened to engulf the country before any of the putative beneficial effects of his economic policies could be felt.

The New State

The New State came into existence after the generals who overthrew the Republic in May 1926 handed over control of the government to civilian politicians headed by António Salazar. After 1929 the economies of Europe and its colonies suffered the devastating effects of the Great Depression and the New State was designed to insulate Portugal and its colonies from the effects of the global economic cycles. Salazar also made much of the chaotic history of the Republic while he stole many of the Republican clothes, particularly in the field of colonial policy.

The New State was formed by a series of constitutional laws between 1930 and 1933, the most important of which was the Colonial

75 W.G. Clarence Smith, *The Third Portuguese Empire*, pp. 129-130; A.B.Hutchinson, *Report on the Economic Situation in Angola*, London: Department of Overseas Trade, 1925, pp. 11-13.

Act. Salazar envisaged the colonies and Portugal forming a single state, which would constitute, if not a great power, then certainly a world power of the second rank. He was determined that this world-wide Portuguese state would be as free as possible from what he saw as the bullying of the great powers and he set out systematically to limit the influence of foreign capital—most notably in Mozambique where the British-owned charter companies were returned to state control and strict conditions were imposed on other foreign-owned businesses. To avoid being blown off course by financial crises, as had so often happened to the Republic, Salazar planned to make 'greater Portugal' as independent as possible of international investment or loan finance. Portugal and the colonies had to live within their means and finance development from their own resources—an objective to which many former colonies were to aspire in the immediate aftermath of independence.

However, Salazar always tempered his dislike of foreign capital with a realism born of the need to earn foreign exchange and have friends in the international capital markets when these should be needed. He never seriously interfered with the WNLA's recruitment of Mozambican labourers to work in the mines of South Africa, with the Diamang mining concession in eastern Angola or with the Benguela railway that had finally been connected to the Katanga copper mines in 1930. These companies were exempted from foreign exchange controls.[76]

Putting an end to the autonomy which had been enjoyed by the Angolan High Commissioners was the first priority. Budgets and development plans now had to be approved in Lisbon and strict financial controls were imposed to eliminate deficits and to create a central foreign exchange fund overseen by the government. Large cuts were made in capital expenditure and imports whilst financial support for white immigration was withdrawn. A new currency unit, the Angolar, was introduced to end the depreciation of the existing currency.

76 W.G. Clarence-Smith, *The Third Portuguese Empire*, p. 147.

Salazar also created a professional colonial civil service with proper supervision and line management, whose personnel replaced locally recruited whites and Afro-Portuguese—thereby removing one of the levers of power which might have remained in the hands of the Angolan settlers. Although provision was made for a Legislative Council to advise the governor, this was effectively made up of nominees and did not provide the Angolan *civilizados* with any institutional framework to pursue their own political interests. Here there is a marked contrast with the situation in the neighbouring British colony of Southern Rhodesia, which had approximately the same number of white settlers. In 1923 the Rhodesians were granted internal self-government and were able to take control of the civil service and the local defence forces.

Salazar's colonial service began the process of bureaucratising life in Angola and in the process succeeded in paralysing any form of local initiative. Henrique Galvão and Carlos Selvagem, writing in 1952, counted twenty-seven separate government departments and complained of the 'corruption that spreads among this group [of colonial bureaucrats] the low level of whose salaries is the cause of a mental and professional mediocrity.' Bureaucratic centralisation was to be one of the legacies passed on by Salazarism to independent Angola. Nothing could be done without complicated, inefficient and intrusive administrative procedures, which stifled local initiative without creating the dynamism that might have resulted from central control and direction.

Galvão also commented on the steady destruction of African authority in the countryside: 'It is one of the most serious mistakes in Angolan native policy of recent years to have favoured the destruction (*pulverização)* of the *sobas* and to have hastened the decline in prestige of the native chiefs.'[77] Nevertheless, although the Portuguese were careful to recognise only those *sobas* who were deemed loyal to the regime, the traditional authorities remained indispensable to the

77 Henrique Galvão and Carlos Selvagem, *Imperio Ultramarino Português,* Vol 3, pp. 213, 230, 236.

New State. They were to play a key role in the final decade of colonial rule and in the post-independence period, creating direct links back to the pre-colonial era of African political life.[78]

Having restored its control over the colony, the New State began to develop a coherent economic strategy, which would integrate the colonies and the mother country in a closed economic system designed to repair the damage caused by the Great Depression. This policy built on the ineffectual experiments of the Monarchy and the Republic. The production of raw materials in the colonies was to be encouraged through a system of guaranteed prices and quotas, which assured access to a captive Lisbon market. In return the colonies were expected to import manufactured goods from Portugal and to pay for any deficit on the balance of trade by remitting hard currency to the mother country.[79]

To ensure the success of this policy labour had to be made available for the increased production of palm oil, maize, cotton, sugar and coffee, which were to be the main contributions of Angola to the colonial project, and local officials were once again allowed to recruit for private employers. Salazar believed that the past failures of colonial agriculture had been the result of fluctuations in world market prices. He now resolved to fix the prices paid for colonial produce centrally in order to achieve stability. During the 1930s institutions were set up to co-ordinate the production and marketing of these crops and to improve quality. Maize, for example, came under the supervision of the Grêmio do Milho Colonial and the Junta de Exportação dos Cereais. Between 1926 and 1960 maize exports from Angola rose by over 300 per cent. [80] In some areas the local population were required to produce quotas of cotton and by 1945, 90,000 peasants were involved in cotton production. However, this

78 Linda Heywood, *Contested Power in Angola, 1840s to the Present,* pp. 85-6.

79 For the working of this policy see W.G. Clarence-Smith, *The Third Portuguese Empire,* Chapter 6.

80 Linda Heywood, *Contested Power in Angola, 1840s to the Present,* pp. 72, 81.

was only ten percent of the number growing cotton in Mozambique and Angola was never as large a producer as its sister colony.[81] In the Malanje province the marketing of cotton was entrusted to a monopolistic company, Cotonang. The unpopularity of forced cotton growing was said to have speeded up the rate at which peasants left the land to seek employment in the towns or in neighbouring Belgian Congo. In spite of the increased output across all the major agricultural sectors, Galvão summed up the effects of twenty years of Salazarist policies in his usual epigrammatic style—'*Angola produz caro e produz mal.*'[82]

The policy pursued by the New State was very similar to that followed by many other societies in the transition from a peasant-based subsistence economy to large scale commodity production. The peasant economy was left largely untouched to support the reproductive costs of the population and to provide a refuge for the old, sick and disabled so that their costs did not have to be borne by the modern sector of the economy. As a result the Angolan peasants largely kept possession of their land, which continued to be allocated and farmed in traditional ways. Peasant society was then expected to provide surplus labour for the capital sector and to pay taxes to support the government. In other words, the modernisation of the economy was, to a substantial extent, to be paid for by the peasant community. 'Portuguese capitalism was nurtured on the labor and agricultural surplus of the African people'.[83] Taxes paid by the African peasant, for example, were made to form an ever increasing proportion of Angola's revenue and in 1948 constituted as much as 68 per cent.[84] This, of course, was the policy advocated in the Communist Eastern Bloc countries and, after independence, continued to be the strategy

81 Antonio Carreira, *Angola: da Escravatura ao Trabalho Livre,* Lisbon: Arcádia, 1977, p. 149.

82 Henrique Galvão and Carlos Selvagem, *Imperio Ultramarino Português,* Vol 3, p. 300.

83 Linda Heywood, *Contested Power in Angola, 1840s to the Present,* p. 63.

84 Linda Heywood, *Contested Power in Angola, 1840s to the Present,* p. 73.

pursued by many African countries (for example Mozambique) in their attempt to accelerate modernisation.[85]

Towards the end of the 1930s, strict mercantilism was adjusted to aid the creation of a modern industrial and market-based economy, though the Second World War prevented the full effects of this change in policy from becoming apparent until after 1945. At the end of the war restrictions on foreign capital began to be removed and permission was granted for limited industrialisation. This was a prelude to the first of the five year Development Plans (published in 1953), covering both Portugal and its colonies. These policy changes produced a rapid and far-reaching transformation of Angola, which by the 1960s had one of the most dynamic economies in Africa. Driving this economic expansion were the state investments in infrastructure, in particular road and port construction and the building of dams for irrigation and hydro-electric power. Between 1954 and the end of colonial rule five major hydro-electric dam complexes were constructed from the Kwanza in the north to the Kunene in the south.[86]

Large concessions were also made to attract investment into the plantation sector. These were the years of the coffee boom with Angola's production rising from 53,400 tons in 1948 to 79,600 tons in 1958, when coffee plantations covered a quarter of a million hectares.[87] Angolan coffee, which was of excellent quality, was a major earner of foreign exchange and Angola rose to become the world's fourth biggest producer. In 1955 coffee constituted 45.5 per cent of Angola's total exports.[88] Table 1 shows the growth of coffee exports.

---

85 Elisete Marques da Silva, 'O Papel Societal do Sistema de Ensino na Angola Colonial (1926-1974)' paper presented at the II Colóquio Internacional em Ciências Sociais sobre África de Lingua Oficial Portuguesa, Bissau, 1991, pp. 3-4.

86 D.M. Abshire and M.A. Samuels, *Portuguese Africa: a Handbook,* London: Pall Mall, 1969, p. 302.

87 Linda Heywood, *Contested Power in Angola, 1840s to the Present*, p. 67.

88 Fernando Andresen Guimarães, *The Origins of the Angolan Civil War*, London: St Martins Press, 1998, p. 21.

This great expansion was mainly achieved by outside investment in large coffee estates but, even at the height of the coffee boom, there was always a significant number of African farmers. The growing of coffee required large inputs of labour and this led to an unprecedented mobility in the labour market. Substantial numbers of migrant workers came north from the central highlands to work in the coffee producing regions where their presence was deeply resented by the local peasant population—a factor considered by David Birmingham to be a major element in the outbreak of rebellion in the north in 1961.[89]

Table 1
Coffee Exports from Angola

Year	tons	% of total exports
1948	53.4	30.9
1952	47.7	41.3
1955	60.1	45.5
1958	79.6	41.7
1961	118.1	36.1
1964	138.7	48.7
1967	196.5	51.9
1970	180.6	31.9

Source: Fernando Andresen Guimarães, *The Origins of the Angolan Civil War*, p. 21

Perhaps most impressive of all was the industrial expansion. Textile production had begun in the 1940s and this was followed by cement and then by a wide range of consumer industries. By the mid-1960s Angola was processing most of the food crops produced in the country and supported a range of consumer industries including tobacco, beverages, soap, paper, motor tyres, bricks, glass, plastics, rubber and

89 Fernando Andresen Guimarães, *The Origins of the Angolan Civil War*, p. 21; David Birmingham, 'Angola' in Patrick Chabal, *A History of Postcolonial Lusophone Africa*, London: Hurst, 2002, p. 140.

electrical products. There were car and bus assembly plants, steel and aluminium factories—all designed to save imports, to meet the demands of the local market or to earn foreign exchange.

While diamond mining continued to grow, with output rising by 50 per cent between 1957 and 1967, it was oil production that experienced the most impressive growth. In 1955 the first crude oil was exported from Luanda and in the next decade a refinery was built to supply Angola with fuel. The massive Cabindan oilfields were brought into production by Gulf Oil.

The growth of the Angolan economy was such that by the end of the colonial era it had reached the 'take off point' beloved of classical economists. Angola had impressive foreign exchange earnings, supplied most of its local food and consumer needs, was self-sufficient in energy and had an economy that was impressively diversified between the various sectors. However, although foreign investment had played a major role, the Portuguese state had always controlled a major part of the economy. As Frank Brandenburg pointed out in 1969 'most basic transportation and communication facilities—roads and railroads, airports and local airlines, port facilities, telephone and telegraph—along with municipal services and some electric-power generation and distribution facilities are now under state ownership'.[90] Moreover, the state had invested in the oil industry through the Petrangol Company and still planned to provide 60 per cent of investment scheduled by the development plans. The government of independent Angola inherited an economy in which the state had a very large stake. The temptation to use the state owned enterprises as sources of revenue and patronage was not resisted, with the result that a once strong and diversified economy was reduced to ruin in only two or three years.

As the modern sector of the economy expanded, the demand for labour increased. The practices pursued in the early part of the cen-

90 Frank Brandenburg, 'Development Finance and Trade' in D.M. Abshire and M.A. Samuels, *Portuguese Africa: a Handbook*, London: Pall Mall, 1969. pp. 221-2.

tury, which had made forced contract labour little better than slavery, had been modified by Republican legislation. Under the New State, however, there was renewed pressure to make sure that the African population fulfilled its obligation to work. These pressures were felt particularly in the central highlands, which were the most densely populated part of the country. In the 1930s about 15 per cent of the adult male population had been regularly contracted but after the war this rose rapidly until in the late 1950s up to 80 per cent were migrants working on the railways, coffee plantations and fisheries.[91] By this time there was some substance to Galvão's famous statement that 'only the dead are really exempt from contract labour.'[92] Large numbers also went to work on the copper belt.

Galvão and Selvagem, in their mordant criticism of the Portuguese regime in Angola, called this a 'demographic haemorrhage' and added 'the inhabitants of Mozambique emigrate; those of Angola flee'.[93] They pointed to the depopulation, particularly of the frontier regions, which registered losses of between 16 and 22 per cent between the 1940 and 1950 censuses. Luanda, by contrast, had grown by 152 per cent.[94] Population mobility on this scale was to lead locally to severe communal tension between black and white but also between different African ethnic groups. Largely unperceived by the Portuguese, the social components of civil war were falling into place. 'The virulence of rivalry between different colonial peoples with different experiences of exploitation was profoundly rational and economic …The bitterness ran so deep that although the diverse peoples of the north, and the many peoples of the south, both became deeply hostile to the Mbundu of central Angola and their

91 Linda Heywood, *Contested Power in Angola, 1840s to the Present,* p. 75.

92 Henrique Galvão, *The Santa Maria: My Crusade for Portugal,* London: Weidenfeld and Nicolson 1961, p. 52.

93 Henrique Galvão and Carlos Selvagem, *Imperio Ultramarino Português,* Vol 4, p. 132.

94 Henrique Galvão and Carlos Selvagem, *Imperio Ultramarino Português,* Vol 3, p. 212.

powerful cousins in the city of Luanda, north and south were never able to collaborate effectively.'[95]

From the mid-1930s white immigration was once again promoted by the government as a way of expanding the modern sector of the economy, although this policy was influenced by the ideological preoccupations of Salazar who entertained fantasies of establishing a rural peasantry similar to that in Portugal. However, immigration from Portugal remained modest until the end of the war (when the white population of Angola stood at 44,000). The development plans of the 1950s set aside huge investment funds to promote *colonatos*, rural farming settlements such as Cela in the central highlands. Although these *colonatos* proved only modestly successful, and were very costly, there was nevertheless a rapid increase in the white population, most of which settled in the towns. During the 1950s the white urban population grew by over 70 per cent, so that in 1960 Huambo had a white population of 28,000 while Benguela and Lobito had 10,474 and 24,000 respectively.[96] Between 1960 and 1973 the white population doubled again and, although most of the immigrants were at best semi-skilled, their arrival in Angola had the effect of denying opportunities to upwardly mobile Afro-Portuguese and *assimilados*, thereby accentuating racial tensions.

Table 2
White population of Angola

1900	9,198
1920	20,700
1940	44,083
1950	78,826
1960	172,529
1970	290,000

95 David Birmingham, 'Angola' in Patrick Chabal, *A History of Postcolonial Lusophone Africa*, pp. 140-1.

96 Linda Heywood, *Contested Power in Angola, 1840s to the Present*, p. 69.

1973	335,000

Source: G. Bender, *Angola under the Portuguese: the Myth and the Reality*, London: Heinemann, 1978, p. 20.

Social development—the missions and education

Until the end of the 1950s the people of Angola formed two parallel societies engaged in two parallel economies. The majority were born and lived most of their lives in traditional lineage-based communities, supported by subsistence farming. They remained subject to traditional African custom administered by African authorities, even when they performed contract labour or when they made the formal step of conversion to Christianity. Alongside traditional society were the towns with their urbanised population, the plantations and the industrial enterprises designed to serve the towns and to produce raw materials for export. The bridge between the two worlds was often provided by the missions.

Protestant missions had worked in Angola since the late 1870s and, as in other parts of Africa, provided a means, at first limited but later increasingly effective, by which some Africans were able to gain the education and skills which helped them to adjust to the changes that were affecting their societies. Initially, the activities of the missions were encouraged by the Portuguese who saw in them instruments for achieving the social and economic transformation of the colony. In 1914, for example, Norton de Matos provided land in the highlands to build the Currie Institute, which attracted children from many of the traditional Ovimbundu elite families. By the 1920s the Protestant churches in the central highlands ran 26 missions and 215 rural schools.[97] The missions not only trained young men and women in the skills of a modern society but played a major part in creating a new identity. The missionaries had turned the Umbundu dialects into a written language, which was taught in their schools, and by the 1920s

97 Linda Heywood, *Contested Power in Angola, 1840s to the Present*, p. 53; for the history of the Protestant Missions see John Tucker, *Angola: the Land of the Blacksmith Prince*, London: World Dominion Press, 1933.

it was common for people in the highlands to refer to themselves, using this linguistic term, as Ovimbundu.

By the 1920s the Republican authorities, whose anticlerical zeal had led to the suppression of the Catholic missions, were becoming increasingly alarmed at the Protestant influence. Protestant converts were frequently targeted by the administration for forced labour or army recruitment and in 1922 the missions themselves were subjected to strong administrative controls. Teaching now had to be conducted in Portuguese, the use of African languages in schools was prohibited and 'the use of native languages, in writing, or of any other but Portuguese in tracts, newspapers, leaflets or manuscripts of any kind is forbidden.' All African teachers had to be licensed by the authorities and had to speak Portuguese. In consequence many small rural schools run by Ovimbundo teachers were closed. In 1938 the government ordered that qualified Portuguese staff should be employed by the schools of the Protestant missions to teach Portuguese language because 'foreign mission stations tend to introduce non-Portuguese characteristics and ... do not maintain close contact with the Portuguese population'. [98] This official pressure only enhanced the prestige of the Protestant churches, membership of which was increasingly seen by the Africans themselves as a form of opposition to the demands of the state.[99]

It may have been a desire to counter the influence of the Protestant missions that persuaded Lisbon to undertake a major reform of education in 1927. This was based on a '*dicotomía funcional*' between education for *civilizados*, which had as its objective the '*unidade intellectual e moral da Nação Portuguesa*, and education for the rest, which was 'to spread among the savage peoples (*povoados selvagens*), the natives, the best precepts of morality and hygiene and the knowledge of

98 Decree 77 9 December 1921 in *Provincia de Angola. Providencias tomadas pelo General J.M.R.Norton de Matos, como Alto Comissário da República e Governador Geral* Lisbon, Sociedade Nacional de Tipografia, 1922, pp. 202-4. Translation from HM Consul to Secretary of State Luanda 5 Jan, 1939. National Archives (London) FO371 24070.

99 Linda Heywood, *Contested Power in Angola, 1840s to the present*, pp. 57-9.

our language, and to teach them a trade which will make them useful to themselves and to the colony.'[100]

In practice educational provision developed very slowly, largely because the New State thought in terms of providing for the skilled and professional needs of the colonies through immigration from Portugal. The growth of school attendance by *civilizados* is shown in Table 3. From these figures it is clear that education was only seriously developed during the 1950s when white immigration was rapid and the expanding economy needed skilled workers. Educational opportunities for whites and *civilizados* in Angola soon became superior to the opportunities available in metropolitan Portugal.[101]

Education for those who did not have *civilizado* status was confined to the mission schools until the 1940s when a system of elementary schools run by the Catholic church was established. In 1959/60, 68,960 children attended primary school (16,400 of them Protestant mission schools). The same year the church claimed that 279,110 children attended catechism schools. Less than 5 per cent of the pupils attending primary schools reached the fourth class and in 1950 it was estimated that less than 1 per cent could read.[102]

Table 3
School attendance in Angola

		Civilizados (primary)	
	1929/30	1949/50	1959/60
Public	3,653	7,403	19,338
Private		3,054	15,729
%white		48*	
%mestizo		31*	

100 Quoted in Elisete Marques da Silva, 'O Papel societal do sistema de ensino na Angola (1926-1974)', pp. 7-8.

101 Elisete Marques da Silva, 'O Papel societal do sistema de ensino na Angola (1926-1974)' p. 10.

102 Figures from Elisete Marques da Silva, 'O Papel societal do sistema de ensino na Angola (1926-1974)', pp. 8-10.

% black		21*	
		Civilizados (secondary)	
Public	333	920	7,752
Private		1,256	3,084
%white			80
%mestizo			17
%black			3
		Civilizados (technical and seminary)	
Public and church			10,836

* figures refer to 1951/2

Source: Elisete Marques da Silva, 'O Papel societal do sistema de ensino na Angola (1926-1974)', pp. 7-9.

Religious and Political movements

Conversion to Christianity offered Angolans of all classes new perspectives and new opportunities. As the role played in daily affairs by ancestral and territorial cults inevitably declined in a more modern society, Angolans were increasingly drawn to other forms of religious expression. The Protestant missions had appeared in parts of the country long before there was any effective colonial rule and often seemed to be very much at odds with the Portuguese authorities. Moreover, in the mission churches Angolans often found ways of reconstituting a close-knit and supportive community in the otherwise alienating environment of the towns and cities.

In the Kongo region there was a long history of prophetic movements, many of which had shown a degree of syncretism. Indeed Christianity, which had been implanted at the end of the fifteenth century, had been adapted by local devotees to Kongolese notions of the spirit world. In the early part of the twentieth century two important religious movements arose among Christian converts in the Belgian Congo, which proved especially attractive to exiles and migrant workers from the northern Kikongo-speaking regions of Angola.

The movement founded by Simon Kimbangu was an offshoot of Baptist missionary activity. Kimbangu taught at one of the mission schools and received his first call during the influenza epidemic of 1918. From the first his church, which was founded in 1921, was focused on the healing powers of Kimbangu himself.[103] Simon Toko was a teacher in the Baptist mission of Kibokolo in northern Angola and his church was much influenced by both the Baptists and the Jehovah's Witnesses. Sometime around 1943 he went to Léopoldville and there formed his own group of followers. He and the members of his nascent church were expelled by the Belgian authorities in 1950 and on their return to Angola were dispersed throughout the country—a measure which had the effect of disseminating their influence more rapidly.

From that time the Tokoist church grew rapidly in numbers, appealing to the young *déracinés* Angolans in the cities. Tokoism emphasised a split between the world of politics and the world of religion and encouraged its followers to concentrate on a religious life and on religious values. Although Toko never espoused African nationalism, and ordered his followers not to resist the colonial authorities, the existence of his church as an independent and nationwide organisation, not under the supervision or control of the Portuguese authorities, was seen as highly threatening, and Toko himself was exiled to the Azores.[104] The influence of the independent churches was clearly apparent in the early stages of the insurrection in the north of Angola in 1961.

Ever since the Concordat of 1940, the Catholic church had acted very much as an arm of the state, particularly in the development of education for the mass of the population. However, Catholicism, like Protestantism, can encourage the emergence of radical ideas and

---

103 Marie-Louise Martin, *Kimbangu: An Africa Prophet and his Church*, Oxford: Basil Blackwell, 1975.

104 Alfredo Margarido, 'The Tokoist Church and Portuguese Colonialism in Angola', in Ronald H. Chilcote ed., *Protest and Resistance in Angola and Brazil,* Berkeley and London: University of California Press, 1972, pp. 29-52

resistance to the state. In 1960 there were 64 African priests in Angola and after the uprising of February 1961 in Luanda nine of these were arrested by the PIDE, including Joaquim Pinto de Andrade, whose brother was one of the founders of the MPLA.[105]

There had always been opportunities, albeit limited, for political expression in Angola. There was a longstanding tradition of local government and in the nineteenth and twentieth centuries the town councils were often the only political institutions where white settlers and *civilizados* could exert any kind of political pressure. However, by their very nature these town councils lacked a colony-wide vision. There were some contested elections for the national Cortes in Lisbon, but these tended to reflect settler concerns. The various towns of Angola developed a lively but very locally focused press. Between 1881 and 1926, for example, twenty-four different papers appeared in the southern towns of Moçamedes and Lubango, which provided a vigorous outlet for settler opinion.[106] With the declaration of the Republic political parties sprang up in some numbers—the best known being the Liga Angolana, which was founded in 1912, claiming to be 'representative of the native peoples of Angola' and which was suppressed by the High Commissioner, Norton de Matos, in 1922.[107]

Throughout the Republican period Angola retained a relatively free press, but under the New State censorship was imposed and public political activity became virtually impossible. Nor were there any trade unions or civic associations except those organised by the regime itself

105 Emmanuelle Besson, *Autour du proces de Joauim Pinto de Andrade. L'église catholique et l'Angola colonial, 1960-1975, Le Fait Missionaire* Cahier no 12, June 2002, p. 61.

106 W.G. Clarence-Smith, *Slaves, Peasants and Capitalists in Southern Angola 1840-1926,* pp. 54-5; Douglas Wheeler, 'Origins of African Nationalism in Angola: Assimilado Protest Writings, 1859-1929' in Ronald Chilcote ed., *Protest and Resistance in Angola and Brazil,* pp. 67-87.

107 Douglas Wheeler, 'Origins of African Nationalism in Angola: Assimilado Protest Writings, 1859-1929', Ronald Chilcote ed., *Protest and Resistance in Angola and Brazil,* pp. 73-4.

like the *grêmios* or the Mocidade Portuguesa. Douglas Wheeler referred to Angola under the New State as 'the kingdom of silence', and indeed the regime was so successful at stifling expressions of discontent from any section of the community that there is very little recorded opposition.[108] It is difficult not to form the conclusion that Angolans were, to an exceptional extent, isolated from the world.

However, discontent there was beneath the surface. During the Second World War the authorities were concerned that rural unrest, or the activities of Angolan separatists, might encourage an invasion by Belgian or Free French forces.[109] After the war the large poor white population flooding into the country was open to Communist propaganda and the Partido Communista Angolana (PCA) was established secretly in 1954. Communists are alleged to have infiltrated government-sponsored organisations like the Liga Nacional Angolana. There were also young intellectuals from among the *civilizado* population who met together and may even have established some rudimentary organisation among themselves. It seems likely that the Angolan electorate voted strongly for Delgado when the general challenged Salazar's nominee for election as president of Portugal in 1958. However, whatever clandestine political activity may have existed was eliminated by the PIDE in a wave of arrests in 1959, which resulted in seventy people of all races being tried before a Military Tribunal in Luanda.[110]

The most striking aspect of political life in Angola in the 1940s and 1950s is the extremely low level of activity. By 1959 in British and French Africa there had already been a generation of political activism in the African press, and in civil associations, churches, trades unions and political parties. This had led to the evolution

108 Douglas Wheeler and René Pélissier, *Angola,* p. 115.

109 Alexander Keese, '"Proteger os pretos": havia uma mentalidade reformista na administração portuguesa na África tropical (1926-1961)', *Africana Studia,* 6 (2003) p. 102.

110 Fernando Andresen Guimarães, *The Origins of the Angolan Civil War,* p. 39-40; Emmanuelle Besson, *Autour du procès de Joaquim Pinto de Andrade,* p. 34.

of nationalist ideologies ranging from the *Négritude* of the French African intellectuals to the African Socialism fashionable in British Africa. There had also been formidable armed uprisings, challenging the French in Madagascar and Algeria and the British in Kenya. Ghana was already independent and Nigeria heading for independence, while the French colonies were experiencing the first taste of local autonomy introduced by the Loi Cadre in 1956.

Although the tradition of Afro-Portuguese republican radicalism lingered in the older generation in Luanda, it was among the few Angolan students who were studying in Lisbon and Paris (Mário de Andrade was later to say '*Paris était véritablement pour nous une capitale africaine*'[111]) that radical ideas took root, and that attempts were made to establish an explicitly nationalist movement. Although these students had links with Portuguese Communists and met on a regular basis with each other and with like minded individuals from the other Portuguese colonies, no coherent political organisation was founded before 1958—the later suggestion that the MPLA was founded as early as 1956 has now been widely discounted.[112]

Eventually a small group, which included Manuel Pinto de Andrade, Lucio Lara, Eduardo dos Santos and Viriato da Cruz, formed an independence party and the following year established headquarters in Conakry. Its members were very much self-appointed leaders who had no real political base within Angola—indeed their politics were formed '*plus ou moins en réunions de café*'.[113] They were representatives of the *civilizado* groups who had once formed the Angolan elite but who had suffered loss of status under the Republic and the New State. Most of them were Marxist inclined—and it has been

111 Mário de Andrade and Christine Messiant, 'Sur la première génération du MPLA: 1948-1960. Mário de Andrade. Entretiens avec Christine Messiant', *Lusotopie* (1999) p. 205.

112 See discussion in Fernando Andresen Guimarães, *The Origins of the Angolan Civil War*, pp. 42-4.

113 Mário de Andrade and Christine Messiant, 'Sur la première génération du MPLA: 1948-1960. Mário de Andrade. Entretiens avec Christine Messiant', p. 185.

pointed out that the mestizos, whites and *assimilados* who formed the MPLA, needed a class-based ideology to deflect the accusations that they were not really African at all. The lack of any organisation or even any firm constituency of support within Angola was to force the MPLA to rely on its international friends, initially among the members of the non-aligned bloc, but later the Soviets and Cubans. This was to be a major factor dictating the pattern of the civil wars that followed independence.

The MPLA barely existed, and had no leader and no organisation to speak of, when in February 1961 an uprising, aimed at releasing inmates from prison, occurred in Luanda. The MPLA played no role in its organisation, but immediately took credit for staging this armed insurrection and thereby won a certain credibility in the international community, among people who wanted to believe in the existence of an active Angolan nationalist movement.[114]

If Lisbon was one centre where nationalist politics could germinate, Léopoldville was another—and much closer to home. The Belgian Congo had always attracted Bakongo from Angola who sought new opportunities in what was the major city of the Kikongo-speaking people. It was the place to which those in trouble with the Portuguese could escape. It was also in the Belgian Congo that the Kimbundist and the Tokoist churches had been born and it is alleged that in the early 1960s there were as many as fifty-eight Angolan political organisations active in Léopoldville. The tone of nationalist politics in the Congo was very different from that in Lisbon. The Bakongo nationalists appealed directly to Kongo cultural institutions and traditions, focusing initially on trying to restore the old Kongo kingdom. As such they belonged to an Africanist strand of nationalism, which can be clearly traced back to the last traditional resistance movements and which had had more recent manifestations in Mau Mau in Kenya and the PAC in South Africa.

114 Fernando Andresen Guimarães, *The Origins of the Angolan Civil War*, pp. 42-8.

The UPNA (later UPA and later still FNLA) was founded by Holden Roberto and his uncle in 1956 and for the next five years was the only high profile African nationalist movement representing Angolans. Although Roberto himself was French speaking and deeply involved in Léopoldville politics, his movement did have strong ties with the people in northern Angola and appears to have instigated the insurrections in Luanda in February and in the coffee growing region of the north in March 1961. From his base in Léopoldville Roberto was able to profit from the March uprising. The UPA leadership was widened to include Mbundu and Ovimbundo members and early in 1962 the UPA was changed into the FNLA, to suggest that it had formed a common front with other nationalist organisations. In April 1962 a government in exile (GRAE) was established, which in August 1963 was officially recognized by the OAU.[115] However, these were all manoeuvres on the international stage and had little meaning inside Angola itself, where the Portuguese remained firmly in control.

Already by this time the pattern on which Angolan politics was to develop can be discerned. Whereas Amílcar Cabral successfully welded together the radical *assimilados* of Cape Verde and the rural peasants of Guiné in support of the PAIGC and Julius Nyerere was able to convince the different nationalist groups in Mozambique to form Frelimo, there was no one able to persuade MPLA and UPA (and later UNITA) to form a common front. Various explanations have been offered for this. The three movements had rival patrons among the newly independent African states. The MPLA came to depend on Congo-Brazzaville, which was bitterly hostile to Zaire whose government patronised the UPA/FNLA. Later Tanzania was to support the MPLA while Zambia offered qualified support to UNITA. Without the support of their patrons none of the movements would have survived, but the patrons had no incentive to create a united movement.

115 Fernando Andresen Guimarães, *The Origins of the Angolan Civil War*, pp. 54-7, 65.

It has been claimed that the MPLA represented an urban constituency while UNITA and the UPA sought the support of the peasant community. Although there is superficially some strength in this argument, it crumbles on closer examination: the leadership of UNITA and the UPA was also drawn from the class of urban and educated *civilizados,* while MPLA was later to obtain the votes of the Mbundu peasantry.[116] It is certainly the case that the three movements took up different positions vis à vis the major powers. The MPLA was fairly consistently supported by the USSR after 1964 while the US lent support to UPA and intermittently to UNITA. Yet, it is fairly clear that the ideological positions of UPA and UNITA were as much the result of the split with the MPLA as the cause of it.

The support for the rival movements certainly reflected strong ethnic rivalries but again this was something that grew more intense over time and was not clear and irrevocable from the start. In the early days there were Mbundu and Ovimbundu members of the UPA. The retreat into dependence on ethnic loyalties grew as the antagonism of the movements deepened, and by end of the colonial era this was a defining factor in Angolan politics. The same can be said of the 'racial issue'. The accusation levelled against the MPLA leadership that it was made up of whites and mestizos was a useful propaganda weapon, and it may well be that the close-knit group of families that came to dominate the MPLA was determined from the outset not to widen the constituency from which its members were drawn. Yet, none of these factors would have been decisive if the three leaders had not been so authoritarian and had set out to be conciliatory.

However, the struggle for the future of Angola was early perceived as being a 'zero sum game.' Angola was very different from either Guiné or Mozambique. The latter were relatively poor and independence would only profit the victors if the resources of the country could be developed. Angola, on the other hand, offered the prospect of vast wealth in oil and diamonds, which would accrue to the vic-

116 David Birmingham, 'Angola' in Patrick Chabal, *A History of Postcolonial Lusophone Africa,* pp. 142-4.

tors without the need for any economic planning or development. The wealth of Angola could be plundered, the wealth of Guiné and Mozambique would have to be earned.

The war of independence

The first outbreak of rural violence occurred in the Malanje cotton growing district in January 1961. This was followed by the February risings in Luanda and the March rebellion in Cassange. These insurrections were clearly triggered by events in the Belgian Congo the previous year when the Belgians had decided precipitately to leave. Encouraged by the collapse of this colonial regime and by discontent following an economic downturn that was affecting agricultural prices and wages, violence erupted. In Malanje the rebellion was instigated by a prophetic movement headed by António Mariano, whose followers fled into newly independent Zaire as soon as the Portuguese army arrived. The rising in Luanda appears to have been an opportunistic event influenced by the presence of foreign journalists and rumours that Henrique Galvão was to bring the hijacked liner *Santa Maria* to Luanda in order to stage a coup.[117] The insurrection in Cassange was crudely aimed at massacring isolated and vulnerable Ovimbundu migrant workers and white settlers. The uprisings showed little organization or sense of strategy, and it seems the UPA believed that a violent revolt would bring about the rapid collapse of the colonial regime and that the settlers would be panicked into leaving.[118] The Portuguese, for their part, took the uprising as an excuse to attack the Protestant missions, which for so long had been seen by them as a hostile foreign body in their midst.[119] Although the

117 John Marcum, *The Angolan Revolution*, 2 Vols., Cambridge, Mass: MIT Press, 1969. Vol 1 *The Anatomy of An Explosion*, p. 124-7.

118 John Marcum, *The Angolan Revolution*, Vol. 1, p. 144-7; Fernando Andresen Guimarães, *The Origins of the Angolan Civil War*, p. 53.

119 John Marcum, *The Angolan Revolution*, Vol 1 149; for a contemporary account of the killing of Protestant pastors see Len Addicott, *Cry Angola* London: SCM Press, 1962.

Protestant churches had not been involved in organising opposition to the Portuguese, there is no doubt that education in the mission schools had proved a seed bed for nationalism and had helped to produce a nationalist leadership.

The insurrections precipitated the war of independence and forced both the MPLA and the UPA to commit to armed action. They also probably hastened the outbreak of war in Guiné and the formation of Frelimo with the aim of launching an armed struggle in Mozambique. However, the Portuguese empire in Africa did not collapse like the Belgian one. Instead the challenge presented by the uprisings hardened the attitude of the regime and committed Portugal to a more determined defence of its colonies. The Portuguese army in Angola was rapidly reinforced and, together with local white vigilantes, suppressed the 1961 rebellions in four months. It had taken the British four years to crush Mau Mau in Kenya.

The outbreak of the rebellions in 1961 precipitated a crisis for the regime. Salazar's authority was challenged by a group of senior generals in what became known as the Botelho Moniz coup. Although the main objective of the conspirators was to remove Salazar from power, it seems likely that they had also intended to initiate a quick withdrawal from Africa. However, Salazar triumphed and the commitment of the regime to hold the line in Africa was reinforced. The Portuguese regime believed that the war had to be won not only through military action but through speeding up the transformation of Angola into a modern industrial society. They were also aware of the importance of the propaganda war and of the need to obtain international backing for their continued presence in Africa.

The war which followed continued with only a few uneasy periods of truce until the year 2002. The first phase lasted until the withdrawal of Portuguese troops from Angola in November 1975. During this period, with the exception of the violent suppression of the 1961 uprising, military operations remained at a very low level and the main struggle was a political one between the rival nationalist parties. The Portuguese adopted tactics that contained the activities of the nationalists and created conditions for the continued rapid growth of the Angolan economy. The nationalists for their part did just enough to keep the war alive and the Portuguese military busy, while they manoeuvred for advantage on the world stage (particularly in the UN and the OAU) and sought the patronage of the main protagonists of the Cold War.

The military side of the war was, from the Portuguese perspective, fairly successful. The Portuguese armed forces in Angola numbered 6,500 at the beginning of 1961 but were heavily reinforced and by the end of the year there were 33,000 men in the colony. This number was gradually increased and at the end of the war the armed forces had a strength of 66,000 including naval units and the air force. In addition, local militias known as *Corpos Voluntários* were recruited to protect plantations, towns and installations. In the early 1970s, 2,000 special forces and a contingent of 1,000 commandos, known as the *Flechas*, were recruited locally. The Portuguese also employed 3,000 former Katangese 'gendarmes' dubbed the *Fieis*.[120] Use was also made of irregular units, including some from the San and Khoi ethnic groups, for tracking and bush warfare. As there were never enough Portuguese conscripts to maintain the manpower levels, there was a gradual Africanisation of the armed forces and in 1974 just under half the Portuguese army was made up of locally recruited Africans.[121] The Portuguese appear to have been more successful than the guerrillas at recruiting fighters and by the end of the war there were nearly three times as many African soldiers in the Portuguese armed forces as in the guerrilla armies.

Until 1966 the majority of the military operations occurred in the north where the guerrillas could operate out of Zaire. However, when Zambia became independent in 1964, a new front was opened and from 1966 onwards most of the armed activity took place in remote

120 Luís A.S. Inocentes, 'Counterinsurgency operations', John P. Cann ed., *Memories of Portugal's African Wars 1961-1974.* Contributions to War Studies No 1, Quantico VA: Marine Corps University Foundation, 1998, pp. 37-44.

121 John P. Cann, *Contra-subversão em Africa* Lisbon; Prefácio, 2005, p. 123.

areas in the east, where good intelligence allowed the Portuguese to raid guerrilla camps or to bomb them from the air. [122] The war never reached the populous zones or endangered vital installations since Zambia prevented attacks on the Benguela railway. Production of diamonds, coffee and oil was relatively unaffected by the bush war. On the other hand, the low intensity conflict continued unabated throughout the thirteen years with no final military outcome in sight. As in Mozambique the Portuguese tried to group the rural population in fortified settlements where they would be free from contact with the guerillas. Large numbers of Africans also took refuge in the Portuguese towns, which were unaffected by the war. These were reactive strategies by the civilian population that were to be repeated during the post-independence civil wars.

Mindful of the unpopular aspects of the colonial regime, which were widely assumed to have been a major cause of the insurrections, the Portuguese formally declared the end of forced contract labour and the status of *indígena.* The government also pushed ahead with capital development projects. The regulations against foreign investment were relaxed and foreign capital increased its activities in the oil, iron mining and coffee growing sectors. The expanding economy was reinforced with the spread of education and the rise of white immigration. Most whites, however, congregated in the towns and schemes to settle military veterans on the land did not yield significant results.

Government propaganda was largely concerned with convincing NATO to support a war that Salazar presented as a struggle against communism. Gradually the United States was won over and NATO began to supply Portugal with aircraft and weapons. South Africa and the Rhodesian regime were also brought into a common system of defence planning. Portugal had less success in convincing a scepti-

122 For an official view of the phases of the war see Joaquim Chito Rodrigues, 'Angola, a Military Victory', John P.Cann ed., *Memories of Portugal's African Wars 1961-1974*, pp. 45-90.

cal world that Lusotropicalism was a reality or that it offered any plausible reason for Portugal to refuse independence to its colonies. On the other hand, the Portuguese did manage to deepen the divisions between the rival nationalist movements and, soon after its foundation in 1966, UNITA began a clandestine collaboration with the Portuguese military against the MPLA.

The least successful part of Portugal's strategy was its failure to create institutionalised support on the domestic front. Although the war was at first seen as patriotic, by the mid-1960s there was growing resistance in Portugal, which took the form of draft evasion and emigration to France and Germany. From 1965 onwards, 19 per cent of those liable for military service avoided the draft each year.[123] In Angola the government was reluctant to devolve any initiative to the local population. Perhaps the Unilateral Declaration of Independence by the white Rhodesians in November 1965 served as a warning that the local settlers were not to be trusted. So the regime offered no form of political opening to counter the nationalists' demand for independence and their moves to attract African allies (for example by encouraging African coffee growers) were at best half-hearted.[124] Nor were any steps taken to train and pass responsibility to the Angolan population. The full implication of these failures was to be made clear in 1974. With the collapse of the central authority after the Lisbon coup on 25 April, there were neither local leaders nor local institutions able to take control of a rapidly deteriorating situation.

For most of the thirteen years of the war the nationalist guerrillas spent as much time fighting each other and manoeuvring for political advantage as they expended against the Portuguese. However, from their point of view, it was only necessary to remain in the field and tie down large numbers of increasingly resentful Portuguese conscripts for the war eventually to be won. Indeed, it was wise not to waste

123 Figures in John P. Cann, *Contra-subversão em Africa,* p. 107.

124 David Birmingham, 'Angola' in Patrick Chabal, *A History of Postcolonial Lusophone Africa,* p. 141.

military strength against a much superior army and to husband resources for the inevitable power struggle that would follow a Portuguese withdrawal.

The rival guerrilla armies obtained their recruits largely from Angolan exiles who had to be trained abroad. Moreover they needed bases from which to operate and patrons to protect them. Much of the war effort was therefore devoted to these vital activities behind the war zone. In the three years immediately after the 1961 uprisings the MPLA struggled to counter the active hostility of the Congo (Léopoldville) government and the FNLA, which issued orders to its military units to eliminate MPLA guerrillas.[125] In early 1962 the MPLA set up headquarters in Léopoldville, in the same city as the UPA, and later that year Agostinho Neto was chosen to head the movement. Neto soon consolidated his hold on the party and ousted his only serious rival, Viriato da Cruz. He then spent a year touring the world's capitals, rallying the support of Angolan exiles and trying to counter Holden Roberto, who had formed the FNLA and set up a government in exile. At this stage the MPLA was not committed to a hard Marxist ideology, but in November 1963 it was expelled from Zaire and set up in the neighbouring Congo Republic.[126] There it found an enthusiastic patron and moved decisively into the orbit of the Eastern Bloc countries. It was also able to mount some military incursions into Cabinda without suffering from FNLA interference. The FNLA meanwhile was becoming increasingly ineffective. It suffered repeated defections and was unable to conduct any serious military activity in northern Angola. It survived only by being propped up by the Mobutu regime in Zaire.

Once the MPLA had committed itself to a Marxist ideology and, together with its allies in the PAIGC and Frelimo, had sought backing among Eastern bloc and non-aligned countries, it launched a

125 Fernando Andresen Guimarães, *The Origins of the Angolan Civil War*, pp. 64-5.

126 Fernando Andresen Guimarães, *The Origins of the Angolan Civil War*, pp. 58-61, 72.

very successful propaganda war with the aid of left wing supporters in the West. It presented itself as a modernising party, opposed to tribalism and racism, which planned to create a new socialist society based on scientific principles, where there would be equality between men and women and in which traditional authorities, traditional religion and practices like polygamy would have no place. In contrast, it branded the FNLA as a tribal party, identified with outdated and backward looking Africanist values. Like Frelimo and the PAIGC, the MPLA claimed to have begun to create the new society in the areas it controlled by setting up modern health and educational services and a newly structured peasant economy.

It is now clear that in practice the MPLA was very different. It was only after 1966, when it shifted the base of its operations to Zambia, that the party could claim to hold sway over any territory or population at all. In the areas it controlled near the eastern frontier, the MPLA commanders implemented a policy of terror in order to cow the local population. There were numerous executions not only of people suspected of having links with the Portuguese but of anyone accused of causing 'disunity'. These political accusations soon merged with more traditional accusations of witchcraft, so that those executed included witches as well as alleged traitors. Many people tried to flee to the safety of the Portuguese controlled *aldeamentos* but those who were caught were killed.[127] The realities of this reign of terror in the eastern region, where most of the MPLA commanders and fighters were strangers, were a foretaste of the bitter social conflict that was to follow the retreat of the Portuguese in 1975. It was far removed from the image of a humanitarian, modernizing socialist party portrayed in the propaganda.

David Birmingham summed up the futility of the MPLA campaign in the East: 'in an unpropitious guerrilla campaign in the lands at the end of the earth ....nationalism as defined by the MPLA drained

127 Inge Brinkman, 'War, Witches and Traitors: Cases from the MPLA's Eastern Front in Angola (1966-1975)', *Journal of African History*, 44, (2003), pp. 303-325.

away into the sands of the great wilderness of eastern Angola.'[128] The lack of success caused deep divisions in the MPLA leadership, which resulted in constant splits and defections. This led Neto and the hard core of his supporters to adopt a more and more Stalinist stance, reducing any element of democracy within the movement and consolidating a leadership that would not tolerate any dissent.

The bitter divisions between the nationalist leaders, their ineffective military activities, their ideological posturing, and above all their failure to engage with the people of Angola itself were all highlighted by the formation of UNITA, the third major nationalist movement. Jonas Savimbi was an Ovimbundu from the Huambo area who had also been a student in Lisbon. Initially, Savimbi joined the UPA, was active in the creation of FNLA and became the GRAE's first 'foreign minister'. However, in 1964 he resigned from the FNLA and in March 1966 he launched UNITA as a third nationalist movement.[129]

Savimbi built his image and personality cult with as much care as Neto or Roberto and in this he, like Neto, was aided by sympathisers in the West. Where Neto was portrayed favourably by Basil Davidson, Savimbi was to be the subject of a major sympathetic biography by Bridgland.[130] Savimbi's propaganda focused on the fact that many of the leaders of the MPLA were mestizos. He accused both the MPLA and the FNLA of being ethnically exclusive and militarily ineffective. Moreover, UNITA claimed to be the only party actually based inside Angola—the founding of the movement inside the country had the same symbolic importance for Savimbi as the holding of the second party congress inside Mozambique in 1968 had for Mondlane and Frelimo.

128 David Birmingham, *Frontline Nationalism in Angola & Mozambique*, London: James Currey, 1992, pp. 40-1.

129 For the founding of UNITA see Fernando Andresen Guimaraes, *The Origins of the Angolan Civil War*, pp. 76-80.

130 Fred Bridgland, *Jonas Savimbi. A key to Africa*, Edinburgh: Mainstream Publishing, 1986.

Although UNITA was able to recruit from those who attended the Protestant mission schools, it soon came to resemble its rivals. It was very dependent on the support, albeit short lived, of a foreign patron, in this case Zambia. It drew its support in Angola from only one of the ethnic groups and it showed a chameleon-like approach to political ideology—espousing Maoism or capitalism according to the direction from which international backing was coming. Although Savimbi posed to the world as a modernising nationalist, his movement sought the support of traditional authorities and, like the MPLA, invoked witchcraft beliefs as a way of disciplining his followers and coercing the population. However, it was the rivalry with the MPLA in the east of Angola that produced the most compromising development. In order to become the dominant nationalist force in that region, UNITA began collaboration with the Portuguese military, paving the way for still closer cooperation with South Africa in the post-independence period. Like Neto and Roberto, Savimbi saw the Angola independence struggle as a 'zero sum game' where the winner would take all—and the 'all' included some of the richest oil and diamond fields in the world.

After 1968 the main developments in the war took place outside Angola. The commitment of the Estado Novo to Africa was weakened by the departure of Salazar from the scene in that year. Marcello Caetano, the new prime minister, surrounded himself with ministers who looked for a closer association with Europe and this trend was followed by Portuguese business, which began to switch its investments from Africa to Europe. Caetano himself began tentatively to look for political solutions to the African wars. Meanwhile a change in the fortunes of the MPLA was signalled when in 1968 the OAU switched its funding from the FNLA to the MPLA, a development Neto owed largely to his close alliance with Frelimo and the PAIGC. Then in July 1970 the Pope officially gave an audience to Cabral (PAIGC), Neto and Marcelino dos Santos (Frelimo) at which he is alleged to have said that the Catholic church was concerned for all those who suffered, particularly the people of Africa and that it supported the struggle for 'justice, liberty and national independence'. Although Vatican officials subsequently claimed that the Pope had not been aware of the identity of the three Africans, the symbolism of this meeting was not lost on the world.[131] Portugal was visibly losing the propaganda war, though it was the events in Guiné and Mozambique rather than in Angola, which were to precipitate the April 1974 military coup in Portugal.

The End of Portuguese rule in Angola

The Movimento das Forças Armadas (MFA), which overthrew the government of Marcello Caetano, stated in its manifesto that it sought a political solution to the wars in Africa. Beyond that it made no commitments and had made no specific plans. General Spínola, installed as head of the provisional government, wanted to retain the empire in the form of a loose federation of states and for two or three months he tried hard to realise this vision. However, his plans, which were for an interim government to rule each colony for two years, followed by a referendum on their future, were undermined by the refusal of the Portuguese army, supported by the MFA, to continue to hold the line against the guerrillas. In 1961 the Portuguese had not abandoned their colonies but had crushed the risings and proceeded with rapid economic development. In 1974 they behaved like the Belgians in the Congo. After Spínola resigned in September 1974, following a failed attempt to neutralise the influence of the MFA, negotiations for a handover of power in Angola were convened at Alvor in southern Portugal. The Alvor Accord that was reached in January 1975 stipulated that the three nationalist movements and the Portuguese would form an interim government and hold elections prior to the Portuguese departure in November.[132]

131 Emmanuelle Besson, *Autour du procés de Joauim Pinto de Andrade,* pp. 79-80.

132 For the Alvor Accord and the decolonization of Angola see Norrie Macqueen, *The Decolonization of Portuguese Africa,* London: Longman, 1997.

During the months that followed the Alvor Accord, the FNLA and MPLA poured men into Luanda and fighting between the factions erupted. The Soviet Union, which had withheld support from MPLA while the party appeared so divided and ineffective, now resumed its aid. Cuba sent military missions and subsequently a large army, thus tipping the balance in favour of the MPLA. The MPLA also had an advantage as it had close connections with many sections of the Luanda population and was favoured by Portugal's governor, Admiral Rosa Coutinho. Coutinho withdrew all Portuguese forces from the eastern regions of the country, though it was UNITA rather than the MPLA which filled the vacuum left by the departing Portuguese army.[133] The Portuguese concentrated on evacuating not only their armed forces but most of the civilian Portuguese, who now packed their bags and fled the country. The last Portuguese governor handed over power to the 'Angolan people' on board a warship on 11 November 1975, leaving behind an incipient civil war, with Zaireans, South Africans and Cubans all poised for armed intervention.

As the outcome of the revolutionary struggle in Portugal had yet to be decided, the rapid evacuation of Angola and the other colonies is hardly surprising. The Portuguese had made no preparations for an orderly handover and had not settled any of the issues affecting the future of Angola. Worse, however, was that none of the three nationalist movements had given serious thought to how they would unite the new nation and take over the running of a complex modern economy. If the Portuguese abandoned Angola, carrying with them as much moveable wealth as they could, the guerrilla armies occupied the land behind them effectively to plunder what had been left. The stage was set for more than twenty-five years of civil war and foreign intervention with the MPLA, the party dominated from the start by the old Afro-Portuguese elite families, eventually emerging as the victor.

133 Franz-Wilhelm Heimer, 'Les Dilemmes de la Décolonisation en Angola', *Cultures et Développement*, viii (1976) pp. 23-4, 28-9.

BIBLIOGRAPHY

Addicott, L., *Cry Angola.* London: SCM Press, 1962.

Andrade, M. de and C. Messiant, 'Sur la première génération du MPLA: 1948-1960. Mário de Andrade. Entretiens avec Christine Messiant', *Lusotopie* (1999) pp. 185-221.

Anstey, R., *Britain and the Congo in the Nineteenth Century,* Oxford: Clarendon Press, 1962.

Arnot, F. S., *Garenganze; or Seven Years' Pioneer Mission Work in Central Africa,* London: James E. Hawkins, 1889.

Axelson, E., *Congo to Cape. Early Portuguese Explorers,* London: Faber and Faber,1973.

Bender, G., *Angola under the Portuguese: the Myth and the Reality,* London: Heinemann, 1978.

Besson, E., *Autour du procés de Joaquim Pinto de Andrade. L'église catholique et l'Angola coloniale, 1960-1975, Le Fait Missionaire,* Cahier no 12, June 2002.

Birmingham, D., *Trade and Conflict in Angola,* Oxford: Clarendon Press, 1966.

——, 'Central Africa from Cameroun to the Zambesi', chapter 5, *Cambridge History of Africa,* volume 4, Cambridge University Press, 1975, pp. 325-83.

——, *Frontline Nationalism in Angola and Mozambique*, London: James Currey, 1992.

——, 'The Coffee Barons of Cazengo', in David Birmingham ed., *Portugal and Africa*, London: St Martin's Press, 1999.

Bridgland, F., *Jonas Savimbi. A Key to Africa,* Edinburgh: Mainstream Publishing, 1986.

Brinkman, I., 'War, Witches and Traitors: Cases from the MPLA's Eastern Front in Angola (1966-1975)', *Journal of African History,*44 (2003), pp. 303-25.

Burr, M., *A Fossicker in Angola,* London: Figurehead, 1933.

Cameron, V.L., *Across Africa,* 2 vols, London: Daldy Isbister, 1877.

Cann, J. P. (ed.), *Memories of Portugal's African Wars 1961-1974*. Contributions to War Studies No 1, Quantico, VA: Marine Corps University Foundation, 1998.

——, *Contra-subversão em Africa*, Lisbon: Prefácio, 2005.

Carreira, A., *Angola: da Escravatura ao Trabalho Livre*, Lisbon, Arcádia, 1977.

Chabal, P., *A History of Postcolonial Lusophone Africa*, London: Hurst, 2002.

Clarence-Smith, W.G., *Slaves, Peasants and Capitalists in Southern Angola 1840-1926*, Cambridge University Press, 1979.

——, *The Third Portuguese Empire 1825-1975*, Manchester: Manchester University Press, 1985.

Dias, J., 'Uma questão de identidade: Respostas intelectuais às transformações económicas no seio da elite crioula da Angola portuguesa entre 1870 e 1930', *Revista Internacional de Estudos Africanos*, 1 (1984), pp. 61-94.

——, 'Angola', in Valentim Alexandre and Jill Dias, eds, *O Império Africano 1825-1890*, Nova História da Expansão Portuguesa vol x Lisbon: Estampa, 1998.

Estermann, C., *The Ethnography of Southwestern Angola, Vol. 1. The Non-Bantu Peoples. The Ambo Ethnic Group*, New York and London: Africana Publishing Company, 1976.

Galvão, H., *The Santa Maria: My Crusade for Portugal*, London: Weidenfeld and Nicolson, 1961.

Galvão, H. and C. Selvagem, *Império Ultramarino Português*, 4 vols., Lisbon, Empresa Nacional de Publicidade, 1952-53.

Garfield, R., *A History of São Tomé Island 1470-1655*, San Francisco: Mellen Research University Press, 1992.

Carson, R.H. , Graham, *Under Seven Congo Kings*, London: Carey Press, 1930.

Guimarães, F. A., *The Origins of the Angolan Civil War*, London: St Martins Press, 1998.

Heimer, F.-W., ed., Social Change in Angola, Munich: Weltforum Verlag, 1973.

——, 'Les Dilemmes de la Décolonisation en Angola', *Cultures et Développement*, viii (1976), pp. 3-42.

Heintze, B., 'Between Two Worlds: the Bezerras, a Luso-African Family in Nineteenth Century Western Central Africa', in Philip J. Havik and Malyn Newitt eds, *Creole Societies in the Portuguese Colonial Empire,* Bristol University (2007).

Heywood, L., *Contested Power in Angola, 1840s to the Present,* Rochester, NY: University of Rochester Press, 2000.

Hilton, A., *The Kingdom of Kongo,* Oxford: Clarendon Press, 1985.

Hutchinson, A.B., *Report on the Economic Situation in Angola,* London: Department of Overseas Trade, 1925.

Hutchinson, R. and G. Martelli, *Robert's People,* London: Chatto and Windus, 1971.

Katzenellenbogen, S.E., *Railways and the Copper Mines of Katanga,* Oxford: Clarendon Press, 1973.

Keese, A., '"Proteger os pretos": havia uma mentalidade reformista na administração portuguesa na África tropical (1926-1961)', *Africana Studia,* 6 (2003), pp. 97-125.

Macqueen, N., *The Decolonization of Portuguese Africa,* London: Longman, 1997.

Marcum, J., *The Angolan Revolution,* 2 vols., Cambridge, MA: MIT Press, 1969.

Margarido, A., 'The Tokoist Church and Portuguese Colonialism in Angola', in Ronald H. Chilcote ed., *Protest and Resistance in Angola and Brazil,* Berkeley and London: University of California Press, 1972, pp. 29-52.

Martin, M.-L., *Kimbangu: An Africa Prophet and his Church*, Oxford: Basil Blackwell, 1975.

Martin, P., *The External Trade of the Loango Coast,* Oxford University Press, 1972.

Miller, J.C., 'Slaves, Slavers and Social Change in Nineteenth Century Kasanje', in F.-W. Heimer ed., *Social Change in Angola,* Munich: Weltforum Verlag, 1973.

Miller, J., *Way of Death. Merchant Capitalism and the Angolan Slave Trade 1730-1830,* Madison: University of Wisconsin Press, 1988.

Newitt, M., 'British Travellers' Accounts of Portuguese Africa in the Nineteenth Century', *Revista de Estudos Anglo-Portugueses,* 11 (2002), pp. 103-29.

Nowell, C.E., *The Rose-Coloured Map,* Junta de Investigações Científicas do Ultramar, Lisbon: 1982.

Norton de Matos, Major [José de] , *A situação financeira e economica da Provincia de Angola,* Lisbon: Tipografia da Coop Militar, 1914.

Paiva Couceiro, H. de, *Angola: dois annos de governo junho 1907-junho 1908. História e Commentários,* Lisbon: 1948.

Pélissier, R., *Les Guerres Grises,* Orgéval, 1977.

Provincia de Angola. Providencias tomadas pelo General J.M.R.Norton de Matos, como Alto Comissário da República e Governador Geral, Lisbon: Sociedade Nacional de Tipografia, 1922.

Radulet, C., *O Cronista Rui de Pina e a 'relação do Congo'. Mare Liberum,* Lisbon: Comissão Nacional para as Comemorações dos Descobrimentos Portugueses, 1992.

Silva, E. Marques da, 'O Papel societal do sistema de ensino na Angola (1926-1974)', paper presented to II Colóquio Internacional em Ciências Sociais sobre a Africa de Língua Oficial Portuguesa, Bissau, 1991.

Thornton, J., *Africa and Africans in the Making of the Atlantic World, 1400-1800,* Cambridge University Press, 1992.

Tucker, J., *Angola. The Land of the Blacksmith Prince,* London: World Dominion Press, 1933.

Vos, J.A., 'The Kingdom of Kongo and its Borderlands, 1880-1915' unpublished PhD thesis, University of London, 2005.

Wheeler, D., 'Origins of African Nationalism in Angola: Assimilado Protest Writings, 1859-1929', in Ronald Chilcote ed., *Protest and Resistance in Angola and Brazil,* Berkelye and London: University of California Press, 1972.

Wheeler, D. and R. Pélissier, *Angola,* London: Pall Mall Press, 1971.

Williams, R., 'Migration and Miscegenation: Maintaining Boundaries of Whiteness in the Narratives of the Angolan Colonial State 1875-1912', in Philip J. Havik and Malyn Newitt eds, *Creole Societies in the Portuguese Colonial Empire,* Bristol University (forthcoming).

3

THE MUTATION OF HEGEMONIC DOMINATION: MULTIPARTY POLITICS WITHOUT DEMOCRACY

Christine Messiant [1]

It is often said that the 1991 Bicesse Peace Accord brought about a triple transition: from war to peace; from an authoritarian Marxist-Leninist state to a multiparty democratic system; and from a socialist centrally managed to a liberal market economy.

It is true that there have been changes in Angola that point in this direction—or at least resemble similar transitions, which have taken place elsewhere. However, the assumption that the Peace Accord ushered in Angola a particular type of transition is not one that can be taken for granted. The supposition that the dynamics engendered by Bicesse would lead to a move in the direction of recognisable changes that would make democracy more likely needs to be re-examined in its proper historical context. Not all peace agreements are the same; nor do they all contribute in the same way to the consolidation of a non-violent political order. Equally, not all authoritarian systems work in the same way, even when they belong to that category known as 'Afro-communist'. Finally, not all socialist economies exhibit the same characteristics, especially when they are differently endowed.

1 Christine Messiant died in January 2006 while Patrick Chabal was translating her chapter into English, so it has not been updated to take account of more recent events.

Understanding the texture of Angola's present transition(s) requires instead a historically grounded analysis. Among the factors that need to be taken into consideration, we would stress the modalities of the country's decolonisation, the importance of its natural resources, the international context within which outside actors intervened, the complexities of regional issues and the evolution of the internal conflict. Above all, however, it is necessary to investigate the nature of the party (MPLA) that has ruled Angola since independence, and of its role within the evolving political system that is now ostensibly moving towards multipartyism.

If my approach is historical, it also falls squarely within the perspective of political economy, as defined by Max Weber—namely the study of systems of domination and inequalities, of the forms of appropriation and redistribution of national wealth, and of the structure of government that makes such a political order possible. Thus, I want to rise above discussions of 'political regimes' or 'economic models' in order to focus attention on the interactions between the political, economic, social and symbolic aspects of the system of governance that prevails in Angola. This will require going beyond the formal aspects of this political and economic order and investigate the informal, or invisible, characteristics of the system as it operates in everyday practice. Only in this way will it be possible to examine the quality of the democracy currently being envisaged without passion and outside the bounds of ideological disputes. Angola's recent history has been marked by two key factors, which are clearly interconnected: the war and international relations. How these have impinged on the evolution of the country since independence is not straightforward and the proper consideration of its future prospects depends on how we come to explain the dynamics that have shaped its postcolonial political order.

In the pages that follow I will restrict my analysis to the state in Angola, since there is no space here to discuss the political economy of the UNITA armed rebellion. Although it is clearly true that a full picture of the evolution of Angola since independence demands an examination of the impact of the war, this chapter will integrate it within a study of the country's political economy. Here the turning point is what I have called elsewhere the 'shift to clientelism'[2]—that is the period in the mid-eighties when the move towards a liberalisation of the economy was initiated *without* a concomitant change in the Marxist-Leninist political institutional framework.

The key to this early transition was the manner in which economic changes were introduced within an authoritarian one-party state, which never envisaged that such liberalisation would result in a politically competitive system. This conversion in turn shaped the framework within which the present political transition must be set. The fact that the war resumed after the first elections in 1992 and that the international attitude towards the Angolan regime changed as a result made it possible for the Angolan rulers to consolidate a political system able to accommodate, indeed to profit from, the move to a liberal economy, whilst consolidating its hegemonic control over the country.

The shift to one-party clientelism

It was around 1985 that Angola's political economy changed, because of a number of factors that I discuss below. Until then, there prevailed in the country what I would call a 'classical' socialist form of government, of which the main characteristics were as follows.[3] The Constitution gave political primacy to the single ruling party, or rather its Political Bureau, and political responsibilities were entrusted to those whose commitment to the party was unquestioning. The so-called mass organisations (Youth, Women, Workers, etc.) functioned as transmission belts and all others were deemed illegal, with the exception of the churches. The organs of justice and repression also followed party orders, leading to double standards, widespread injustice and discrimination.

2 See Christine Messiant [hereafter CM] 1994b.

3 I develop this notion in CM1998.

This resulted in the *de facto* political and economic supremacy of the *nomenklatura*, which enjoyed virtual impunity—apart from the risk of the President's displeasure. Such a system led to widespread corruption—perhaps best symbolised by the ubiquitous *candonga*, or illegal transactions—and to passive resistance on the part of those who did not benefit from such arrangements. Over time this state of affairs brought about an expansion of the MPLA: from below, since party membership was the only means available to access resources and influence; from above, because there was a deliberate will to create a vanguard party separate from society.

From the beginning, Angolan 'socialism' was distinct because it was shaped by two key determinants: oil wealth and an internationalised civil war. These two factors explain why the MPLA regime combined strong support from a large section of society with a policy of exclusion and repression. The latter fell not just on the regime's political and military enemies, rejected from the nation, but after the attempted 1977 coup it also affected all those who dissented. For its part, the bulk of the population was simply discarded: first in the rural areas, which were afflicted by war and had become irrelevant ever since the oil rent made it possible to buy food abroad; then in the cities, where poverty grew over time and political support dwindled.

The polarisation of the country into two enemy camps, each with its own 'civil' society, conspired to mitigate the effects of such repressive, divisive and iniquitous policies. Because people had to choose their side, if only to receive a modicum of protection against the other, or simply to avoid starving, they did not register their discontent openly and did not challenge the political system. This is why there was little opposition to the MPLA regime during most of the postcolonial period and little shifting of allegiance from one camp to the other.

These particular characteristics resulted in a quite singular specific evolution. The dictatorship of the single party strengthened. There was a vast expansion of corruption, which was fuelled by a profusion of petrodollars and the setting of an artificial exchange rate that favoured the *nomenklatura* and its clients. After 1985, therefore, the political system mutated, not just because of these changes but also because of the regime's reaction to such developments. In effect, the state sanctioned the takeover by its agents of the informal market, thus giving cover to the elite's appropriation of the proceeds of the fraud made possible by the liberalisation of the economy. The rest of the population suffered ever greater poverty.

From that period onwards, a transition occurred to what I would call 'savage socialism', combining the dictatorship of the single party, the 'dollarisation' of the economy—in effect, the sanctioning of illegal practices—and the transition to a political economy of clientelism. In such circumstances, what was 'savage' was the degree of illegal enrichment made possible by arbitrary impunity on the part of the ruling elite. This move came as a result of the ever-tighter control the President exercised over the oil revenue—the accounting for which was totally opaque and very largely bypassed government and party scrutiny. Presidential rule increasingly escaped the supervision of the Political Bureau and came to rest in the hands of a few trusted collaborators.

This new 'liberalism' enabled the *nomenklatura* to take advantage of their position massively to invest in the illegal market, which brought them colossal returns. It is from that period that the 'socialist' dictatorship made possible the emergence of a new class—or rather a new class in the making since the state, which promoted and protected it, remained in nominal control of the means of production and accumulation.

The unalloyed domination of the single party was critical to this process of enrichment for two important reasons. First, it was able 'legally' to prevent any political competition. Second, it helped to check possible popular opposition to these moves, which produced ever-greater inequalities and tied the hands of those outside the presidential circles, whose very survival was now entirely dependent on the proceeds of a highly volatile informal economy. Corruption, which was already endemic, now became systemic and came to define both the new political economy and the new form of governance. Although the state's legal framework had not changed, this transition brought about a system of clientelism that was able to operate with full impunity.

It is by means of this system—the operation of which was made easier by the war, generalised destitution and a high level of repression—that the regime sought to re-anchor itself socially among those who were increasingly tempted by employment in the private sector or outside the country. Of course, such a political economy went hand in hand with a slackening of repression of the illegal activities of the so-called *candongueiros*, or 'black marketeers', which entailed some danger. However, the strength of the single party lessened the risk since it alone made possible social advancement and the socio-economic improvement of its membership. The new political dispensation, in which party and *candongueiros* began to work in harmony, rendered obsolete the ideological commitment hitherto required of party membership. The party became the engine of clientelism.

This transition took place at a time of significant regional and international changes: the end of the Cold War, Angola's constructive engagement in the advent of Namibian independence (followed by the withdrawal of the Cubans), the end of apartheid and increased US pressure for a resolution of the conflict. Yet, this was also a period when the civil war intensified and the regime found itself militarily vulnerable. Faced with the risk of military defeat and the necessity to deal with the enemy, the regime sought to fashion policies that would not threaten the single party, which was the foundation of its survival. It deployed the 'Gbadolite option'—that is, it chose negotiation with UNITA over democratisation. This entailed negotiation without recognition but with co-optation, the best way of incorporating individuals from the other side without jeopardising single-party rule.[4]

4 See CM1993 & 1994, which discuss in some detail this policy of co-optation.

From 'democratic transition' to a political economy of war, 1991-2002

Within the limits of a chapter, it is difficult to present in detail the changes that took place during this critical decade. I will confine myself to a discussion of some key moments in the emergence of the political economy and form of governance that still prevail today. During this period the two main contextual factors were the continued civil war and the growing weight of international pressure. I now analyse separately the four key moments of this period.

The paradoxes of the 'democratic transition'. The first important moment turns around the period between the 1991 peace accord and the elections.[5] If this first transition appeared to resemble those taking place in the rest of Africa at that time, it was in fact quite distinct.[6] Despite the oil revenues, the transition occurred within the context of economic crisis, social disorder and general discontent with the government. The regime was under sustained military assault in most of the country and was losing legitimacy within the socialist camp. However, the war had polarised politics into a clearly demarcated division between two opponents, which had made impossible the emergence of any 'national' civil society. It was also plain that the transition had taken place as a result of international pressure and not primarily because of the demands of Angolan society. The so-called transition was less concerned with the actual wish on the part of the protagonists to bring about a form of democracy than with the need to strike a peace agreement. As a result, it remained constrained within the terms of the Bicesse Accord—an internationally brokered agreement that also, quite naturally, reflected the interests of the external actors involved.

5 For an analysis of various important aspects of this period, see CM 1993, 1995 and 1999b. For an analysis of the international aspects, see CM1994a and 2004.

6 I developed this comparative theme in CM1999b.

The international community involved in the peace process (the UN and the so-called troika—that is, the USA, Russia and Portugal) was dominated by the USA, which supported UNITA and saw the elections as the means of ensuring its victory. However, the paradoxical outcome of the polls, even if the second round of presidential elections was never completed, was the UN-sanctioned victory of the MPLA. The tragic result of this situation was a resumption of war, which was not surprising given that the Bicesse Accord officially sanctioned the absolute bipolar political division of the country. This amounted to the sidelining of any party not involved in armed warfare and the *de facto* disenfranchisement of civil society. Indeed, the Accord encouraged a 'winner-take-all' attitude. Finally, the UN and the troika were criminally negligent in that they tolerated UNITA's refusal seriously to demilitarise and allowed the MPLA to abuse its control of the full resources of the one-party state for the purpose of party campaigning.

The MPLA's continued domination of state power was decisive, not just for its electoral success but also for its ability to test, and adjust to, the vagaries of multiparty elections. In order to ensure continued ascendancy in case of electoral defeat, the regime set in train a massive process of (legal and arbitrary) privatisation. In doing so, it used the resources of the state to broaden clientelistic redistribution, targeting in particular the most influential strata. Beneath the disguise of a reassuring discourse of peace, which contrasted with UNITA's aggressive and militaristic tone, the MPLA was able to use its supremacy to win the elections whilst at the same time arming paramilitary and police forces, in anticipation of a renewed conflict.

It is clear that the elections were held without the requisite political and military guarantees and, because of this, the UN verdict that they had been 'free and fair' was never really tenable. One can speculate about the effects of a UNITA government, given that this organisation was blatantly totalitarian, militaristic and revenge prone. Yet, the MPLA's victory effectively legitimised a one-party form of regime and the government's decision to use force against its opponent in Luanda—provoking the death of thousands. More significantly, it completely transformed the international environment and led to a complete reversal of fortune for the two protagonists. Indeed, the elections effectively brought about official and business support for the MPLA government and a concomitant ostracising of UNITA. In effect, this transition helped the regime to come to terms with multiparty politics and to test the limits of international support for democracy.

The post-electoral war: coercion, predation and impunity. The war that followed the elections was, on both sides, without mercy. The two parties sought to punish the 'enemy' civilian population that had voted 'wrongly'. They thus indulged in an excess of violence and cruelty, which provoked massive destruction throughout the country and contributed seriously to atomising society. The government armed its people into militias. UNITA, which rejected UN intervention, sought to undo the electoral results by force of arms. As a consequence, the US-led international community switched its support from the 'rebels' to the 'legitimate' government.

This conflict brought about the demise of the new 'democracy', a swift rise in coercion and predation—with its attendant destitution and impunity—and the consolidation of a brutal police and military state. Predation continued to be controlled by the President but it now incorporated more fully the armed forces and internal security forces, which ensured that coercion worked. It made possible the extension of a system based on illegal transactions (from top to bottom of society), the privatisation of public assets to the benefit of a designated elite and the development of private enterprises underpinning the war effort (air transport, imports, security, etc.). At the same time, the resumption of war enabled the regime to neglect ordinary 'citizens', whose support was now no longer required.

The re-militarisation of society and the strengthening of oppression took place in a climate of total impunity. Since the MPLA had an absolute majority in the National Assembly and also controlled the judiciary there was no institutional, political or legal check on a process of predation that favoured the President's networks. The party, once emptied of most of its power, regained its place within the political system and its members quickly took advantage of the new dispensation. Those who had distanced themselves from the MPLA before the elections, when the result seemed in the balance, now had to make amends in order to benefit from its prebends.

The post-electoral situation polarised society between those who had supported UNITA or had failed to support the MPLA and those who had remained faithful to the ruling party. The President, who himself had sought to mark his distance from the MPLA before the polls, now made it clear that it was again at the centre of the circle of power—into which he co-opted those who had supported him during the elections. The MPLA was once again the instrument of domination, which the President controlled. With the political map thus redrawn, the regime was now in a position to use military means in order to force UNITA to accept in 1994 the terms of the Lusaka Accord, which it had rejected in 1992/93.

'Neither war nor peace': a strategy for consolidating domination. The Lusaka Accord was signed under both military and international pressure. The solution agreed upon consisted in the formation of the Governo de Unidade e Reconciliação Nacional (Government of Unity and National Reconciliation), or GURN, which had been rejected after the first round of elections but which now served to demonstrate the 'illegality' of UNITA if it failed to join. The Accord enshrined the imbalance between the two sides: UNITA had to demobilise *and* demilitarise as a condition of joining the GURN, whereas the government was naturally entitled to maintain the national army intact.

The Accord was essentially stillborn in that neither signatory had the slightest intention of honouring it.[7] UNITA refused to demilitarise before gaining access to power; the regime refused to share power, thus turning the GURN into a pretence. Furthermore, sanc-

7 For a discussion of the reasons why the Accord was in a 'structural' impasse, see CM2001, CM2003b and especially CM2004.

tions were imposed on one party only—UNITA—since the rebel movement sought continuously to evade the terms of the Accord. As a result, the country remained divided into two parts and the war continued—UNITA violating the Accord during the day and the MPLA during the night, as Issa Diallo, the UN's Special Envoy, is rumoured to have said. After the establishment of the GURN in April 1997, the regime was able to increase pressure on the UN to strengthen sanctions against UNITA. At the same time, it was able to intervene militarily in the sub-region (most notably in Congo-Brazzaville and the former Zaire) without incurring any penalty from the international community.

During this post-Lusaka period, the regime consolidated the domination gained by military means. It ensured that UNITA failed to get a toehold, either in politics or within society, which might have been threatening to the MPLA. It also made sure that no political opposition was allowed to surface and that civil society remained unable to challenge the prevailing predation, destitution, injustice and impunity. Nor were civil organisations able to link up with outside organisations critical of the way things were developing in Angola. Civil society remained weak.

This situation of 'neither war nor peace' enabled the regime to consolidate its political and economic hegemony. Economically, this was the period when a large number of joint ventures, associating outside interests with the Angolan elite, were set up—to the benefit of the ruling circles. Paradoxically, the formation of the GURN—which resulted in the allocation of some portfolios to UNITA members and allowed UNITA deputies to take their seats in parliament—resulted in the political emasculation of the rebel party. With the MPLA holding an absolute majority in the National Assembly, opposition deputies had no influence over policy. Given the tightening of censorship, they even had difficulty in putting their message across, though there developed a more independent press in the second half of the 1990s.[8] The regime made certain that the media praised the MPLA and attacked a 'war-mongering' UNITA.

The President for his part took measures to ensure that discontent within the party about policy decisions did not affect his personal standing. He appointed his supporters to the key governmental positions and reinforced the control capacity of the presidential office. Furthermore, he made sure to check the activities of those areas of civil society (press, churches, NGOs) that sought not just to relieve the misery of the population but also to challenge governmental decisions. The threat of coercion, or sometimes the use of brute force (a journalist was murdered in 1994 when he started investigating corruption within the ruling circles), prevented recourse to judicial protection.

Furthermore, the President went beyond the clever use of prebends for potential opponents in order to defuse possible political challenges to the regime. He sought to neutralise Angola's autonomous civil society—the activities of which might by implication have exposed government failures—with an ambitious scheme to create his own 'civil society'. To that end, he set up the José Eduardo dos Santos Foundation, whose main aim was to ensure that support for social, health and educational activities would be credited to him, not to the extensive independent NGO sector, which was financed by donors.

The growing antagonism between the GURN 'partners', and the realisation that foreign interests were becoming ever more closely associated with the regime, contributed to the population's disillusionment with the transition to democracy in Angola. In the end, even if it did not manage to gain society's support, the regime was able to maintain acquiescence by means of a judicious mix of clientelism and coercion.

The return to war: defeat UNITA militarily in order to subdue it politically. The patent failure of the Lusaka Accord was best illustrated by

8 The broadcasting of parliamentary sessions was soon ended.

the impossibility of achieving the demilitarisation of UNITA, and this situation led the international community to approve the government's remilitarisation. The UN vote for new sanctions against UNITA's diamond trafficking inevitably brought renewed legitimacy to the MPLA regime and made it easier for it to reject further negotiations, opting for a return to war. Ostensibly justified on the grounds of neutralising UNITA's military threat, the new strategy was in fact politically bolder.

In the first instance, the President sought to eliminate UNITA's political threat by forcing its elected representatives to join a new party, UNITA-Renovada, the only one recognised as the legitimate 'opposition' by the government. This made it possible for the regime to claim that, even in the face of a renewed armed threat by UNITA, it was willing to honour its commitment to 'democracy and the rule of law'. But dos Santos' aim was more ambitious. The military elimination of UNITA was intended to give a clear signal that the regime would not tolerate any political dissent, either from political organisations or from civil society. The government would tightly control whatever transition was to take place after the war.

The return to war against a well-armed UNITA (that was rich in diamonds) prompted the international community to support the government more openly: applying sanctions to weaken the rebel movement and, against all humanitarian principles, agreeing to the supply of vital aid only to that segment of the population aligned with the MPLA. With outside assistance, the government's army, the Forças Armadas de Angola (FAA), were able to regain the initiative on the ground and launch an all-out attack on UNITA, regardless of the widespread concerns about the consequences of such drastic military action.

In fact, for the first time in Angola there were internal protests, from the Church among others, about the unsuitability of the 'presidential' constitution as well as in favour of a return to negotiation and dialogue as the only viable path to peace.[9] These complaints,

9 See CM2003b.

which were dangerous for those who made them, disturbed the international community but did not deflect it from supporting the government's policy of seeking total military victory. Many deplored the excessive force used by the FAA, its 'scorched earth' policy for example, but in the end the regime was able to continue the war until it had eliminated Jonas Savimbi and defeated UNITA.

The consequences of this policy of a war to the finish were enormous. The two protagonists committed untold war crimes and destroyed huge swathes of the country. The regime for its part resorted to renewed repression against all dissenting voices and distributed resources with the sole aim of gaining political support. It made every effort to silence those who called for peace and it infringed press freedom (jailing journalists if necessary) despite strong condemnation from the international community, for which a free press is considered a requirement for democracy.[10]

The consolidation of hegemonic power, 2002–2004

The government's military victory brought about a peace for which Angolans had longed over thirty years but, paradoxically, it failed to rekindle hope for the future. The defeat of UNITA, made possible by the acquiescence of the international community, effectively gave the regime license to shape the post-war political transition as it chose. In the first instance, it no longer had to negotiate with UNITA and was able to design its management of political opposition as it saw fit. Concretely, this meant that the government was able to monopolise power, organise demobilisation in the way that suited it best, interpret the Lusaka Accord to fit its interests and in this way consolidate further its political hegemony.

Except in Cabinda, where armed conflict continued largely free of international interference, there were some improvements in the life of the population at large. The end of the war finally enabled Angolans to live free of the fear of killing and in the hope of rebuild-

10 On the war and its consequences, see CM2001, 2002, 2003a and 2003c.

ing their lives. The regime ceased to use the conflict as the overriding excuse for its inability to improve conditions in the country. It now sought to project a more caring and constructive image, in large measure to ensure renewed international support, and the President now stressed his stature as a 'peace maker'. The official discourse spoke of reconciliation and democracy.

However, these changes did not lead to any substantive transformation, either politically or economically. The ruling elite continued its appropriation of the country's resources, the regime consolidated its hold on politics, the government did not become more accountable and no improvement occurred either in terms of democratic legality or with regard to citizens' rights. In sum, there was no notable change in the country's political economy, even if there was greater reference to the potential benefits of 'democratisation'.

Predation or the control of national economic assets. Despite a certain number of goodwill gestures on the part of the government, oil revenues remain tightly controlled by the ruling elite. If the regime has allowed the publication of some data, notably in respect of its oil financial accounts, there has been no convincing account of the glaring discrepancies between official accounts and documented oil income.[11] Although there have been some genuine administrative difficulties in furnishing convincing financial tallies, the truth is that it has so far been impossible to achieve accounting transparency or even to satisfy the IMF's basic demands for data on oil revenue.

Although it is technically more difficult for the government to control diamond production, the absence of parliamentary oversight has enabled the regime to ensure that revenues are also used for clientelistic purposes. It is the President's (civilian or military) clients who have been the beneficiaries of the diamond rent. Moreover, the

11 To illustrate the scale of the problem, there has hitherto been no explanation given to the IMF of what has happened to the extra $600 million of additional oil income that accrued in 2004 because of rises in the price of crude oil that year. Furthermore, the government has been in receipt of billions of dollars, lent by Western banks, and more recently China, on account of future oil exports.

wholesale privatisation of state activities (banks, telecommunications, air industry, import businesses, fishing, real estate, etc.) has also benefited primarily the ruling elite and its dependents. The creation of new enterprises, particularly in strategic sectors, has taken place without proper transparency or competitive bidding and even outside the existing legislation.

The template for this has been the setting up of partnerships between public enterprises and national or international private companies. The domestic companies are linked to the President, or receive his support; the foreign ones bring capital and know-how. Given the present relative scarcity of oil on the world market, there is intense competition within that industry. A new factor is the huge reconstruction market within the country, which foreign companies crave to enter. The regime is thus able to balance outside pressure for political democratisation with outside interests in the Angolan economy and is often able to ensure foreign links that enhance the position of the President.[12]

What has happened in the last few years has been a transfer of state assets to the private sector as well as the allocation of business sinecures to, and the appropriation of large sectors of the economy by, those who hold power and their clients. This has been done for political reasons in the sense that favours have been given to those who have been willing to support the regime. This system of co-optation and 'economic reward' is entirely in the hands of the President, who dispenses patronage according to political expediency regardless of whether the recipients of his largesse are members of the party or not. He has in this way created vast networks of personal dependency that provide unconditional support to the continuation of his rule.

This has made possible the emergence of a wholly unaccountable but powerful oligarchy, which controls both the political levers and

12 What is happening to the diamond industry is emblematic of this process: the President's daughter is associated with an Angolan company that has links with outside partners—among them Arkady Gaydamak, who has acted as the President's intermediary for arms purchases and the renegotiation of the Angolan debt.

the main areas of the economy. Such a system has contributed to a sharpening of social and economic polarisation, the emergence of ever more extreme inequalities and the widespread extension of a patrimonial logic to the whole country. Because there are insufficient resources devoted to reconstruction, rebuilding of social services, improvement of the infrastructure and alleviation of poverty, there is no alternative to clientelism for those (even within the so-called middle classes) whose quality of life has failed to improve since the end of the war.

Control of the State. In and of itself, such domination of the economy and of the means of co-optation would not be sufficient to guarantee political hegemony. The ability to evade accountability additionally requires control of both the legal process and parliament. It needs to rest on the regime's ability to get its way, regardless of the formal institutional checks and balances in place.

It so happens that since 1992 the MPLA has enjoyed an absolute majority in the National Assembly. This has meant that parliament has not really been able to play its constitutional role, regardless of the tenor of the debates it has held. Except when it needs to give the right image to the international community, parliament has not even sought to exercise supervision over government policies or budgets. It does not have, nor does it seem to have sought, the means to call the government to account or to take any legislative initiative. Government essentially rules by decrees, over which the National Assembly has nothing to say. Its role is merely to rubberstamp the political and financial decisions made, whether or not they serve the national, as opposed to merely factional, interest.

With rare exceptions—such as the 1999 legislation on the press, which the government eventually chose to withdraw—parliament approves legislation that restricts political rights and furthers social inequalities. The following illustrates what is at stake. The law on land ownership stipulated that so-called communal land ought to belong to those who 'develop' it—in the rural areas through agriculture and in urban centres through house building. This has resulted in massive expropriation and the displacement of poorer communities. The law regulating oil production stipulates that the parties concerned refrain from making public the terms of their involvement, which obviously makes transparency impossible. Finally, the MPLA's majority enables it to block any parliamentary inquiry or opposition legislative proposal.

Although such dominance in the National Assembly is crucial, it would not be sufficient to protect the ruling elite's hegemony without the widespread abuse of the judicial system. Except at the very apex, where the top hierarchy belongs to the inner presidential patrimonial circle, the judiciary is starved of funds and cannot function properly. The long-heralded organs designed to ensure state legality and protect the rights of Angolans have never come to life. The only functioning institution—the Tribunal de Contas (or Court of Accounts)—is presided over by someone who was selected by the President and is accountable to him.

The Prosecution Service comes under the supervision of the Ministry of the Interior. Consequently, it almost never launches inquiries into the alleged misdeeds or crimes of state officials; but when it does these never result in any conviction. On the other hand, those (most frequently from the media or NGOs) who bring to light alleged violations of the law are commonly harassed. It is rare that the judiciary upholds the rights of ordinary citizens, especially when those clash with the interests of the holders of state power. In short, it can readily be seen that what prevails in Angola is the negation of justice.

A clear indicator of the judiciary's real authority within the existing power structure is what happens to those officials who, having been accused of corruption or embezzlement, are seen to embarrass the regime. Here, the sanction comes from the President and not from the courts. Conversely, officials are exonerated not on the basis of a judicial inquiry but following political intervention from the top. This direct political interference discredits the judiciary since it undermines the basic principles of justice and ensures that the evidence is never brought out.

As for the armed forces and the police, they are essentially at the service of the rulers rather than of the nation. Although a number of UNITA soldiers were integrated into the FAA in 1991, and again in 2002, these constitute a very small minority. Both army and police are highly politicised and the proportion of their numbers that is intimately linked to the presidency is growing all the time. Furthermore, the government has failed to disarm many of the militias that had been set up during the war, ensuring that a large number of weapons have remained in the hands of civilians who take orders directly from the regime. Finally, the government has ensured that parliament votes its proposed budget for the Defesa Civil, or Civil Defence Force, which should have been dissolved after the end of the war. The coercive arm of the state is thus entirely controlled by the regime.

The MPLA has filled since independence virtually all administrative posts in the country—at all levels, in all sectors and in all regions—thus ensuring complete party domination over the civil service. Although after the 1992 elections and after the creation of the GURN in 1997 a small number of posts was to be allocated to non-MPLA personnel, this remained symbolic. It is only since 2002 that the regime has been confronted with the need to allocate agreed numbers of portfolios and administrative offices to UNITA. The regime has responded to this new pressure in two ways. As regional and local administration becomes increasingly important to reconstruction and privatisation, it has ensured that the top sub-national officials, of whom the regional governors are the most important, continue to be appointed. Second, it has made certain that those selected are accountable only to the President.

The refusal to allow the election of regional and local organs makes it impossible for the local population to force accountability on a governor and his subordinates. Since it is those very administrative organs, along with the security forces, which ensure 'law and order' locally, there can be no challenge to the MPLA's control of the bureaucracy and the services it is supposed to deliver. Although the ruling party's dominance is sometimes challenged in the urban centres, the deployment of increased numbers of security personnel in 'difficult' areas, who are not shy about using violence when needed, has usually managed to contain any opposition or protest.

The regime's immense reluctance to appoint UNITA staff to key (or 'sensitive') administrative positions, particularly outside the main urban centres, allied with the obstacles that are placed in the way of those who are nominated, has conspired to limit their impact. With very few exceptions, it is clear that civil servants work to further the aims of the MPLA and to undermine those of all other political or civic organisations. The overlap of administration and party (i.e. the MPLA), which goes back to independence, is so complete that ordinary people will readily approach either when in need of services or favours. It is a priceless asset for a regime that can now no longer evade international pressure and must accept multiparty elections.

Freedom of expression has been, and continues to be, severely constrained owing to the advantages enjoyed by the state. The official media, controlled by the regime, are the only ones able to operate freely across the country. Only state television and state radio are allowed to broadcast nationally. The private broadcast media, of which the most authoritative is the Catholic Church's Rádio Ecclesia, have until now failed to obtain licenses to operate throughout the country. Added to this, non-state media face innumerable obstacles—ranging from the lack of financial support and the dearth of private printing firms to straightforward harassment, all of which make the work of their journalists difficult, if not dangerous.

The combined weight of such political and economic hegemony ensures that the regime has the means to silence the opposition and check demands for social or civic rights. In Cabinda, where there is a covert conflict, there is a *de facto* state of war.† In the rest of the country, particularly in the provinces where there is little international presence to observe the behaviour of officials, there are continuous violations of the most basic human rights. Force and impunity are

† A peace accord has now been signed, officially bringing this conflict to an end.

the twin pillars of the regime, making the prospect of 'democratisation' quite unrealistic.

The 'problem' of the autonomy of civil society. The final obstacle to the assertion of hegemony was the putative autonomy of civil society. Given that both the basic principles of the rule of law and the pressures of the international community demanded a 'vibrant' civil society, the regime faced a dilemma. On the one hand, it was in the process of strengthening party control over all aspects of political life and wanted now to extend this to civil society. On the other, it was expected by outside donors to make good its promise of greater democratisation, a process that is predicated on the autonomy of civil society organisations. It chose, therefore, to apply the Lusaka Accord in a way that would not threaten its dominance.

This involved a two-part policy. The first part was to re-establish direct party control over the mass organisations (such as the women's and youth organisations) that had acquired some autonomy since the advent of multiparty elections. It also involved the creation of a number of new organisations, now coming under the umbrella of the 'Movimento Espontâneo', or Spontaneous Movement, closely linked to the President, which sought to move into new, less political areas of civil society. The second consisted in setting up a number of officially sponsored NGOs to rival those international and domestic NGOs (including Church organisations) that, for obvious reasons, could not be abolished or cut down to size. The aim here was to turn these 'official' NGOs into substantial sources of patronage, which would be directly linked to the regime. The dire need for NGO funding in all social areas ensured that such largesse had direct political value.

As a rule, the regime is vigilant about international NGOs, which were prevented during the conflict from assisting those people living in UNITA areas. Confronted with the fact that many sought to assert their independence after the end of the conflict, the government made it clear that it would not hesitate to tighten up the conditions under which they were allowed to operate. What this means in practice is that the regime, though keen that NGO support should continue, is prepared to curtail their activities unless it can be seen to benefit politically from what they do.

Another area in which the regime has been active is that which concerns the role of professionals who are, or can be seen to be, 'opinion makers' within the country. It has increased its control of key independent professional organisations, such as those of lawyers and journalists, by making sure that they are run by individuals close to the President. More generally, it has sought to co-opt large numbers of professionals either by patronising their businesses or by offering them consultancies and other lucrative contracts. This ensured that many of them became dependent on the regime, of which they have in effect become 'organic intellectuals'.

Indeed, the government's efforts to limit the autonomy of civil society have surpassed those habitually found in authoritarian African countries. Since the Lusaka Accord, the President has launched a most ambitious plan: namely, to create his own 'civil society'—one that will be more powerful and better endowed than its autonomous rival. In point of fact, it was intended from the first that the Fundação Eduardo dos Santos (FESA) and its myriad affiliated organisations would be lavishly funded from the proceeds of the oil revenue and the donations of major public enterprises. With further financial support from the state and many other contributions offered in the name of the President, FESA has now become a significant player in the support of 'welfare' activities.[13]

This policy has spawned a large number of local NGOs and associations, now designated as Governmental NGOs (or GONGOs), which come together in a vast regime-linked network of civil society organisations that has become essential to the lives of ordinary people on the ground. Such a scheme has extended clientelistic dependence to the bulk of the population, ensuring thereby support for the ruling party. In this way it is made clear that continued health, welfare and social provisions are intimately tied to the enduring rule of the MPLA and that support for the President is the price to pay for a

13 On FESA's enormous importance within the country, see CM1996.

better life, or the avoidance of a worse life. Additionally, the government has moved to strengthen its links with a vast array of local and grassroots organisations, such as neighbourhood groupings or the councils of traditional authorities, cementing thereby an alliance with politically influential 'resident' associations.

The combined effects of a weak autonomous civil society, a well-endowed official network of GONGOs and enduring poverty have created a situation in which there was very little scope for opposition. Indeed, four years after the end of the conflict Angola still ranked amongst the most deprived countries on all UN indices. This was not just the result of the war but also the consequence of government policies. The insufficient resources devoted to national reconstruction and social welfare, allied to a widespread system of clientelism, generalised corruption and predation, favoured an environment in which development came second to the maintenance of the regime. The cumulative effects of such dynamics reduce the risks of violent opposition and minimise the need for overt repression (as is, for example, found in Zimbabwe).

Political domination. It is the same logic that guided the regime's political action. The aim here was to neutralise the opposition and to control the 'transition' to democracy. Its hegemony thus rested on its ability to exclude competitors from acquiring any real power and to manage the preparation and organisation of the forthcoming multiparty elections. This was a key aspect of the regime's political economy that was even more closely controlled by the President, who had long planned a strategy designed to maintain MPLA dominance and the continuation of his rule.

It is indeed the MPLA—the lynchpin of regime control over the state—which benefited most from clientelism. However, the management of the transition to more 'democratic' politics required that the party remain disciplined, so as to preserve a united front against political competitors within a multiparty National Assembly. This meant that the MPLA could not possibly be run democratically, which explains why it became notably more authoritarian after the advent of multiparty elections. The last few years have witnessed a tightening of the President's control over both party personnel and policies, making certain that no dissenting voice is allowed to garner support within the MPLA. Despite a discourse that speaks of transformation and new beginnings, there has been less and less scope within the party for the discussion of policy changes that would open up the political system. Hence, the latest Fifth Party Congress (2003) revealed no dissent from the official regime line.

The near-total dependence of the MPLA on the President had two important consequences. The first was that dissent was only allowed when it did not question the regime's dominance. Internal debates were limited by the knowledge that any challenge to the President's hegemony would be severely punished—which in a patrimonial system such as Angola's meant removal from the clientelistic networks. The second was that, contrary to the widespread view that only an experienced MPLA can usher in the new democratic age, there is no reason to believe that continued MPLA dominance can ever be compatible with democratic governance.

Although the party's control of the National Assembly enabled it to guarantee the passage of its chosen legislation without demur, the regime's preferred strategy was to neuter democracy by means of co-optation rather than coercion. To that end, the GURN was an ideal instrument. From its creation, but even more so since the defeat of UNITA in 2002, the GURN has been a tool of the government. This is so not just because it was the only way that the small parties could hope to partake of a modicum of clientelised power but also because it was an effective means of neutralising UNITA. Participation in the GURN was the only way for UNITA to benefit from the funding it needed in order to function as 'opposition' party. This was all the more critical since it had strictly limited access to the economic sector, which was the preserve of the regime. But UNITA also needed the GURN to mark its official standing within the current multiparty dispensation.

The price to pay for participating in the GURN was high. UNITA ministers had no real power and were compelled to implement official MPLA policies. Furthermore, UNITA participation in government did not even ensure that those policies negotiated between the two parties were implemented. The key in this respect was the reluctance of the government to finalise the appointment of UNITA members as ambassadors, provincial governors and other important local officials. Even when they were appointed, their autonomy was severely constrained by their own officials (and staff) who continued to take their orders directly from the government or the President. UNITA was constantly torn between the desire to gain its rightful place within the state apparatus and the fear that too aggressive a position on its part would lead to a further deterioration of its position.

The regime's intentions were clear. On the one hand, it aimed to prevent UNITA from either becoming more independent or joining forces with other opposition parties. On the other, it sought to weaken UNITA in two different ways. One was that UNITA remained linked with government policies and found it difficult to position itself in overt opposition. The second was that the regime's co-optation of individual UNITA members, who were allowed to join the appropriate clientelistic circles, created internal divisions within the party. Not every UNITA politician gained equally from the party's participation in the GURN. And it was the Luanda-based politicians who benefited most, not the party's local activists in the provinces.

After Savimbi's death and military defeat in 2002, UNITA showed that it was able to survive as an independent political organisation with a well-grounded local organisation. Indeed, in the congress that followed it opted for democracy rather than the continuation of its subordinate role within the regime's political dispensation. So long as it stayed in the GURN, however, the party's autonomy and its capacity to set out on its own or to join forces with other political organisations remained severely limited. Indeed, UNITA's continued membership of the GURN had the potential to tear the party apart—an outcome that would evidently not have displeased the MPLA.

But the regime did not limit itself to manipulation of the GURN in order to preserve its political domination and undermine the rules of democracy. Indeed, when the democratic institutions did not deliver the 'right' results, the ruling elite simply bypassed them. One way of doing this was to resort to direct 'consultations' with the necessary interlocutors—political parties, civil society organisations, churches community leaders, opinion makers, etc. This made possible the 'spontaneous' voicing of views, opinions and policies that went against those who opposed official government policies and justified legislation that limited further fundamental democratic rights or liberties—as occurred in respect of the laws on the press and on land use.

Such a political strategy also lay at the root of the management of the next elections, and in particular the question of when the polls should be held. Soon after the end of the war, the opposition proposed that elections should take place in 2004 or 2005. As the government failed to respond, the opposition decided in May 2004 to suspend its participation in the Constitutional Commission until the President announced the date. In this instance, international pressure forced dos Santos finally to make a move. He chose to consult the Conselho da República, which advised that the elections should be held in 2006. However, the President failed officially to endorse this advice, a requirement to trigger preparation for the polls, thus leaving unclear whether this was the final date. His statement in February 2006 that the country's road infrastructure was unsuited to holding elections confirmed what many already expected, that is, a further postponement of the elections.

Another example of undemocratic practice concerned the question of constitutional change. The opposition had long argued that the approval of a new constitution should be the purview of the newly elected National Assembly—since parliament had last been elected in 1992. The regime for its part favoured the opposite, since it had an absolute majority in the present National Assembly and was confident of gaining support from enough UNITA deputies to reach the two-third majority it required for constitutional amendment. Although the President gave some ground on this issue, the matter was never satisfactorily settled. Until the much-delayed elections are held, this is unlikely to be settled by negotiation between government and opposition.

The fact that, as of the end of 2005, the government had not yet set in motion the key preparations required for the elections to take place simply confirmed the suspicion that it was determined to control the pace of 'democratisation' in order to ensure that it remained in power once the polls were held. Quite clearly, the delays in the compilation of a proper electoral register made it impossible to fix a time for the polls. Even more crucially, the failure to agree the formation of a genuinely independent National Electoral Commission was bound to hold up the process even longer. Unless all political parties agree on the composition of that Commission, the elections will never be accepted as 'free and fair'. The latest presidential statements in early 2006 seemed to indicate that the regime was not yet prepared to subject itself to electoral scrutiny.

Of course, time was not wasted. Whilst waiting for the election dates to be fixed, the MPLA had started seriously to prepare itself for the campaign. Because it had decided to abandon its 'workplace cells', the party was busy setting up 'residential cells' in all urban/suburban neighbourhoods and rural communes. These political networks were being used not just to garner support for the party but also to guarantee that there were means by which 'useful' votes could be rewarded. The aim here was not just to win the elections but to obtain a two-third majority, which would make it possible to introduce those constitutional dispositions that would ensure continued MPLA supremacy.

Such a strategy is to be understood within a context in which the regime does not enjoy any 'democratic' legitimacy but relies instead on a well-oiled system of clientelistic legitimacy. What this means is that Angolans do not have political and social rights as such but only the right to be part of patrimonial networks, which make it possible to access certain resources and avoid certain penalties. It is the very arbitrariness of the system that ensures compliance, not its legitimate authority. The regime can only contemplate a transition to multiparty politics that fits the *de facto* single party strictures of the present political arrangement.

Finally, it is worth pointing out that the regime can no longer resort to ideology in order to unite and mobilise the country. It certainly cannot credibly claim that it represents a national 'bourgeoisie', which alone is in a position to ensure social, economic and democratic 'progress'. No one in the country believes for one instant that the current ruling oligarchy is working towards a form of development that will deliver such 'progress'. Nor is it plausible to claim that the present rulers represent a 'national' bourgeoisie, tied as they are to outside economic interests that have little concern for social and economic development.

This ideological vacuum is filled with talk of 'sovereignty regained', a nationalist discourse that is primarily geared to reject outside interference with the current political 'transition'. The emphasis on unity and reconciliation is not, as some might infer, meant to bring all political forces together for the sake of bringing about democratisation. It is, rather, meant to call all groups to rally behind the banner of the MPLA, still today conceived as synonymous with the Angolan nation. What this means in practice is that in this new multiparty situation the regime conveys the clear impression that support for the MPLA *is in and of itself* a sign of commitment to 'national' unity and reconciliation. The focus on such an interpretation of reconciliation is obviously at the expense of a serious debate about the meaning of democracy in a country like Angola—a country emerging from 40 years of war and 30 years of single-party authoritarian rule.[14]

This in itself shows that the regime is far from accepting the logic of 'democracy'. What it is doing, as it prepares for elections, is to attempt to revive the early postcolonial ideology of equating the MPLA with the 'people'. This obviously implies that those who do not support the party are in effect disqualifying themselves from the new political roadmap. At a stroke, therefore, they become 'dissidents', a sobriquet that implies they ought not to be entitled to the political rights that would be theirs in a genuinely competitive multiparty system. Such an attitude on the part of the regime is nefarious to greater accountability and entirely against the spirit of a genuine transition towards greater democracy.

Conclusion

An analysis in terms of political economy, such as the one offered above, aims above all at going beyond a superficial definition of the so-called democratic transition, which equates 'democracy' with economic and political 'liberalisation'. From this viewpoint, therefore, it is simply impossible to contend, as the regime does, that Angola is a 'young and fragile' democracy. What has happened in Angola is in effect the conversion of the political system from a single-party dictatorial structure to an authoritarian hegemonic dispensation adapted to multiparty electoral politics. This means that the oligarchy in power uses and abuses both the democratic process and constitutional legality in order to ensure the continuation of a clientelistic system that will deliver electoral victory.

It is thus impossible to conclude that there is in Angola an 'emerging' democracy, as though this were the beginning of a process that

14 The creation of a 'Citizenship and Civil Society Office' under the aegis of the MPLA is symptomatic of the regime's approach since it contributes to the confusion between State and Party and ensures that this important question is debated within the ambit of a *de facto* political campaign aimed at garnering support for the ruling party.

would eventually result in 'democratisation'. On the contrary, the obstructions placed in the way of such democratic transition and the consolidation of the regime's political and economic hegemony are the very foundations of a political economy that is designed to make democracy well nigh impossible. These impediments are structurally inherent in that system, which makes plain to the population that the 'future' lies with the MPLA. The feelings of political impotence thus generated are an integral part of the strategy that aims to make certain—in so far as this is ever possible—that the regime stays in power after the elections.

BIBLIOGRAPHY

Christine Messiant [CM] 1993, 'Social and Political Background to the 'Democratization' and the Peace Process in Angola', in *Democratization in Angola*, Leiden: African Studies Centre, pp. 13-42.

CM1994a 'Angola: le retour à la guerre ou l'inavouable faillite d'une intervention internationale', *L'Afrique Politique 1994,* (Paris: Karthala/Bordeaux, CEAN, 1994, pp. 199-229.

CM1994b 'Angola, les voies de l'ethnisation et de la décomposition. I. De la guerre à la paix (1975-1991): le conflit armé, les interventions internationales et le peuple angolais', *Lusotopie* (Paris: L'Harmattan/Bordeaux: Maison des Pays ibériques), 1-2, 1994, pp. 155-210.

CM1995 'Angola. Les voies de l'ethnisation et de la décomposition. II Transition à la démocratie ou marche à la guerre? L'épanouissement des deux 'partis armés' (mai 1991-septembre 1992), *Lusotopie*, 3 (Paris: Karthala), pp. 181-212.

CM 1997, 'Angola, The Challenge of Statehood', in David Birmingham and Phillis Martin, (eds.), *History of Central Africa*. Vol. III: The Contemporary Years, London: Longman, pp. 131-165.

CM1998 *Une capitale dans la guerre: ordre politique et violences à Luanda* (ed. Centre d'études et de recherches internationales,

Direction des affaires stratégiques), Projet de recherches sur les 'villes en guerre', duplicated.

CM1999a 'La Fondation Eduardo dos Santos (FESA): à propos de l'investissement de la société civile par le pouvoir angolais', *Politique Africaine*, n° 73, March 1999, pp. 82-102.

CM1999b 'A propos des «transitions démocratiques». Notes comparatives et préalables à l'analyse du cas angolais', *Africana Studia* (Oporto), 2, 1999, pp. 61-95.

CM2001 'The Eduardo dos Santos Foundation: Or, How Angola's Regime is Taking over Civil Society', *African Affairs*, 100, March 2001, pp. 287-309.

CM2001 'Une "petite guerre" dans "l'endroit le plus excitant au monde". Angola: une "victoire" sans fin ?', *Politique Africaine,* 80, March 2001.

CM2002 'Fin de la guerre, enfin, en Angola. Vers quelle paix?', *Politique Africaine*, 86, June, pp. 83-95.

CM2002 'Angola. A Caminho de que Paz ?', *História* (Lisboa), 51, November, pp. 26-32.

CM2003a 'Des alliances de la guerre froide à la juridisation du conflit', *in* P. Hassner & R. Marchal, (eds.), *Guerres et sociétés. Etat et violence après la Guerre froide,* Paris: Karthala, 2003, pp. 491-519.

CM2003b 'Angola. 'Malheur aux vaincus!'. Les coûts d'une 'guerre pour la paix', in MSF, *A l'ombre des guerres justes*, Paris: Flamarion, pp. 119-143.

CM2003c 'Les Églises et la dernière guerre en Angola (1998-2002). Les voies difficiles de l'engagement pour une paix juste', *in* 'Religion, guerre et paix/Religion, War and Peace', *Le Fait missionnaire. Missions et Sciences Sociales*, n°13, October 2003, pp. 75-117.

CM2004 'Why did Bicesse and Lusaka fail? A critical analysis' *in* G. Meier, (ed.), *From Military Peace to Social Justice. The Angolan Peace Process*, London: Conciliation Resources.

4

THE ANGOLAN REGIME AND THE MOVE TO MULTIPARTY POLITICS

Nuno Vidal

Introduction

During the ten years between 1992 and 2002—from the first multiparty elections to the signing of the Luena memorandum—the Angolan transition to a multiparty system that began in 1990 was more or less suspended, held hostage by the civil war. Restrictions on the proper functioning of a multiparty system continued throughout the nineties, especially as concerns civil and political rights. After the death of Savimbi and the end of the war in 2002, many hoped for the rapid and effective opening up of space for political opposition, which would serve an emerging civil society and bring about a thorough transformation of the Angolan political system.[1] This did not happen. Why?

1 Research for this study was financed by the Portuguese Foundation for Science and Technology and developed under the aegis of the Faculty of Economics at the University of Coimbra. It is the result of field research over a period of three years and of the cooperation of the author with a number of international research teams operating in Angola. Around three hundred and fifty in-depth interviews were held during this period in Luanda and in the provinces of Huambo and Malange, with people from a broad social and professional spectrum, including national and local members from all political parties represented in the National Assembly as well as representatives from a few parties outside parliament; national and local government members; presidential aides; Catholic and Protestant religious leaders; members of the national army; journalists from radio, television and the press, both state and private; academics;

A major assumption for opposition parties and for much of the emergent civil society is that peace and elections—legislative, presidential and local—might bring some significant change to the Angolan political system. This assumption is based upon three main arguments: firstly, that the dynamics of an electoral process closely monitored by international organisations will open more space for political debate; secondly, that the possibility of having a parliament in which no party has a majority will be an opportunity to institutionalise political negotiation; and thirdly, that local elections, to be held after the legislative, might start a gradual process of development beyond the oil sector as well as a process of political inclusion and participation—thereby eroding the current centralisation of power and administration that excludes the majority of people from politics.

This chapter tests these assumptions by analysing the political process through which the Angolan political system emerged over time. It is in three parts: the first examines the so-called socialist period; the second discusses how these same characteristics survived throughout the nineties, during the so-called transition to multiparty politics; the third studies how these features are so many obstacles and constraints to effective democratisation.

The analysis is centred on the way the political system facilitates the regime's patrimonial and clientelistic operation despite the formal model in place—be it single-party socialism or multiparty capitalism—allowing a specific type of domination to prevail, which combines selective distribution and cooptation with repression, social fragmentation, and the political and economic neglect of the majority of the population.

---

trade-union leaders; managers and workers of national and international NGOs. A full list of interviewees is available by request to the University of Coimbra. A different version of this chapter was published in Portuguese as Nuno Vidal, "Multipartidarismo em Angola", in Nuno Vidal and Justino Pinto de Andrade, *O processo de transição para o multipartidarismo em Angola,* Luanda and Lisbon: Firmamento, 2006, pp. 11-57.

The construction of the Angolan political system after independence

As in so many other African countries, the Angolan post-colonial political system assumed a clearly neo-patrimonial character.[2] The state and its resources were used from the start by the elites in power to achieve political and economic hegemony. A re-distributive scheme of privileges and benefits operated by means of the allocation of party, governmental and other public offices, blurring the distinction between public and private spheres. The juxtaposition of party and state structures and the political and economic centralisation typical of a Marxist model were well suited to the needs of a patrimonial operation.

Regardless of the regime (civilian or military) and regardless of the political model (socialist or capitalist), all neo-patrimonial states have in common a strategy for concentrating political power and centralising administration in those strategic areas that provide primary access to state resources, so as to centralise the general distribution of benefits and privileges. This strategy is crucial for the survival of patrimonialism because if the system of redistribution is politically scattered and administratively dispersed, the patrimonial organisation risks disruption. Even if economic privileges can still

2 For a characterisation of modern patrimonialism, see Jean-François Médard, 'The Underdeveloped State in Tropical Africa: Political Clientelism or Neo-Patrimonialism?' in C. Clapham (ed.), *Private Patronage and Public Power,* London: Frances Pinter, 1982, pp. 162–92; Jean-François Médard, 'L'État néo-patrimonial en Afrique noire' in Jean-François Médard (ed.), *États d'Afrique noire,* Paris: Karthala, 1991, pp. 323-53; Jean-François Bayart, *The State in Africa, the Politics of the Belly*, London: Longman, 1989; Jean-François Bayart et al., *The Criminalization of the State in Africa,* London: James Currey, 1998; Patrick Chabal, *Power in Africa,* London: Macmillan Press, 1994; Patrick Chabal and Jean-Pascal Daloz, *Africa Works,* London: James Currey, 1999. For an analytical comparison of these works and their characterisation as a neo-patrimonial perspective see Nuno Vidal, *Post-modern Patrimonialism in Africa: the Genesis and Development of the Angolan Political-Economic System 1961–1987,* PhD thesis, London: King's College, 2002, ch. 1.

be obtained, there is no longer a clear dependency on hierarchical distribution.[3]

Post-independence Angolan patrimonialism started off, during Neto's administration, by being partisan in nature; it soon became presidential. At first, during the second half of the 1970s, simple party membership gave access to state distribution. Yet, in the face of decreasing revenues owing to the war effort and the disruption of the productive sector of the economy outside the oil industry, the lower and (even certain middle) echelons of the party began to lose a good part of their benefits. The majority of the population, in or outside the party, fought to establish clientelistic links with the higher levels of the patrimonial pyramid, usually appealing to primary solidarities such as family, region of origin or even ethno-linguistic bonds—all of which contributed to the fragmentation of the social tissue. The inequality between rulers and ruled in their access to resources was gradually aggravated. Angolan patrimonialism became increasingly elitist at the same time as it became more solidly presidentialist, especially during the dos Santos administration in the mid-80s.

The system of distribution that was supposed to bring rulers and ruled together, link centre and peripheries, urban and rural areas, simply collapsed. It became extremely concentrated at the top, in the hands of a select few: in effect, the President and a restricted clique. Insofar as it was the political and administrative system that gave access to material benefits and privileges, such a phenomenon drastically restricted access to the channels of resources and led to the neglect of the population at large. The enclave and *rentier* nature of the main source of revenue, oil, facilitated this phenomenon. It allowed the ruling elites to ignore the need to care about the ordinary population, who were virtually excluded from any effective political and economic participation. Politically, they had no votes to exchange for benefits; economically, they were not a source of income to the state. I have characterised this process as post-modern patrimonialism in order to

3 Jean-François Médard (ed.), *États d'Afrique noire*, Paris: Karthala, 1991, p. 360.

distinguish it from the neo-patrimonialism that prevailed during Neto's administration.[4]

State services such as public administration, social security, health and education, gradually collapsed.[5] Within such a context, where freedom of expression and the operation of civil society or legal opposition were not allowed, inefficiency and corruption thrived. The increasing intensity of the internal conflict in the 1980s reinforced the characteristics of the whole system: war served as a justification, or excuse, for the decline of redistribution and poor state delivery of services. It justified a strong internal state security apparatus and fierce authoritarianism. It required political control and unified command, thereby strengthening centralisation and the concentration of power. It disrupted internal production and increased economic dependence on oil revenues. Finally, it intensified social fragmentation.[6]

The process of increasing centralisation and elitism began with the first President, Agostinho Neto, and was later developed to an extreme by dos Santos. As early as 1976, Neto had progressively started to absorb the powers of the Prime Minister and to reinforce his authority over the provincial commissioners, who are now called provincial governors. In August 1977, he assumed the role of head of government.[7] In December 1978, he abolished the posts of prime minister and vice-prime minister.[8] This process of centralisation was boosted by the reaction to the attempted coup, led by Nito Alves, that took place in May 1977. Seen as the consequence of poor internal discipline and power dispersal, it led to an increase in presidential powers, the setting up of a strong state security apparatus and a 'rec-

4 For such a characterisation see Nuno Vidal, *Post-Modern Patrimonialism in Africa*; also Nuno Vidal, 'Modern and Post-Modern Patrimonialism', in *Community and the State in Lusophone Africa,* ed. Malyn Newitt with Patrick Chabal and Norrie MacQueen, London: King's College, 2003, pp. 1–14.

5 See my chapter on social issues in this volume.

6 Nuno Vidal, 'Modern and Post-Modern Patrimonialism', pp. 1–14.

7 See Law 71/76 in *Diário da República*, I, 266, (11 November 1976); also Law 13/77, in *DR*, I, 194 (7 August 1977).

8 See Law 1/79, *DR*, I, 14 (16 January 1979).

tification movement' that drastically reduced party membership. There followed the establishment of strong political control over the judicial system, which juxtaposed civil and military courts with an increasing supremacy of the military over the civilian.[9] These were all characteristics that became central to the Angolan political system and have survived to this day, as will be shown.

Right after the attempted coup, a radical campaign for the 'cleansing' of society and the political apparatus degenerated into a savage and terrifying witch-hunt throughout the country, which struck particularly young activists, intellectuals and cadres, generally believed to be close to Nito Alves' ideals. The purge and its traumatic memory, along with the consolidation of a fearful state security service, became a powerful inhibitor of organised popular protest against the MPLA's leadership. In parallel, a movement of party 'rectification' was launched, whereby rigid criteria were introduced for party membership, which consequently dropped from 110,000 to a mere 31,000 members.[10] In an estimated population of 8 million in 1980, the new party members represented around 0.4 per cent of that population, a tiny number considering that it was a single party system.

Selection criteria for membership privileged 'the more aware elements of the working class'—usually taken as the more educated.[11] This discriminated against peasants since most of them were illiterate and 60 per cent of the whole labour force, working in agriculture mostly as peasant farmers, was simply ignored—this in a context where 74 per cent of the population still lived in rural areas.[12] After the 'rectification campaign', peasants represented merely 1.9 per cent

9 See Nuno Vidal, 'Multipartidarismo em Angola', pp. 11-57.

10 In *Relatório do Comité Central ao I° Congresso Extraordinário do Partido, realizado em Luanda de 17 a 23 de Dezembro de 1980,* Luanda: Secretariado do Comité Central, 1980, pp. 17–18.

11 In *Relatório do Comité Central ao I° Congresso do MPLA, realizado em Luanda de 4 a 11 de Dezembro de 1977,* Luanda: DEPI, 1977, p. 22, pp. 18–19.

12 In Keith Somerville, *Angola: Politics, Economics and Society,* London: Frances Pinter, 1986, p. 91 and pp. 96–7.

of that membership.[13] They became ever more distanced from the party. Since the party was the main provider of benefits and goods and since agricultural production abruptly dropped because of the war and centralised socialist management, peasants were now on the margins of patrimonial distribution.[14] The party was showing its first signs of elitism.

Bearing in mind the problems caused by a young generation involved in political activities—some having resisted the MPLA's dominance or joined the 'Nitista' movement—a new control over education was established by the party. Through his presidential despatch dated February 1979, Neto determined that the Council for Student Grants Abroad and the Scholarship Fund (Internal and Abroad) should now be accountable to the Central Committee's Department of Party Cadres, itself directly answerable to the President.[15] Thus, for scholarship students, Neto created a mechanism of economic and educational dependency on the party's supreme organs, which was used, albeit informally, to reward or punish the students' political behaviour and was soon to become part of a wider system of distribution of privileges and benefits.

The new policy had its results: on the whole, the generation that followed that of the politically active youth committees understood and respected the new rules that regulated access to professional education and upward mobility. This new generation provided politically accommodating young members for the party, loyal to any given protector, and expecting benefits in exchange for dependability and political correctness. Those who fitted these parameters went on with their education and did well. In the early 1980s, they were given senior positions in the state administration, both in government and in state enterprises, and those within the armed forces—FAPLA (*Forças Armadas Populares de Libertação de Angola*)—were promoted to higher ranks. A few of them were later recruited by the new Presi-

13 In *Relatório do Comité Central ao I° Congresso Extraordinário*, p. 18.

14 See Nuno Vidal, *Post-Modern Patrimonialism in Africa*, chapter 7.

15 Legal Despatch, *DR*, I, 29 (3 February 1979).

dent, Eduardo dos Santos, to become part of the powerful presidential shadow government.[16]

The process of centralising and controlling the political system evolved further with the restructuring of the judiciary. The death penalty was approved to punish vaguely defined crimes against state security and military courts were given broad competence, which coincided with those of the civilian courts, thereby blending ever more the civilian and military areas.[17] Political control of the two judicial systems, the military and the civilian, was enshrined in law on the grounds that the legitimacy of both tribunals arose from the MPLA, the supreme state organisation.[18] These two judicial systems and their respective tribunals were subordinated to the party, and ultimately to the President.[19] This situation still prevails today.

By the time Eduardo dos Santos assumed the presidency in September 1979, the MPLA and its regime had clearly taken on an authoritarian and much feared character. During the Marxist phase of dos Santos's administration (up to 1987) authoritarianism, restricted party membership and political control of the judicial system were all strengthened. The process of political and administrative centralisation continued unabated.

Owing to party discrimination and centralisation, together with escalating public expenditure on the war, the lower social strata (including even those party members at the bottom of the party structure, the party cells) were increasingly removed from the sys-

---

16 See Nuno Vidal, *Post-modern patrimonialism in Africa.*

17 See laws: 7/78, *DR*, I, 136 (10 June 1978); 8/78, *DR*, I, 137 (26 May 1978); 16/78, *DR*, I, 15 (24 November 1978); 17/78, *DR*, I, 15 (24 November 1978).

18 See in this sense the introduction to law 7/76, *DR*, I, 102 (1976); also introduction to law 8/78 in *DR*, I, 137 (26 May 1978); also article 1 of law 17/78 in *DR*, I, 15 (24 November 1978).

19 The president of the military tribunal and the judges of the Civilian Tribunals were all nominated or removed from office by the National Security Commission of the MPLA's Central Committee, which was presided over by the President of the Party, also President of the Republic; see art. 6 law 17/78 in *DR*, I, 15 (24 November 1978); also art. 7, nº 1, law 8/78 in *DR*, I, 137 (26 May 1978).

tem of distribution. At the start of the 1980s, this kind of grassroots membership no longer enjoyed any special material privileges by comparison to non-party members.[20] The result was the paralysis of party-cell activity, especially at provincial level.[21] A campaign for the recruitment of new members began in 1983 with the declared objectives of doubling membership from 30,000 to 60,000. However, insofar as the 'rectification principles' were maintained, the results presented at the 1985 congress accounted for only 3,500 new members.[22] Once again selection criteria kept on favouring the urban and literate to the detriment of the rural and illiterate. In fact, out of the 628 delegates to the second congress in 1985, only 12 were peasants whereas administrative office-holders and civil servants numbered 269.[23] In short, the party had reinforced its elitist character and the lower 'orders' had entered into a 'pernicious state of apathy', as recognised by the President himself.[24] The party remained tiny until 1990, still including less than 0.5 per cent of the population.

Continuing to concentrate power, the President was constitutionally consecrated as President of the People's Assembly in August 1980 and as such was entitled to control and revoke all executive and legislative acts of the new organisations, be it at central or local level.[25] In practice, the People's Assembly was reduced to a ratifica-

---

20 Michael Wolfers and Jane Bergerol, *Angola in the Frontline.* London: Zed Press, 1983, p. 177.

21 See *Relatório do Comité Central ao I° Congresso Extraordinário*, op. cit., 1980, p.21; also comments on the CC meeting of December 1982 on the *Angolan National Radio* (9 December 1982), in *Survey of World Broadcast* (13 December 1982).

22 In *Relatório do Comité Central ao II Congresso do Partido, realizado em Luanda de 2 a 10 de Dezembro de 1985,* Luanda: Edição do Secretariado do Comité Central, 1985, pp. 22–3.

23 See *Relatório do Comité Central ao II° Congresso*, pp. 22–3; also Keith Somerville, *Angola*, p. 105.

24 See 'Opening Speech of the President of the Republic to the Ist National Conference', in *Documentos da Iª Conferência Nacional do MPLA–PT de 14 a 19 de Janeiro*, Luanda: Edição do Secretariado do Comité Central, 1985, pp. 13–17.

25 See amendment to Constitutional Law, *DR*, I, 225, (23 September 1980).

tion chamber of the President's decisions; the situation is not much different today.

With regards to the party, in 1980 dos Santos began to isolate certain areas within the presidency that had previously been under party control, such as foreign economic affairs where the President's Cabinet was now entrusted with establishing business contacts with public or private foreign entities.[26] The President's intention was beginning to show: it allowed him to have autonomous control over external sources of income, such as oil revenue, itself the main pillar of the Angolan patrimonial system. Although the origin of these changes dates back to the early 80s, they were only uncovered in the late 1990s by the media.[27]

Taking advantage of new South African incursions into southern Angola in November 1982, dos Santos demanded from the Central Committee new and sweeping emergency powers, including military ones. A new national political, military and administrative infrastructure was created—the Regional Military Councils, or CMRs.[28] These were hierarchically above all other (local, provincial or central) governing and administrative bodies and were accountable to a Council for Defence and Security, a form of martial government under the President in his role as Commander-in-Chief of the armed forces. It had almost unlimited powers across the territory, including control of all financial dealings with the outside.[29] The President personally

26 Article 1 in Presidential decree 25–A/80, *DR*, I, 72 (1 April 1980); statutes of the President of the Republic's Cabinet.

27 See the reports by Global Witness that name several members of the presidential clique involved in networks of arms dealing, missing funds from oil income to the state, among other scandals: 'A Crude Awakening: the Role of the Oil and Banking Industries in Angola's Civil War and the Plunder of the State Assets', a report by Global Witness, December 1999; 'All the President's Men', a report by Global Witness, March 2002; 'A Rough Trade: the Role of Companies and Governments in the Angolan Conflict', a report by Global Witness, December 1998; published on www.oneworld.org/globalwitness .

28 Law 5/83, *DR*, I, 179 (30 July 1983).

29 Article 4 of law 3/84, in *DR*, I, 22 (26 January 1984), creating the CDS; also Decree 6/84, *DR*, I, 79 (3 April 1984), regulating the CDS.

took charge of foreign affairs, dismissing the minister and assuming his portfolio from mid-1984 to 1985.[30] The whole ministry was then placed under the President's direct tutelage, as shown in the Central State Structure diagram (fig. 1).

In parallel to the new emergency powers, there now developed a bitter struggle between historical political figures inside the Political Bureau, the Central Committee and the government.[31] The young President became more politically aggressive and gradually deprived the government and party structures of effective executive power, transferring such powers to dependent subsidiary organisations—such as the Secretariat of the Council of Ministers, the Cabinet of the President of the Republic and the Cabinet of the Head of Government. These institutions comprised mainly young people, issued from the post-27 May generation, with good technical preparation, coming from the faculties of Engineering, Law and Economy. They belonged to those who had been purged and 'rectified' earlier and had thus become submissive to the President, to whom they owed their social, professional and, above all, economic advancement.

With power now concentrated in those institutions surrounding the presidency, these young cadres became inherently powerful although they were deprived of political legitimacy other than that bestowed by the President. Their relatively young age, their technical education and their weak ideological convictions also made them more permeable to new socio-economic ideas and, according to official party documents, they were the main protagonists of the 1987 economic reform.[32] It is also important to stress that, insofar as

30 The President held the portfolio of foreign affairs until April 1985 when a new minister was appointed, Afonso 'M'Binda' Van Dunem, a man of absolute confidence to the president (a 'loyalist' as defined), who had been until then the head of the President's cabinet; in *Africa Research Bulletin–ARB* (April 1985), p. 7565.

31 So-called incident of the picture and the play; see Nuno Vidal, *Post-Modern Patrimonialism in Africa*, 10.1.

32 See *Biografia Oficial de José Eduardo dos Santos, Presidente da República de Angola* (Luanda: np, nd), pp.vi and vii.

the access to the President became ever more restricted, these young technicians came to act as gatekeepers and were used by Western diplomats to transmit information to the presidency.

Finally, regarding the judicial system, dos Santos intensified the process initiated by his predecessor. The attorney-general was considered subordinate to the President.[33] The same applied to the whole Ministry of Justice (see fig. 1). Following the creation of the CMR, the competence of the military courts was broadened and the new organs of military justice were explicitly granted juridical preponderance over civilian tribunals.[34] The presidents and professional judges of the regional military tribunals were to be directly nominated by the President of the Republic.[35]

In the mid-80s, the regime had reached the peak of power concentration and administrative centralisation: it was run by President Eduardo dos Santos, exercising to the full his functions as President of the Party, Head of State, Head of Government, Commander-in-Chief of the Armed Forces and, above all, head manager of the system of distribution, directly controlling oil, the major source of state revenues. Nevertheless, it would be an exaggeration to suggest that President dos Santos established a personal dictatorship during this period. He and other MPLA leaders had to play complex games of consensus politics, alliance building and patronage within the party.

Beyond the presidency, the connections between the military, the state and the party's top organs prevented the military from becoming an autonomous source of power as has happened in other African countries such as Nigeria.[36] The presidential structure, sometimes

33 See articles 1 and 2. of decree 25/80, *DR*, I, 70 (24 March 1980), approving the organisational regulation of the Office of the Procurator General of the Republic.

34 Law 14/84, *DR*, 168 (17 July 1984), on the regulation of organs of military justice.

35 In article 7, para. 2 of Law 14/84, *DR*, I, 168 (17 July 1984), on the regulation of organs of military justice.

36 On the case of Nigeria, see Jean-François Bayart, *The State in Africa*. This state of affairs in Angola was supposed to change with the peace after 2002, the military demobilisation (and reduction of the armed forces) and the effective integration of UNITA's military structures into the national army.

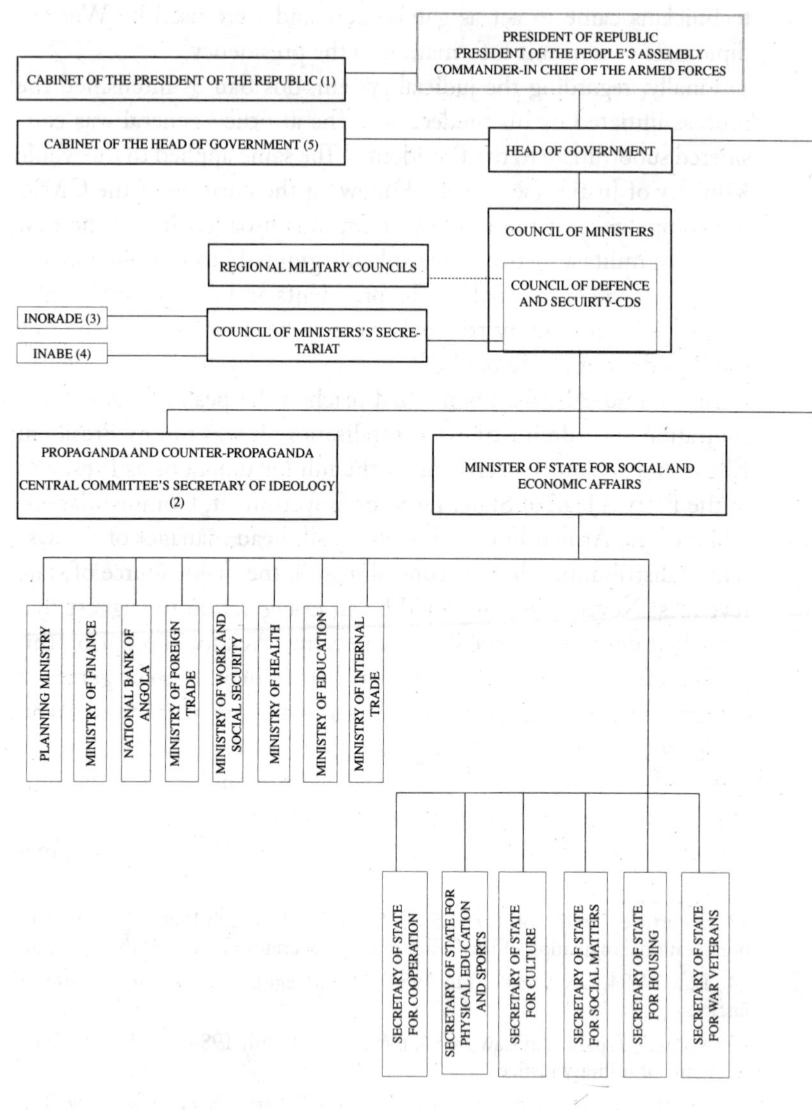

Fig. 1 Angola's central state structure in mid/late 1980s

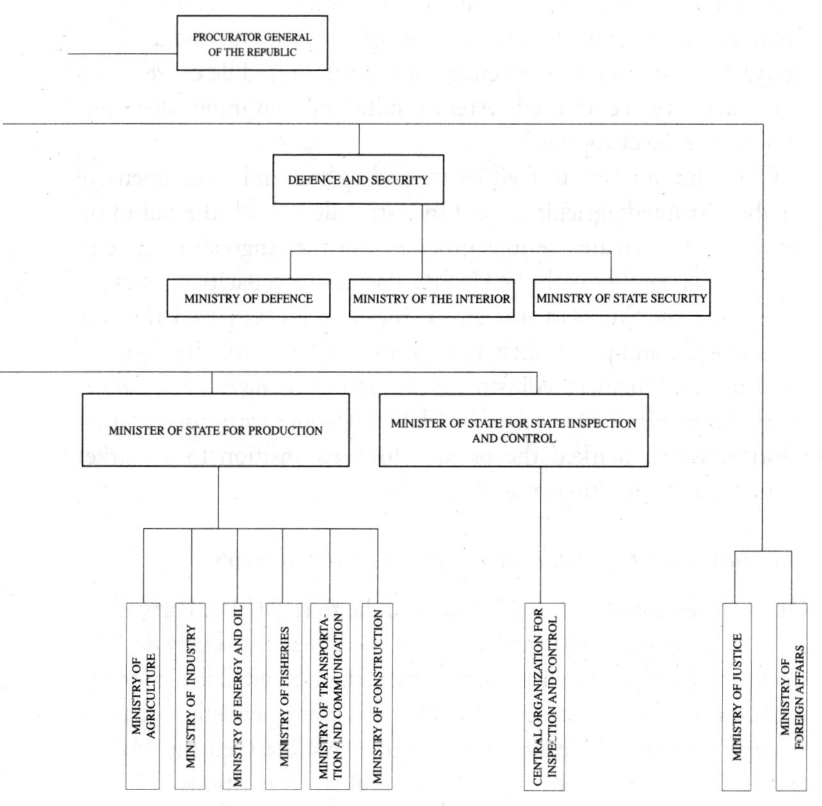
PROCURATOR GENERAL OF THE REPUBLIC
DEFENCE AND SECURITY
MINISTRY OF DEFENCE
MINISTRY OF THE INTERIOR
MINISTRY OF STATE SECURITY
MINISTER OF STATE FOR PRODUCTION
MINISTER OF STATE FOR STATE INSPECTION AND CONTROL
MINISTRY OF AGRICULTURE
MINISTRY OF INDUSTRY
MINISTRY OF ENERGY AND OIL
MINISTRY OF FISHERIES
MINISTRY OF TRANSPORTATION AND COMMUNICATION
MINISTRY OF CONSTRUCTION
CENTRAL ORGANIZATION FOR INSPECTION AND CONTROL
MINISTRY OF JUSTICE
MINISTRY OF FOREIGN AFFAIRS

supported by the top party leadership, made the strategic policy decisions, but it was not easy to ensure delivery because of an increasingly dysfunctional state bureaucracy, resulting from the war and a Marxist-type bureaucracy with an enormous deficit of middle cadres. This top-heavy, over-centralised system resulted in even minor decisions needing top-level approval.

Increasing imports to feed an expanding war and to compensate for the disrupted agriculture and industry, along with the fall in oil prices in 1986, created serious problems for the Angolan balance of payments. Together with the USSR's decreasing capacity to carry on supporting the Angolan war effort, these problems paved the way for economic and political changes from 1987 onwards. By then the economic and financial adjustment programme (*Programa de Saneamento Económico e Financeiro,* or SEF) introduced cautious market reforms, which marked the prelude to the transition to a market economy and a multiparty system.[37]

The transition to a multiparty system in the nineties

Officially the socialist model lasted until the third MPLA Party Congress of December 1990, but by 1987 it was already in steady decline. Complex negotiations with South Africa, the US and Cuba led to the withdrawal of Cuban troops and Namibia's independence—paving the way for the 1991 Bicesse peace agreement between the MPLA and UNITA followed by the first ever multiparty elections in 1992.

A constitutional revision of law 12/91 in 1991 simply approved the basic principles of a multiparty democracy, defining Angola as a democratic State based on the rule of law, enshrining the key civic and human rights as well as the basic principles of a market economy. The new political and legal framework opened a space for the emergence of opposition political parties and so-called civil soci-

37 On these issues, see Manuel Ennes Ferreira, 'A política de recuperação económica na República Popular de Angola', *Política International*, 1, I (1990), pp. 107–32; Manuel Ennes Ferreira, 'La reconversion économique de la nomenklature pétrolière', *Politique Africaine*, 57 (1995), pp. 11–26.

ety organisations—church groups, private media, independent trade unions and professional unions, and NGOs. Government radio and television became somewhat more pluralist and a wave of strikes took place in 1991 and 1992.

Within such a climate, and having to prepare himself for the first elections in independent Angola, the President realised the need to rehabilitate the party machine, not only in terms of effective power, but also in terms of a revival of the local structures that had been forgotten and marginalised over the years. Several former leaders from the nationalist period, such as Lopo do Nascimento and Lucio Lara, were again called to prominent positions and the party was effectively revitalised. Grassroots structures and hierarchical set-ups were rehabilitated through a major reorganisation. According to the third MPLA extraordinary congress of May 1992, it was now time to reunite the party's 'big family', namely all those who considered themselves to the belong to the MPLA even though distanced from party militancy. There was a large distribution of material benefits and traditional authorities were politically rehabilitated. Party membership was enlarged from 65,362 members in 1990 to 544,639 by the end of 1992.[38] A significant amount of funds became available for party activities and for a professional electoral campaign managed by Brazilian experts.

The MPLA gained in dynamism but it is important to stress that a revived party did not mean an emerging autonomous entity. Several of the young cadres surrounding the Presidency had been occupying positions in the party's top echelons since the second congress (1985) and had remained there, preventing the party from becoming a parallel power to the Presidency. Later, during the fourth congress (1998), when war resumed after the 1994–98 Lusaka peace period and power was concentrated once again, former party leaders were again degraded in favour of the younger cadres: Lopo do Nascimento

38 See *Relatório do Comité Central ao IV Congresso do MPLA—Firme, rumo ao século XXI*, Luanda: Publicações do MPLA, 1998, pp. 5–10.

gave up his place as Secretary General to João Lourenço and Lúcio Lara was dismissed from the Central Committee.

A strong electoral dynamic progressively emerged within the MPLA ranks, helped significantly by UNITA's bellicose, *revanchiste* and frustrated electoral discourse, which effectively helped to bring together within the MPLA all those who feared UNITA's victory.[39] In Angola's first nationwide multiparty elections, a turnout of more than 91 per cent (4.4 million) registered voters gave the MPLA candidate, President dos Santos 49.57 per cent of the vote against 40.07 per cent for Savimbi, and the legislative elections resulted in UNITA getting 34.10 per cent of the vote against 53.74 per cent for the MPLA. The elections were considered generally free and fair by the UN and other foreign observers and according to the law there should have been a presidential election run-off, but UNITA refused to accept the results and resumed war.[40]

By then, a lot of criticism had been raised against the international community for not having sufficiently supported the implementation of the Bicesse agreement. In the face of UNITA's significant military gains—taking control of more than two thirds of the territory and isolating several urban centres—it became clear that Savimbi's forces had never disarmed as they should have under the supervision of the UN. The problem was not only the insufficiency of means—financial and human—allocated to the process, but also the weak reaction of the international community in general, and of the West in particular, after the elections to the patently false political claims made by

39 For the characterisation of this UNITA attitude towards the MPLA and all those who might be close to the MPLA, see Christine Messiant, 'MPLA et UNITA, processus de paix et logique de guerre', *Politique Africaine*, 57 (1995) pp. 53-4; also Christine Messiant, 'Angola les voies de l'ethnisation et de la décomposition. II. Transition à la démocratie ou marche à la guerre? L'épanouissement des deux "partis armés" (Mai 1991, Septembre 1992), *Lusotopie*, 3 (1995) pp. 181–221.

40 On the election results see Sofia Marques, *Angola: da Guerra à Democracia,* Luanda: Edipress, 1993.

UNITA. The international community was perceived by observers inside and outside Angola as having let the country down.[41]

The political liberalisation that had occurred during the electoral period (1991–92) was reversed and power was once again concentrated within the presidency, especially when it came to the purchase of arms, financed with oil revenues. In spite of the appointment of a new Prime Minister, Marcolino Moco (nominated mainly for the politically expedient reason that he came from the same regional-ethnic background as Savimbi), the main political decisions were still made at the level of the Council of Ministers presided over by dos Santos. Once again, the distribution of resources came under the control of the top echelons of the party/state/presidency (these organs remained intertwined). At the same time, the majority of the population most affected by the war was left to the care of international organisations now arriving en masse to offer emergency aid.[42] The activism and dedication of party members during the electoral campaign gave way to passivity.[43]

With a gradual military reversal in favour of the MPLA, the US finally conceded diplomatic recognition to the Angolan government in May 1993. Increasing US pressure seems to have led to the Lusaka peace agreement of November 1994. A new period of political openness then started with the integration of some of UNITA's military forces into the national armed forces (the FAA) under UN supervision, with UNITA's deputies taking their seats in parliament in 1997 and the creation of a so-called Government of Unity and National Reconstruction, or GURN, which integrated elements of several opposition parties represented in parliament.

Despite several minor military incidents, the protocol was partially implemented until 1998, when the Government decided to suspend

41 See. among others, Christine Messiant, 'Angola: le retour à la guerre ou l'inavouable faillite d'une intervention internationale', *L'Afrique Politique* (1994), pp. 201–29.

42 See my chapter on social issues in this volume.

43 See *Relatório do Comité Central ao IV Congresso,* p. 8.

it because of UNITA's repeated failure to hand over the administrative control of municipalities in the areas it still dominated. Since both sides had continued rebuilding and rearming their military forces during the peace period, the military conflict resumed with unprecedented intensity. The government resorted to the oil rent to finance its war effort while UNITA used the diamonds extracted from the areas under its control.

The resumption of war meant another contraction of the political and civil space opened during the 1994–98 Lusaka protocol implementation period. As ever, concentration of power, authoritarianism and political control followed. The President took over as head of government in January 1999 and abolished the post of Prime Minister (by then occupied by França Van Dunem). Political pressure upon the private media was reinforced through state security and judicial activity resulting in several arrests and lawsuits against journalists.[44] A multitude of opposition political parties had to face the challenge of internal factions (the so-called phenomenon of '*renovadas*'), which according to all opposition leaders dealing with the problem were instigated and sponsored by the MPLA. Such internal 'factionism' weakened the opposition and strongly reduced its ability to play a more active role during that period. The party most affected was obviously UNITA, whose deputies in Luanda were split between those who supported Savimbi and those who did not. Among the latter, a clearly government-sponsored group of defectors was formed (UNITA-Renovada or Renewed UNITA), which took the parliamentary seats reserved for Savimbi's party but had no internal or external credibility.

On the MPLA's side, the decision was clear: this time no concession would be made and a military solution was definitely to be sought—as confirmed by the President at the fourth congress in De-

44 See *Angola, Freedom of Expression under Threat*, Amnesty International Index AFR 12/016/1999 (1 November 1999); also Amnesty International, *Angola: Unfair Trial of Rafael Marques* (Amnesty International, 31 March 2000). URL: http://web.amnesty.org/library/index/ENGAFR120161999.

cember 1998. That goal was achieved with the progressive disruption of UNITA's military forces and the killing of Savimbi in February 2002. Despite attempts made by the international community and the Angolan social movements supporting peace, the ceasefire and the ensuing Memorandum of Luena were signed without any external or internal participation apart from the victorious MPLA and the defeated UNITA.[45] Such unequal relation of forces would from then on characterise the multiparty system in Angola.

Constraints to an effective multiparty system on the eve of elections

After the cease-fire negotiated in Luena in April 2002 and the resumption of the Lusaka protocol, many hoped for the rapid opening up of space for civil society and political opposition—as had occurred after the Bicesse agreement until the 1991–92 elections and again during the first stage of implementation of the Lusaka protocol between 1994 and 1998. However, more than five years after the memorandum, there were still no significant signs of change. The presidency and the MPLA's top echelons retained tight control over the state, its institutions and resources, using them to maintain their political and economic hegemony, and significantly restricting liberalisation. Opposition parties and civil society organisations faced severe constraints and were fragile or highly dependent. I detail here

45 During the socialist period, Churches, both Catholic and Protestant, were the isolated voices defending human rights, but during the last stages of the civil war, they were greatly helped in their initiatives by Civil Society Organisations–CSOs, which had grown stronger since 1991. In the late 90s, a myriad projects and initiatives for peace emerged between Churches and CSOs: Pro Pace movement; Angolan Group Reflecting for Peace, or GARP; Programme for Peace Building, or PCP; and a number of others. For a detailed analysis of these initiatives, see Michael G. Comerford, *O Rosto Pacífico de Angola,* Luanda: published by author, 2005, especially end of chapter 2 and chapter 4. See also Christine Messiant, 'Les églises et la derniére guerre en Angola (1998–2002). Les voies difficiles de l'engagement pour un pays juste', in *Le Fait Missionaire. War, Peace and Religion,* nº 13, October 2003, pp. 75–117; see also my chapter on social issues in this volume.

the MPLA's political strategy to retain power and the main constraints, obstacles and problems faced by the opposition.

The safeguarding of political and economic hegemony. Elected in 1992 for a four-year period, the National Assembly has been active but its credibility has been affected by the lack of a renewed mandate since then. With the end of the war in 2002, new legislative and presidential elections were expected to occur, first in 2004, then in 2005, soon replaced by 2006, then 2007 and later 2008.[46]

Unlike the opposition, the MPLA was well advanced in its preparation for elections, with clear directives established at its fifth congress in 2003. Returning in part to the strategy used in the third extraordinary congress of 1992, the fifth congress called for greater party militancy and the general mobilisation of all its members, reaffirming the importance of traditional authorities and the need to address the needs of the rural areas and its populations—all in an attempt to revive the party's grassroots support base. Once again, the distribution of resources was expanded and former party members were called back—such as Lúcio Lara, who was re-elected to the Central Committee. The usual measures were then put in place to restructure the party and control all the political process, always taking advantage of party dominance over the state and its structures—that is, the executive, the legislative and the judicial.[47]

One of the first measures was, again, to increase party membership. A massive and aggressive campaign was launched all over the country to recruit new members and party membership reached 2 million in 2006 against 544,639 in 1992, 998,199 in 1998 and 1,862,409 by the end of 2003.[48] MPLA membership has grown sharply since the end of the war, especially in the central highlands, traditionally seen

46 See Eduardo dos Santos' statements at the Central Committee meeting on 27 January 2006, in *Jornal de Angola* (28 January 2006); also in *BBC* (28 January 2006).

47 See also Nuno Vidal, *Angola: Preconditions for Elections*, a report for the Netherlands Institute for Southern Africa—NiZA, Amsterdam: NiZA, 2006.

48 See *Relatório do Comité Central ao V Congresso Ordinário*, p. 6.

as UNITA's stronghold: Bié has now over 300,000 members, while Huambo and Huíla provinces are not far behind and even the sparsely populated Kuando Kubango province, where UNITA's headquarters were located, now boasts 100,000 MPLA members. Membership in Luanda rose sharply from 80,000 to around 1 million in 2006.

A process for the restructuring and revitalisation of the party's base structures followed. Preparing itself for the forthcoming elections and addressing the requirements of the new democratic rules, the party established more transparent mechanisms for the election of members at all levels of the hierarchy, from local cells to the Central Committee—requiring more than one candidate for every position. Equally the party began transferring its cells from workplaces to neighbourhoods, where they were integrated into the previously existing network of neighbourhood cells—coordinated by the (one per neighbourhood) Action Committees. New elections to these committees were supposed to occur and with the newly elected members this transfer process would be completed.[49] The process started in February 2004, but according to several opposition leaders it was just a cosmetic operation, which left the workplace cells untouched. At the same time, neighbourhood cells were being restructured and coordinated with their counterparts in the workplaces, thus rendering the party's social control more effective. Finally, a campaign of political seduction aimed at traditional authorities began, with gifts and respect offered whilst party political activities all over the country intensified in what was clearly perceived as a pre-electoral campaign.[50]

---

49 Above the neighbourhood Action Committee is the provincial party committee, topped by the national Central Committee.

50 See references to such seduction campaigns on traditional authorities and comparison with the same procedures in 1992 in 'Seduções pré-campanha', in *Agora* (10 December 2005), pp. 8–9; see also the book resulting from the 2002 national meeting on traditional authorities promoted in Luanda, 20–22 March 2002 by the Ministry of Territorial Administration and supported by the President, *1º Encontro Nacional Sobre a Autoridade Tradicional em Angola*, Luanda: Ministério da Administração do Território-MAT, 2004.

As usual in patrimonial type regimes, where there is no clear distinction between the public and the private, commitment to delivery of services by ministers and provincial governors was personalised. Electoral periods seem to be the exception to this rule. On such occasions, delivery of services becomes mandatory. That happened in 1992 and again after the fifth congress, which clearly set the strategy towards the 2008 elections. Accordingly, the rehabilitation of infrastructure became a major objective. The party drew up long term economic development plans with heavy investment in infrastructure and technology transfer, aiming at accelerated economic growth. This was to be financed by new and more favourable oil-backed loans such as the one from China—two loans of US $2 billion on conditions similar to the aid credit conceded by international financial institutions[51]—and the use of record-high oil revenues, which in 2005 rose to around US $6.88 billion.[52] There were plans to support a myriad economic sectors and regional development clusters.[53] This development perspective was exclusively planned, debated and put in place within the MPLA. Besides investing in new or rehabilitated infrastructure, there was also an appeal to membership voluntary effort in service delivery to the community—activities such as painting neighbourhood schools or medical centres, neighbourhood cleaning, helping the government with the rubbish disposal problem, to mention but a few.

51 See the official characterisation of these loans by the Ministry of Finance, available at www.minfin.gv.ao ; on these loans, see also Arlindo Miranda, *Angola 2003/2004, Waiting for Elections,* a report for the Christian Michelsen Institute (2004), p. 18.

52 See Global Witness Press Release: *Western Banks to Give Huge New Loan to Angola in Further Blow to Transparency* (23 September 2005).

53 Such as large intensive agricultural projects in several regions with special emphasis on the central plateau; a new oil refinery in Lobito; three new railway lines stretching east from the coast at Luanda, Lobito and Namibe, followed by north-south railways in eastern Angola; an international airport in Luanda and maybe another in Kuando Kubango province; and a natural gas factory in Soyo with export capacity to Namibia and South Africa.

As it did prior to the 1992 elections, and taking full political advantage of the control over the legislature, the party sought as much as possible to restructure the legal framework before the elections to suit the political strategy and interests of those in power. To that end it restructured the Land Law, the Law on Territorial Organisation and Town Planning, the Oil Law and, whenever possible, the Constitution.[54] It also prepared to 'engineer' a resounding majority of members within the new electoral organs. The majority party and the President directly or indirectly appointed 8 out of 11 members of the National Electoral Commission—the institution responsible for the organisation, management and supervision of the whole electoral process—and also ensured a majority in the provincial, municipal and communal electoral commissions.[55] It attempted to regulate the electoral register through the Council of Ministers, creating new electoral organs such as executive commissions, with members exclusively appointed by the majority party, to take over responsibilities initially attributed to the National Electoral Commission—thus circumventing the electoral law and granting absolute control over the registration process to the party in government.[56] This position led the main opposition party to question the legitimacy of any future elections, considering that they could not be internationally considered democratic, free and fair.[57]

Benefiting from dominion over the executive, the MPLA ensured that its ministers, provincial governors and administrators (who in

54 For now the opposition seems to have managed to postpone the approval of a new constitution to the new legislature.

55 See electoral law, Law 6/05, *DR, I*, 95 (10 August 2005), title IX.

56 Compare the electoral law approved by the National Assembly, Law 6/05, *DR, I*, 95 (10 August 2005) with the Council of Ministers Decree 63/05, *DR, I*, 111 (16 September 2005) and the Council of Ministers Decree 62/05, *DR, I*, 107 (7 September 2005).

57 Statements and arguments produced by UNITA's secretary for information, Adalberto da Costa Júnior, in a press conference entitled 'Alert on the legitimacy and dangers of the electoral process', Luanda: Hotel Trópico, 7 December 2005.

several cases were also top members of the party at national and regional level) were seen to inaugurate public infrastructure projects financed with public money in ceremonies where state and party symbols were often mixed. Such events were manipulated by the state media in order to give as much political credit as possible to the party in power. Television and national radio broadcasting remained a monopoly of the state.[58] Severe constraints were imposed on the private media. The government was able to block the only relatively independent radio station—the Catholic Church's radio Eclésia—from broadcasting outside Luanda and continued to intimidate journalists into practicing self-censorship while buying off some and co-opting others into the state media.[59]

Political control over the judiciary remained as strong as ever and was clearly a major advantage for the party and its regime. The President of the Republic, who is also the President of the MPLA, preserved significant powers over the appointment to the judiciary, including the power to appoint Supreme Court judges without confirmation by the National Assembly. There were several reports of political pressure from the presidency affecting the outcome of cases. One of the most recent and enlightening examples was the Supreme Court decision, on 22 July 2005, not to consider dos Santos' terms of office since 1992 as presidential mandates, in order to circumvent the constitutional disposition that limits presidential mandates to

58 A new press law was approved in 3 February 2006, abolishing the state monopoly over television broadcasting, but from the example of commercial radio stations in 1992, one should not expect politically independent television channels; new private commercial radios started broadcasting in 1992, but were all, without exception, controlled by the MPLA: LAC in Luanda, Rádio 2000 in Lubango, Rádio Morena in Benguela and Rádio Comercial in Cabinda. The Catholic Church's radio station Eclésia re-opened in Luanda in 1997, after having been closed down since 1977.

59 See Human Rights Watch report, *Unfinished Democracy: Media and Political Freedoms in Angola* (14 July 2004); also news report, 'Director of Government News Agency threatens to shoot journalist', Media Institute of Southern Africa, 23 February 2005; also *Human Rights Watch World Report 2006,* New York: HRW & Seven stories press, 2006, pp. 74–9.

three five-year terms. Otherwise, the presidency initiated after the first elections in 1992 would have counted as three five-year presidential mandates (1992-2007) and would therefore have prevented him from standing again.[60]

Central control over the public and private sectors of the economy remained extremely tight. The political dominance over the public sector is as old as the regime and was extended to the private sector as soon as the transition to a market economy started in the early 90s. Privatisation throughout the 90s served the elites in power and resulted in an oligopoly in politically crucial private sectors like banks, communications, diamonds, insurance and transport, all managed within the prevailing patrimonial and clientelistic logic. Directly or indirectly, the President and the party kept a tight grip over each and every significant business activity in the country, public or private, and it was simply not possible for a medium or large business to operate without political consent from the top.[61] Material benefits and financial privileges for those occupying political positions were significantly increased.[62]

Despite an obvious excess of low-qualified public servants, who overcrowded state administration during the socialist regime, resisting each and every IMF and World Bank restructuring programme in the late 80s and throughout the 90s, it was announced in 2006 that an extra 5,000 positions would be open in public administration and salaries would be raised.[63]

---

60 In power since 1979 and currently aged 65 (born 28 August 1942), dos Santos may well remain President for life.

61 See Manuel Ennes Ferreira, *La reconversion*, pp. 11–26; Renato Aguilar, 'Angola's Private Sector: Rents Distribution and Oligarchy', in Karl Wohlmuth, Achim Gutowski, Tobias Knedlick, Mareike Meyn and Sunita Pitamber, *African Development Perspectives*, Germany: Lit Verlag, 2003; Renato Aguilar, *Angola: Getting off the Hook*, a report for SIDA, Gothenburg: Gothenburg University, 2005, in particular pp. 13–18.

62 See Decree-law on *DR*, I (12 April 2006), establishing new privileges for those occupying political positions within the state structure; see also *Semanário Angolense* (13 to 20 May, 2006), pp. 6-7.

63 See *Jornal de Angola*, 19 January 2006; also *Semanário Angolense*, 'Migalhas

In sum, the President and the party in power reinforced their control over the state apparatus, carefully preparing for the forthcoming elections. Since the regime's *modus operandi* had not changed, political power was still concentrated in the person and institution of the President and the administration remained centralised. Access to the President was highly restricted and key policy decisions were made by presidential aides, who are mostly technocrats. The post of Prime Minister was reintroduced in December 2002, with the nomination of Fernando 'Nandó' Dias da Piedade, along with the appointment of a reformist economic team. Nevertheless, the prime ministerial post remained weak and President dos Santos continued to chair the powerful Council of Ministers, which effectively made him head of government and gave him control over the management of governmental affairs. Power was still managed according to a distribution mechanism of state resources operated through the rotation and cooptation of key-figures for the top jobs in party and state structures. Positions such as those of ministers, provincial governors and ambassadors, and especially those in the myriad services surrounding the presidency (under the supervision of the Civil and Military Cabinets of the Presidency), were some of the most prized posts and their political importance continued to depend upon proximity to the President.

Opposition political parties. Although in 2006 there were 125 registered political parties in Angola, fewer than a quarter were in fact operational. The MPLA held an outright majority with 129 seats out of 220 at the National Assembly while UNITA had 70 seats and other parties the remainder.[64] Opposition parties were politically and institutionally fragile and faced severe constraints.

---

para o povoléu', 13 to 20 May, 2006; on public administration, post-colonial development and policies up to the 2000s see Nuno Vidal, *Post-Modern Patrimonialism in Africa*, in particular the conclusion.

64 PRS - Partido da Renovação Social/Party of Social Renewal, 6 MPs; FNLA-Frente Nacional de Libertação de Angola/National Front for the Liberation of Angola, 5 MPs; PLD - Partido Liberal Democrata/Liberal

Financial difficulties were the main problems for the opposition. In contrast to civil society organisations,[65] opposition parties could not readily access external funding. Membership fees were merely symbolic at around $1 per month and even then most of the members usually did not pay their dues.[66] Those opposition parties represented in parliament before the elections essentially survived on funds coming out of the state budget ($10 per vote obtained in the 1992 election), which in 2006 worked out at around $14 million for UNITA per year and between $100,000 and $900,000 for the rest of the opposition, with the majority situated within the $100–200,000 range.[67] Opposition parties without exception complained that this was far from being sufficient and was paid irregularly, and sometimes even withdrawn so as to disrupt their activities or apply pressure on them at key moments, such as during the constitutional deadlock in 2005.

In view of these financial restrictions it was extremely difficult for the opposition to expand activities outside provincial capital cities. UNITA was the only opposition party with an effective national presence. Some parties, such as PDP-ANA and PAJOCA, were still struggling to get representation in Luanda. The situation was far worse for parties without parliamentary seats and without access to

---

Democratic Party, 3 MPs; PRD - Partido Renovador Democrático/Party of Democratic Renewal, 1 MP; PAJOCA - Partido da Juventude Operários e Camponeses de Angola/Party of Youth, Workers and Peasants, 1 MP; PDP-ANA - Partido Democrático para o Progresso da Aliança Nacional/Democratic Party for Progress of the National Alliance, 1 MP; PNDA - Partido Nacional Democrático de Angola/Angolan National Democratic Party, 1 MP; FDA –Forum Democrático Angolano/Angolan Democratic Forum, 1 MP; AD-Coligação, Aliança Democrática-Coligação/Party of Democratic Alliance, 1 MP; PSD - Partido Social Democrata/Social Democratic Party, 1 MP.

65 See last chapter in this volume.

66 According to the dominant mentality it is the party that has to support its members and not the other way round; see Nuno Vidal, *Post-modern Patrimonialism in Africa*, especially conclusion.

67 For the exact number of votes obtained by each party in the 1992 elections see Sofia Marques, *Angola…*, p. 43.

state budget funds.[68] In absolute contrast with the opposition stood the MPLA, with an impressive collection of buildings, widespread throughout the country, with a presence in each and every village, with no financial difficulties whatsoever, having the largest state subsidy of around $21.5 million, with membership fees retained at source from salaries in some state companies, and directly or indirectly controlling the most significant private companies.

Opposition parties widely complained about the permanent political advantage accruing to the MPLA from the manipulation of state structures. As an example, some ministers were MPLA Central Committee members and several provincial governors were MPLA first provincial secretaries. The same happened with municipal and communal administrators and it was sometimes difficult to distinguish between party and State activities insofar as party events mobilised state logistics, and vice-versa. MPLA flags were everywhere in the provinces and were very similar to the Angolan Republic's flag. In many rural areas it was easier to find an MPLA flag than the flag of the Republic.

With the GURN, several opposition leaders accused the majority party of pre-empting the responsibilities of every governmental position occupied by their representatives. According to these accusations, no matter what position was given to the opposition—minister, vice-minister, governor, administrator—each and every politically sensitive competence was immediately transferred to the nearest office occupied by an MPLA member. Thus, if the governor was from UNITA, the effective powers such as budget management rested with a vice-governor belonging to the MPLA. This being so, the obvious question is, why did the opposition remain in such a government?

Generally speaking, the reasons for remaining had to do with the effectiveness of the patrimonial system and the fear of retaliation from the majority party in terms of cancellation of state budget funds

68 An exception can be found in PADEPA, (Partido de Apoio Democrático e Progresso de Angola/Party of Democratic Support and Progress of Angola), which has been more active than many parties inside parliament.

and the loss of other benefits that were usually related to positions occupied within the governmental structures. There was also difficulty in obtaining a consensus within opposition parties and more widely in favour of a move that could be seen as being radical, anti-institutional and anti-reconciliatory. Without much success, UNITA's leader, Isaias Samakuva, tried to replace some of his party's representatives in parliament and in government since they had got their posts in the days of UNITA-Renovada.[69]

Access to the state media (national radio, television and daily newspapers) also constituted a problem for the opposition, which experienced censorship through manipulated reporting and the 'editing' of news that ignored them while giving full and premium coverage to even the most innocuous MPLA or government activities. The government clearly used its control of the media to influence public opinion, both domestic and international. In some provinces, opposition parties occasionally took out commercial radio advertisements to get publicity, but this represented an enormous financial effort considering the parties' budget limitations. They were also severely affected by the fact that private media organisations routinely suffer pressure or 'inducements' and are in any event restricted to Luanda. Private weekly newspapers, in their low thousands, only circulated in Luanda and the same restriction applied to Radio Eclésia.

The judicial system was also subject to opposition criticism, accused of serving the general purpose of dividing and weakening the opposition and being manipulated in cases involving factions within opposition parties, often resulting in the suspension of state subsidy. Even the head of the Lawyers' Bar Association, Raúl Araújo, an MPLA member, accepted that judges should be held accountable and retire at a given age instead of being kept in post indefinitely—thereby implicitly recognising that meritocracy is not the main

69 On this subject, see 'Substituição de parlamentares aquece debate na Assembleia Nacional' ('Replacement of MPs warms up debates in the National Assembly'), *Jornal de Angola* (1 February 2006); 'Sem consenso' ('Without consensus'), *Jornal de Angola* (1 February 2006).

criterion for occupying such positions.[70] Moreover, there was still the dual and confused judicial system—civilian and military[71]—which contributed to maintenance of the authoritarian and greatly feared character of justice in politically sensitive areas, keeping alive the memory of the bloody post-27 May purge.

A particular disappointment for the parliamentary opposition was directed at the international community, in particular the World Bank and the IMF, for reducing the pressure that was being exerted on the government in terms of accountability and transparency in the management of public funds and respect for human rights. This was likely due to the increased demand for oil that came from the new Asian partners of the Angolan government—China, India and possibly South Korea—oil that the West also desired.[72] The 'Angola-gate' Falcone case also stands out as a clear example of the leverage exerted by the Angolan government on Western powers such as France.[73]

70 *Jornal de Angola* (28 September 2004).

71 See Luís Paulo Monteiro Marques, *Labirinto do sistema judicial angolano, notas para a sua compreensão,* Luanda: edição do autor, 2004, especially part II.

72 See *More than Humanitarianism: a Strategic US Approach toward Africa*, a report by an independent task force sponsored by the Council on Foreign Relations, New York: Council on Foreign Relations, 2005, especially pp. 32–3, 49–50; also *Human Rights Watch World Report 2006,* pp. 74–9; Renato Aguilar, *Angola*, especially pp. 2, 13–18; also John Reed, 'Angola: o capitalismo dos petrodiamantes', *Courrier International,* (25 November 2005), n. 34, pp. 22–3.

73 Pierre Falcone (arms dealer) was nominated Angolan ambassador to UNESCO in order to be granted diplomatic immunity to travel around Europe and escape French justice, namely the judicial process dealing with corruption and illegal arms deals involving Angolan top government officials and their French counterparts. The French authorities were not willing to recognise such immunity and wanted to detain him for questioning; however, as soon as the Angolan government retaliated by withholding the recognition of the French ambassador and refusing to renew Total's oil contract on block 3/80, the French government dropped its initial intentions and recognised Falcone's Angolan diplomatic immunity in a humiliating move that jeopardised the whole judicial process, given the central importance of Falcone's testimony. On the Falcone 'Angola-gate' case see *Financial Times, 6* August 2004; *World Markets Analysis,* 8 September 2004; *International Oil Daily* 26 October 2004; *Voice of America, 1* November 2004; *ANGOP, 2* November 2004.

Signs of authoritarianism remained. The MPLA still had an active paramilitary militia, the Organisation for Civil Defence, funded by the state budget, and operating in city neighbourhoods. Even though direct intimidation of opposition members and officials was rare in Luanda, it was more common in the provinces where political openness and tolerance depended on the goodwill of provincial governors and municipal administrators. This probably explains why there were still reports of political intolerance in the provinces, such as beatings, threats and harassment of opposition delegations in rural areas: witness what happened in Luwemba in July 2004, Mavinga in March 2005 and Chongoroi in April 2006. Investigations into the murder of opposition leader M'Fulupinga Landu Victor on 2 July 2004 remained inconclusive. The murder might have been a straightforward criminal act but it spread great fear among the opposition and civil society organisations.

It is also important to stress that members of M'Fulupinga's party—the PDP-ANA—were persecuted in the North and East of the country, where they were pejoratively designated as 'Bakongo returnees'—a reference to the fact that they or their parents had returned from Zaire, where they had emigrated in the 60s—and were discriminated against outside their provinces of origin of Uíge and Zaire.[74] They complained of systematic abuse committed against them by the police, such as beatings, extortion, illegal arrests, confiscation of documents and denied access to formal labour markets.[75]

According to several opposition leaders, just as in the old days of the one-party regime, the state was used mainly as a mechanism for patronage, 'feeding' political clients and trying to bribe and/or co-

74 On the issue of 'Bakongo returnees', see Jean-Michel Mabeko-Tali, *Les Bakongo et la Transition Démocratique en Angola: Démocratie ou Représentation Ethnico-Regionale?* Paris: Centre National de la Recherche Scientifique, 1993; 'Rapport Scientifique de la Mission à Luanda; Groupe de Recherches', 846, *Afrique Australe*; also Jean-Michel Mabeko-Tali, 'La chasse aux Zaïrois à Luanda', *Politique Africaine*, 57 (1995), pp. 71–84.

75 Complaints were presented to the author and supported with documentary evidence of judicial processes.

opt potential opponents. They say that promotion to senior levels or access to state jobs remains dependent on MPLA membership; the same is alleged in academic circles, where progress might be affected by an individual's decision whether or not to join the party in power. Similar constraints applied to most of the private sector. According to several UNITA leaders in Luanda and the provinces, such political conditioning was extended to UNITA ex-combatants, who joined the MPLA to the tune of 12,000 in 2004 alone.[76] This was in order to access the support promised to help them integrate back into civilian life—support that in fact was their due in accordance with the Lusaka protocol and the Luena memorandum.

One of the most enlightening examples mentioned by opposition leaders and members of CSOs regarding the degree of political patronage within party and state structures is found in an interview with the Angolan ambassador to Brazil, Alberto Correia Neto.

> 'A major part of the Angolan money comes from oil, but does not enter the financial system [...] State money is not in banks in Angola. Oil companies deposit tax in foreign banks, American, French, etc. The chairman of the Central Bank and other people manage that money according to orders given by juridical persons they represent [...] Capitalism engenders corruption. Why do you think there are people fighting to become ministers, MPs, Senators? Is that because they care for the country or the people? No. It's because of *bufunfa*, money.'[77]

Furthermore, as publicly stated by a member of the National Electoral Commission:

> We must be realistic and say that what we have in Angola is a patrimonial state and not a democratic state [...] we have a country where public funds are not controlled.[78]

76 *Jornal de Angola*, 28 September 2004.

77 *O Globo*, 21 November 2005.

78 Declarations of Cláudio Silva, member of the National Electoral Commission, proposed by UNITA, but formerly a member of the Front for Democracy (FpD), a party joining the AD-Coalition, on the *Voice of America* and the *BBC* on 12 October 2005, during a visit to Washington.

Given all the above mentioned constraints, the opposition in general found its meagre energies and resources absorbed by its own internal problems, involved in legal and bureaucratic disputes with the MPLA, demonstrating a serious inability to mobilise the electorate with political programmes to meet the needs and wishes of the people. In the legal disputes with the MPLA, it usually came out losing, not only because the party in power held the majority of seats in parliament and in every parliamentary working commission, but also because it had more and better qualified cadres and was well resourced financially and better organised to prepare legislation. Moreover, among several of the less well represented parties, there was the reproduction of the same patrimonial practices: favouritism according to primary solidarities, clientelism and the blurring of boundaries between party and personal assets.

Within such a context it is not hard to understand why the National Assembly remained a rubber-stamp institution for laws approved by the Council of Ministers presided over by the President.[79]

In sum, the analysis provided in this chapter clearly reveals the daunting task for all those aiming to bring about socio-political change and therefore defy the regime. The magnitude of such a task is summed up by a saying of Agostinho Neto, in 1977, inscribed on a big placard in front of the provincial committee of the MPLA in Huambo: '*O MPLA é uma barreira intransponível*' (the MPLA is an unsurpassable barrier).

Nevertheless, certain opposition parties and civil society organisations came to believe that the forthcoming elections held the potential to bring about socio-political change. Why?

Could the elections transform the Angolan political system?

Most opposition parties and a number of civil society organisations believed that the dynamics set up by peace and new elections represented a major opportunity to achieve some significant change in the

79 In the same sense, see *Some Transparency, no Accountability,* pp. 76–7; also Arlindo Miranda, *Angola 2003/2004,* pp. 25–6.

Angolan political system towards greater openness and democratisation. Such a point of view was essentially based on three arguments.

First, the MPLA needed domestic and international political relegitimisation through an electoral process. In order to achieve this, it had not only to win the expected new elections but also to have them considered free and fair according to international standards. This implied effective, rather than superficial, openness of the public political space (for example, freer access to the state media by opposition and CSOs and fewer constraints on the private media, public political meetings, speeches and demonstrations, etc.).

Second, if the MPLA lost its parliamentary majority it might be pushed to 'institutionalise' the practice of political negotiation with the opposition and also to be more receptive to civil society pressures.

Finally, there was an expectation that direct local elections might trigger strong regional pressure for effective decentralisation and therefore bring non-oil development, political inclusion and participation—thus eroding the current oil dependency as well as the excessive centralisation of power and administration. Each of these three arguments is analysed in turn.

Opening the political space. This expectation was based on the 1992 experience. At that time, under strong international and domestic pressure for political openness, the MPLA ended up making significant political concessions to the opposition and to a newborn civil society. It became obvious that the dynamics of an electoral process made it impossible to control all the political variables. As the electoral campaign developed, the regime opened much more political space than expected and, even though that space contracted as soon as the war resumed, it was not possible to return to the *status quo ante*. Such experience was still remembered in 2006 and, just as in 1992, there were hopes that the electoral process would increase political and social openness and democratise the regime.

Although it is easy to agree with the argument that electoral dynamics open a space for political discussion, it must also be noted that the domestic and international context in 2006 was vastly different from that of 1992. At that time, the MPLA was in a difficult position: its earlier socialist model had collapsed and the country was exposed as a political and economic failure, oppressing people and retarding development. On the other hand, its major opponent, UNITA, had strong internal leverage, emerging from the civil war in control of significant parts of the national territory, and was strongly backed, both politically and financially, by the US and other Western countries. It was portrayed by the international media, even if inaccurately, as the Angolan force for Western style liberal democracy. Domestic pressure for change also benefited from the arrival of a large number of international organisations. The MPLA, for its part, had had to make massive changes quickly, as demonstrated by the three consecutive party congresses held in the short period of 1990–92, intended to help the party come to terms with the new multiparty framework and the market economy before the elections.[80]

In 2006, the internal and external situation seemed much more favourable to the MPLA than ever before. It had reinforced state control and gained governing experience under the new multiparty framework. It had defeated UNITA, which could no longer count on international backing as in 1992. Indeed UNITA was virtually as weak and funding-dependent as the rest of the opposition. The regime had strengthened control over CSOs, tightened control over the state media and imposed severe restrictions on the private media. It had complete dominion of the new market economy. Furthermore, it had good political and economic relations with the US and other Western countries, which are now eager to please. And, finally, the MPLA was well advanced in its preparation for the elections.

A number of opposition leaders and civil society activists interviewed seemed to realise this and, in order to overcome these liabilities, stressed the need for major coordination between internal and external international CSOs sharing the same principles and values, such as political democratisation and respect for human rights. There

80 Third congress in 1990; second extraordinary congress in 1991; third extraordinary congress in May 1992.

seemed to be no illusion about the leverage that could eventually be exerted over the Angolan regime by donors or International Governmental Organisations, given what had happened during the 'Angolagate' case, (the Falcone episode) and given the change of attitude of the World Bank, the IMF and even the EU.[81]

A loss of parliamentary majority would institutionalise negotiation. The MPLA's absolute majority in parliament allowed it to pass most laws unhindered, except for the Constitution, for which a two-third majority is required. According to several opposition leaders and certain civil society activists, the likely loss of its parliamentary majority would force the regime to institutionalise negotiation. This expectation arose from the constitutional discussion initiated after the 1994 Lusaka protocol.

The existing constitution was approved in 1991 and revised in 1992, prior to the elections mentioned above, but it was assumed at that time that a new constitution would be negotiated after the elections. The resumption of war in 1992 postponed the approval of a new constitution. Discussions were restarted after the signature of the Lusaka Protocol in 1994 but again suspended in late 1998 when war resumed.

During the period 1997–98, and in accordance with the Lusaka Protocol, UNITA deputies took their seats and, for the first time in Angola's history, an effective multiparty political life started to emerge. In 1997 and 1998, the National Assembly was humming with political activity, broadcast live on national radio and television. Negotiations and alliances between parties were at the top of the agenda. Constitutional revision was the main concern. UNITA, FNLA and PRS had already agreed to cluster their votes—forming one third of the total—in order to force the MPLA to negotiate. Discussion about what type of political dispensation to choose for the future stirred the imagination of many Angolans.

81 See my chapter on social issues in this volume; also Nuno Vidal, *Angola: Preconditions.*

Two models emerged from these debates.[82] On the one hand, there was the MPLA project: a French-style, unicameral, semi-presidential system, with a weak prime minister and a central role for the president; some enhancement of provincial autonomy, with direct elections to regional bodies, excepting provincial governors, who held the most powerful position within the provinces. On the other hand, there was the FNLA/UNITA/PRS project: greater provincial autonomy, effective decentralisation with provincial management of local resources, somewhere between regionalism and federalism, with all positions directly elected. The intention was obviously to enlarge autonomy in the core zones of these parties—FNLA in the North, UNITA in the central plateaux and PRS in the North-East.

At that time the second project seemed to be widely favoured; there was a broad consensus among opposition parties, private newspapers, international organisations, national and foreign NGOs and even some sections of the MPLA. The idea was that decentralisation could promote economic development outside the oil sector, allow political participation at grassroots level and defuse secessionism in provinces such as Cabinda and the Lundas. The MPLA appeared ready to make concessions.[83] Savimbi, then still alive, controlled large swathes of territory and therefore had immense leverage.

The suspension of the Lusaka protocol in late 1998, followed by the walkout of UNITA deputies from parliament and the resumption of war, put an end to this process. After the death of Jonas Savimbi, the new constitutional project was negotiated bi-laterally between the MPLA and UNITA (under General Gato's leadership), and was approved in January 2003. This became known as the Alvalade agreement and, although it was presented as a new model, in fact it basically endorsed the original project of the winners of the civil war,

82 Nuno Vidal, 'The Genesis and Development of the Angolan Political and Administrative System from 1975 to the Present', in Steve Kyle, *Intersections between Social Sciences* (Cornell: Institute for African Development of Cornell University, 2004), especially pp. 12-14.

83 At that time the author was in Angola conducting field research for his PhD thesis.

the MPLA. According to the Alvalade model, the president enjoyed discretionary powers to appoint and dismiss the Prime Minister. The provincial governors, although recommended by the party with the largest share of the vote in the province, were chosen, appointed, nominated and dismissed by the President. The President also retained the power to dissolve the National Assembly.

However, soon afterwards, the new UNITA leader, Isaías Samakuva, who took over from General Gato after a congress party vote in June 2003, expressed his concern with the agreement and tried to postpone constitutional approval of this law to the next legislature by allying UNITA with a coalition of smaller opposition parties. These parties were also against the Alvalade agreement because it approved a model they rejected and also because the negotiation had simply ignored them, taking advantage of a weak and defeated UNITA. In May 2004, all opposition parties withdrew from the constitutional commission that had been in charge of the final draft to be presented for approval at the National Assembly. The MPLA was accused of manipulating the commission and holding elections hostage to constitutional approval. In reality, the opposition believed that the MPLA would lose many parliamentary seats in the next election and that the new parliament would be more advantageous to them.

The opposition demanded a date from the President for legislative and presidential elections, after consultation with members of civil society and opposition political parties. They also asked for an electoral calendar with a clear outline of all steps in the electoral process, with due respect for electoral law—electoral registration, monitoring, funding of political parties, electoral campaigns; and the removal of any linkage between elections and the approval of a new constitution.

This move coincided with the President's visit to the US, where President Bush raised the question of elections, which seems to have had a clear impact on the MPLA and the presidency. Returning home, dos Santos called selected members of civil society organisations to see him on 28 July 2004 for bilateral meetings about the elections. COIEPA, ADRA and AJAPRAZ were consulted.[84] Four days later he called the Council of the Republic and listened to the opposition parties represented there. In both meetings there was consensus in favour of holding elections in 2006.

After dos Santos' meeting with civil society, the MPLA's Political Bureau issued a statement saying that elections should take place before September 2006, and it dropped the link between elections and the approval of a new constitution. The opposition appeared to have made a compromise with the MPLA. The MPLA did not follow its usual procedure of ignoring opposition opinion and imposing laws for approval by its parliamentary majority at the National Assembly. This time there was negotiation and the main reason for this was the requirement of a two-third majority, which the MPLA did not have, for such a fundamental constitutional revision.

This example supported the argument of those who thought elections might provide an opening for a more effective multiparty system, especially if there was no majority party in parliament after the elections and if electoral results were respected. The MPLA would constantly have to negotiate with the opposition, thus introducing the practice of democratic dialogue. Even considering the possibility of a coalition between parties after the election, there would still be a need for greater political diversity and discussion within the government.

However, it was not in any way obvious that the MPLA's majority would be at risk. Unlike the opposition, the MPLA was advanced in its preparation for the elections and the internal and external context seemed now much more favourable than in 1992. Moreover, contrary to the suspicion of the opposition, the continuous postponement of the elections since 2004 by the MPLA might have been

84 The Inter Ecclesial Committee for Peace or COIEPA is an ecumenical organisation linking Catholic and Protestant Churches, created in 2000; ADRA is the Action for Rural Development and Environment, the biggest Angolan NGO; AJAPRAZ is the Association of Angolan Youth returned from Zambia and is commonly known as a government-friendly Angolan NGO. See my chapter on social issues in this volume.

related not to the fear of losing its parliamentary majority but to the need for more time to prepare. At the top of the party and within the presidency, there was a strong conviction that what had happened in Mozambique in the second legislative elections and in South Africa with the ANC—a two third majority in parliament—could now happen in Angola. The MPLA would then have absolute control over the legislature, especially in the long-awaited approval of a new constitution. The President's objective of going to elections with a clearly defined set of powers that would ensure his supremacy over the other state organs could still be achieved as long as legislative elections were separated from the presidential ones.[85] Dos Santos' statements in 2006 on the need for more time for the rehabilitation of infrastructure before elections could be held seemed to support this thesis.[86]

Decentralisation: participation, inclusion and non-oil development. This argument was based on the idea that the extreme centralisation characterising the Angolan political and administrative system was a major obstacle to political participation, inclusion and development outside the oil sector. As of 2005, the decentralisation process had been in its very early stages. It involved four main players: the government, the UNDP, the party and the presidency.

At government level there were three ministries concerned: the Ministry of Territorial Administration (or MAT), involved in research, vocational training and co-operation with the UNDP; the Ministry of Finance, dealing with technical aspects related to fiscal and financial autonomy of provinces and municipalities; and the Ministry of Planning, indirectly involved in decentralisation through

85 The intention of separating those two elections was publicly expressed by the President; see *Agence France Press,* 11 and 12 November, 2004.

86 … the party must encourage the government to conclude its rehabilitation program of primary road and rail links in 2007 so that participation in the next polls is considerable… Speech of Eduardo dos Santos at the opening of the CC meeting on 27 January 2006; *Jornal de Angola,* 28 January 2006; also broadcast on the BBC, 28 January 2006.

two projects, namely the *Fundo de Apoio Social* (or FAS), the Social Action Fund, and the *Programa de Apoio à Reabilitação* (or PAR), the Programme to Support Rehabilitation.

Apart from providing technical support to those three ministries, the UNDP also undertook to facilitate the coordination between ongoing projects and to lobby for a more decisive political and legislative move towards the implementation of decentralisation. The party and the presidency had monitored and controlled the whole process, researching and analysing similar cases in other countries such as Mozambique, whilst trying to adapt the process to their overall political strategy—bearing in mind parallel processes like the approval of a new set of laws directly related to decentralisation, such as the Constitution, the Land Law and the Law on Territorial Organisation and Town Planning.

The reasons behind the UNDP's involvement are clear: it believed that decentralisation might bring about political inclusiveness and development. However, the motives behind the government involvement with decentralisation were not. Opinions were not consensual: some argued that the government understood the usefulness of decentralisation, as it helped solve local development problems and could also defuse secessionist pressure in provinces such as Cabinda and the Lundas; others said it could be part of a cynical plan to extend state control to municipalities and communes now that the administration was expanding throughout the whole territory. Although at this stage the whole process was essentially a plan still to be implemented, some useful conclusions can be drawn from the analysis of the regime's plans for decentralisation on the one hand and of the field experiences of PAR and FAS on the other.

The party and presidency strategic views on decentralisation. In a speech on the occasion of the first National Meeting on Local Administration on 30 August 2004, President dos Santos stated that the government planned a two-phase programme for local government: a first phase to reform the state administration and a second to create the conditions for institutionalising autonomous local power structures after the elections. The process had to be gradual and slow, and the reasons for that become obvious from the presidential speech, which explained that around fifty per cent of the administrative capacity of the state was concentrated in just three of Angola's eighteen provinces: Luanda, Benguela and Huíla.[87]

According to presidential advisers and senior party officials, before the creation of 'autarchies'—the final step in the decentralisation process —it would be necessary to consolidate the state at local level. Deconcentration of competence and responsibilities would have to be gradual since Angola has 18 provinces, 163 municipalities and 532 communes, all in a sparsely populated territory. The 'autarchic system' would start with pilot projects that would expand gradually, according to specific needs and demands. Mozambique was the model to be followed. Pilot areas would be started in Luanda, Cabinda, Huambo and the Lundas. The system of 'autarchies' would be implemented in parallel with the existing arrangement of provinces, municipalities and communes. In contrast to the existing administrative system, the new one would not be hierarchically rigid: 'autarchies' would all have equal status within the province, with autonomy in relation to each other and in relation to the centre.

This argument in favour of the creation of 'autarchies' was that it would help solve two types of political problems: secessionist pressures such as those of Cabinda and the political struggle at the centre, related to the management of resources. According to the plan for decentralisation, 'autarchies' would have access to the management of important resources, dealing directly with investors for local development projects, able to retain local taxes and managing funds allocated directly by the national budget. Expanding economic activities would mean higher tax revenues for the 'autarchy'. Therefore,

87 Of this total, 79 per cent of human resources were concentrated at provincial level, with 19 per cent at municipal level and just 1 per cent at communal level. In addition, only 3 per cent of the administrators had received higher education and, of these, 97 per cent were concentrated at the provincial level; see Speech of the President of the Republic to the First National Meeting on Local Administration, Luanda, 30 August 2004.

as soon as 'autarchies' started to manage increasing revenues, they would reduce political tussle at the centre related to the competition for the management of resources.

According to these views, decentralisation was needed to dilute secessionist feelings and lessen the political competition over public resources. Coincidentally or not, a look at the chosen pilot areas where the decentralisation process was supposed to start—Luanda, Huambo, Cabinda and Lundas—shows that these are the most problematic electoral areas for the MPLA. Cabinda and Lundas are known for their rejection of the MPLA on the grounds that it plunders their natural wealth in oil and diamonds, respectively. Huambo is the historical stronghold of UNITA and Luanda exhibits growing popular discontent, mainly in the shanty towns, owing to the harsh living conditions.

Such arguments were clearly patrimonial in nature and it is in no way clear that decentralisation—with or without elections—can bring non-oil development, political inclusion and participation. In several other cases across Africa, decentralisation has merely replicated patrimonialism at a regional level, sometimes degenerating into warlordism as a means of taking advantage of regional resources.[88] There simply was no guarantee that a slow and gradual process as intended by the MPLA would help to avoid such problems by enabling the government to manage the transition carefully and to assess the results of pilot projects on an ongoing basis.

Nevertheless, it was stressed that an effective implementation of decentralisation required the approval of a new constitution, which should include the political programme for decentralisation. Local elections were only expected to take place at least one year after the national elections, but with the stated intention of having presidential elections one year after legislatives, no one knew when local elections would take place.

88 William Reno, *Warlord Politics and African States*, London: Lynne Rienner, 1998.

Decentralisation experiences in the field—PAR and FAS. Two projects of the ministry of planning have been dealing with the decentralisation issue in very practical terms. Although these programmes were basically concerned with the rehabilitation of social and economic infrastructure, they became indirectly related to decentralisation owing to the operating structures in the field. These experiences have been used to argue in favour of decentralisation and seen as a first good example that such reform could bring change.

The *Programa de Apoio à Reabilitação* (Rehabilitation Support Programme), or PAR, was funded by the European Union and targeted thirty-one municipalities in the four provinces of Huambo, Huíla, Benguela and Bié. In each province, municipal implementation was entrusted to national and international NGOs, which acted as *Operadores de Referência Municipal* (Main Municipal Operators), or ORMs. Contracts with ORMs specified three main stages: between 2002 and 2003, the diagnosis of the municipality and its requirements; between 2003 and 2004, the design of a programme for the rehabilitation of the municipality, known as the *Programa de Reabilitação Municipal*, or PRM; and, finally, in 2005, the implementation of the programme as previously designed.

From the perspective of decentralisation, the main interest of PAR was its operating structure with its three types of organs, of which the third was completely new. The main decision-making organ of PAR was the provincial committee presided over by the provincial governor, including all ORMs and supervising the implementation of the programme in the whole province. The municipal committee was the second body with decision-making powers on problems specific to the municipality, presided over by the municipal administrator and including the ORM along with the remaining members of the municipal administration. The third and most innovative organ was the Advisory Forum, intended to assist local administrations and ORMs and, above all, to make the implementation stage more participative. These Forums were to be created in each of the targeted provinces and municipalities; the *Quadros de Concertação Provincial*, or QCPs, and the *Quadros de Concertação Municipal*, or QCMs, were to be presided over by the provincial governor and the municipal administrator at the municipality level. They would also include other members of the administration, the ORMs, national and international NGOs operating in the municipality, businesses, political parties and community representatives.

Although PAR was mainly a rehabilitation programme, its innovative structure at the level of Advisory Forums implied the strengthening of its institutional capabilities and effectively brought about pressure for decentralisation and the democratisation of local politics. The direct involvement of national and international NGOs in ORMs resulted in additional pressure for decentralisation. The dynamics created by PAR, it was argued, buttressed decentralisation. However, funding for the third stage and effective implementation of rehabilitation programmes was halted by the European Union. This premature termination frustrated expectations for rehabilitation projects, and wasted resources and efforts spent in drawing up diagnostic studies and programme outlines. The whole project only made sense with the implementation of this third phase and the Advisory Forums were bound to disappear as soon as the project ended.[89]

The *Fundo de Apoio Social* (Social Action Fund), or FAS, is an autonomous programme of the Ministry of Planning, financed by the World Bank and operating directly in the municipalities. The programme was then in its third stage, or FAS III, and had two main components, not much different from those of PAR: community development, aimed at building social and economic infrastructure; and municipal development, aimed at assisting municipal governments with capacity development and financial resources for the provision

89 It must also be stressed that the Advisory Forums did not exist in all four provinces: Huambo province did not have such a Forum although there was one in the municipality of Bailundo; the forum existed in the province of Huíla, and in Benguela, but not in Bié. The explanation for this variability has to do with the governor's personal attitude towards the programme and its structures, considering they do not have legal existence. See Decree-law no. 27/00, *DR*, I, 20 (19 May 2000).

of social and economic services to communities. Like PAR, it also comprised an advisory body to the municipal administration, namely the *Conselho de Concertação*, or Consultative Forum, which included representatives from communities and civil society.

Again, as for the PAR, the dynamics set in motion by FAS seem to have strengthened the demand for effective decentralisation insofar as it built capacity and accountability mechanisms in local government, communities and civil society. Although there was no funding problem, in contrast to PAR, the programme itself acknowledged the limitations of the role of social funds in the decentralisation process. According to a project appraisal document of FAS III, without the actual institutional and fiscal devolution of authority and resources to local levels, the efforts of FAS would not be sustainable in the long term. At some point, local government would need to take over. [90]

Once again there was a major problem with the lack of legislation for the Consultative Forums; this was a central concern of FAS, which had been pressuring for new legislation within the recently created governmental 'Informal Group on Decentralisation', coordinated by the Ministry of Territorial Administration and grouping several players involved with the decentralisation issue, such as the Ministry of Planning, the Ministry of Finance, the UNDP, the EU, USAID, GTZ (the German aid agency) and FAS, among several others.

When taking into account both programmes—PAR and FAS—it is best to remain realistic about this indirect approach to decentralisation. After all, these experiences were still dependent on external funding and on the approval of a government programme of national decentralisation, which would ensure the mechanisms for an effective transfer of decision-making and financial autonomy to local levels. It

90 World Bank, *Project Appraisal Document on a Proposed Credit for the Third Social Action Fund Project, FAS III* ('World Bank report nº 25671-ANG, June 27, 2003), pp. 10–20; for the characterization of FAS, see also *Avaliação Participativa de Beneficiários* (Luanda: FAS, Novembro 2003); *Relatório Anual de Actividades* (Luanda: FAS, 2004); *Relatório Final de Actividades FAS III* (Luanda: FAS, 2004).

is in no way clear either from the analysis of the government perspective on decentralisation or from the programmes running in the field, that decentralisation *per se* would bring about inclusion, participation and development beyond the oil sector—as is plain from other African experiences.[91]

In Angola, as in many other African countries, there seemed to be two different perspectives on decentralisation. On the one hand, there was the *reformist* view of the donor community and NGOs—both national and international—who saw decentralisation as a dynamic process stimulating citizenship, participation, inclusion and development. On the other hand, there was a *conservative* position, whereby decentralisation serves the political and economic interest of the centre, being designed, implemented and controlled at all levels by the central power—a centralised approach to decentralisation, as it were.[92] The most recent statements by the Head of State seemed to support this second position, once again confusing state and party structures and functions.[93]

91 See among several other evaluations on decentralisation programmes throughout the eighties, J. Wunsch, "Institutional Analysis and Decentralisation: Developing an Analytical Framework for Effective Third World Administrative Reform", *Public Administration and Development*, 11, 1991, p. 433; Dennis Rondinelli and S. Schema, *Decentralization in Developing Countries: a Review of Recent Experience*, Washington DC: The World Bank, 1984.

92 For a theoretical discussion on different decentralisation perspectives see among others John Ayee, 'The Measurement of Decentralisation: the Ghanaian Experience, 1988-92', in *African Affairs*, 95, 1996, pp. 31-50; Amnisur Rahman, *People's Self-development*, London: Zed Books, 1993.

93 'The MPLA needs dynamic and focused managing bodies in all its echelons that are dedicated, with militant and mission spirit, to solve problems, to the political and civic education of all citizens and to the organization of community life. Since national independence was proclaimed, we have organized the management system in both the party and the State, from top to bottom. The war did not allow us to conveniently organize our grassroots structure, that is, the villages, the communes, wards, and the rural and urban municipalities. Thus we have two courses of action to proceed. The first is to continue with the studies and reflection under way in the context of de-concentrating and decentralizing administration based on the organizational and functional model of administration in the municipalities and communes in rural and urban areas.

Conclusion

Despite the new multiparty framework, the Angolan political system retains its basic characteristics as constructed after independence and throughout the eighties. The President and the top party echelons are still in control of the state and its resources—especially the revenues from the oil and diamond sectors, which are still used to maintain the political and economic hegemony of the mainly urban elites in power according to a patrimonial logic. Juxtaposition of presidential, party, state and governmental structures continues, as does the blurring between the private and public spheres. Political power is still concentrated and the administrative system still centralised, presided over by an overstaffed bureaucracy inherited from the colonial period and from the Marxist model of state organisation—and still operating according to the so-called democratic centralism. There is still a deep interpenetration between the judicial, legislative and executive systems, with tight political control over the judiciary. The state security apparatus remain effective, under close presidential and party guidance. The lack of political participation by the majority of the population persists, with a remarkable distance between rulers and ruled. This may explain the forecasts of an increase in the abstention rates and in the number of Angolans who believed in 2003 that elections would not bring about change.[94]

Opposition political parties are weak and face severe constraints such as the lack of funds, cadres and organisational capacity, along

---

The second is to reconcile and overhaul the party chain of management from top to bottom so as to bring about renewal to the managing bodies at a commune and municipal level in terms of the statutes. In this context members to be chosen or elected for, need good political and technical training. Having established this management chain, we need to make perfect our system of information that analyses and handles data on the reality in the provinces and respective municipalities in order to improve our ability to be prepared and to respond.' Speech of Eduardo dos Santos at the opening of the Central Committee meeting on 27 January 2006, in *Jornal de Angola,* 28 January 2006; also broadcast on the BBC on the same day.

94 See Report, *Resultados do Inquérito de Opinião 'Percepções dos Angolanos em relação às próximas eleições'*, Luanda: International Republican Institute, 2003.

with an inability to mobilise the electorate. They and the CSOs also suffer from the widespread culture of fear and intimidation. The state media are tightly controlled and manipulated, and there are numerous restrictions on the private media. Despite all these obstacles, most of the opposition parties and some CSOs continue to think that elections have the potential to bring about change, especially if International Civil Society Organisations link up with their Angolan counterparts to monitor the polls and push for the reinforcement of transparent and democratic procedures and mechanisms.

However, it is not at all clear how such expectations could be fulfilled. Faced with the repeated adjournment of elections and serious problems with the electoral process—among others, the debate about the responsibilities given to executive electoral commissions and the unbalanced composition of the National Electoral Commission—International CSOs inside and outside Angola remained relatively silent. This lack of reaction seemed to confirm the suspicion that outside attitudes were conditioned by the international economic standing of Angola. So-called international activists in the areas of development, civil society, human rights and others did not seem willing to risk their careers and positions in Angola, having clearly understood the politically acceptable limits of their activity.[95]

Finally, it is important to remember that multiparty politics does not necessarily or automatically mean democracy. In Latin America, Asia and Southern Europe, where regular multiparty elections are

95 According to these views, the main drive for change would have to come from within; but, as stressed by a minority of Angolan intellectuals, African opposition parties in general and CSOs in particular must stop their customary tendency of looking abroad and over-emphasising the role of external agents, whilst disregarding internal discontent and populations at large as the main source for social and political change. According to this argument, this is exactly what has been happening in Angola since 2002, after the death of Savimbi, and in Zimbabwe, after the 2001 election fraud, with opposition parties and CSOs expecting the international community, through some kind of task force, to lead the demands for change and to exert pressure for the reinforcement of civil as well as Human Rights. This interpretation can be found in the article by Rafael Marques, 'Os povos da linha da frente,' in *Semanário A capital* (16 July 2005).

held, those political systems that stem from patrimonialism show that the participation of the people remains fragmented and personalised and tends towards a form of *status quo*. In such contexts it can be argued that patrimonialism has an inhibiting effect on the emergence of democratic procedures.[96]

96 For a comprehensive discussion of this subject see Luis Roniger and Ayse Gunes-Ayata, *Democracy, Clientelism and Civil Society*, London: Lynne Rienner, 1994, chapter 2; see also Judith Chubb, *Patronage, Power and Poverty in Southern Italy*, Cambridge University Press, 1982; Nuno Vidal, 'Modern and Post-Modern Patrimonialism, op. cit. pp. 1-14.

5

THE ECONOMIC FOUNDATIONS OF THE PATRIMONIAL STATE

Tony Hodges

This chapter discusses how mineral wealth, in particular the revenue from the rapidly developing oil industry, provides Angola's presidency with ample resources to lubricate a system of patronage that can successfully buy off or co-opt potential rivals and opponents. The scale of these resources, which will soar to new heights as Angola doubles oil production between 2004 and 2007, reaching a level close to Nigeria's, gives the exercise of patrimonialism an order of magnitude that has few parallels elsewhere in Sub-Saharan Africa. The forms by which patronage has been dispensed vary widely. Some of the most important are related directly or indirectly to oil or diamonds, others not. Together, however, they have served to consolidate and sustain presidential power while also nurturing the accumulation of wealth by the politico-business elite. Both the scale of interests involved and the capacity to resist change are immense, making a fundamental change in economic governance unlikely in the foreseeable future.

Economic resources and performance

Few countries in Africa are so favoured with natural resources as Angola. Besides being the second largest oil producer south of the Sahara (after Nigeria) and the fifth largest producer of diamonds in the world, Angola has numerous other minerals: iron ore, for example, was an important export until the war that erupted during the transition to independence in 1975. With a range of different climatic zones and soil types, numerous crops can be grown, including coffee on the humid slopes of the north-western escarpment, cotton on the drier plains further inland and sugar cane in low-lying coastal areas. Angola was self-sufficient in cereals and other basic food crops until independence. The arid south-west is particularly suitable for cattle raising and the Atlantic waters off the southern coast are among the best for fishing in Africa, although they have been depleted by over-fishing over the past two decades because of weak controls on foreign fleets.

The rise of the oil industry has been the most striking development. First discovered inland (in the Kwanza basin) in 1955, oil became a major industry after the start of production in shallow waters off the coast of Cabinda in the late 1960s. By 1973, oil had overtaken coffee to become Angola's leading export. Although there was a brief downturn in production during and after the transition to independence, the licensing of new shallow-water offshore blocks led to a steady increase in production from the early 1980s. The next phase of development came in the 1990s, when international oil companies started to apply the new deep water technology pioneered in oil provinces like the North Sea. A quick succession of major discoveries in deep water fields sparked off intense competition among international oil companies for a slice of the action, prompting them to offer ever higher signature bonuses in their bids for new acreage. By 1999, the first deals were being struck for so-called ultra-deep water blocks with water depths of more than 1,500 metres.

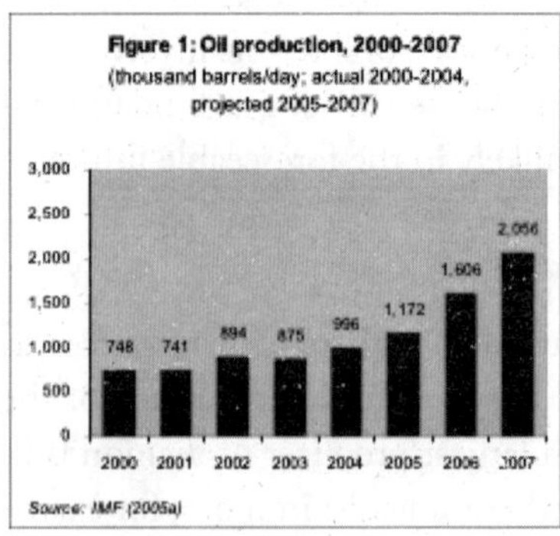

Figure 1: Oil production, 2000-2007
(thousand barrels/day; actual 2000-2004, projected 2005-2007)

Source: IMF (2005a)

The large investment committed to developing the new fields discovered off the Angolan coast, first in shallow waters and then in deep waters, resulted in production rising seven-fold in the quarter-century from 1980 to 2004: from 136,000 barrels a day (b/d) to 996,000 b/d. Angola is currently in another phase of rapid expansion, with oil sector investment exceeding $4 billion in 2003-2004, and production is expected to double between 2004 and 2007, reaching over 2 million b/d (see Figure 1), and then continue to climb thereafter.[1] In short, Angola will soon be achieving levels of oil production close to those of Nigeria, which pumped 2.45 million b/d in 2003—with enormous potential implications in a country with only one tenth of Nigeria's population.

Furthermore, a prolonged period of robust global economic growth, resulting partly from the rapid development of the Chinese economy, has strengthened oil prices on the world market. As a result, Angola's oil export earnings doubled between 2001 and 2004, rising from $5.8 billion to $12.6 billion, according to IMF data (2005a). With world oil demand remaining strong and supply capacity limited in the medium term, oil prices are expected to remain high for several years, raising Angola's export earnings and government revenue to unprecedented levels. The IMF projects that gross oil export earnings will rise above $25 billion by 2007 (see Figure 2), although it should be borne in mind that net oil exports are slightly less than half of gross earnings because of the industry's high level of imports of goods and services (including profit repatriation), particularly during a period of heavy investment.

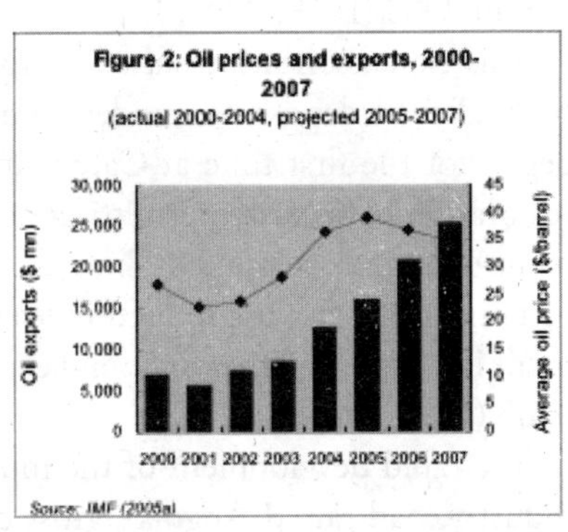

1 The IMF forecasts that production will reach 2.1 million b/d in 2007 and rise further to 2.2 million b/d in 2009 (IMF, 2005a). One of the major oil industry analysts, the UK company Wood Mackenzie, expects the rise in production to be slightly slower at first, reaching 1.8 million b/d in 2007, but then to rise steadily, reaching 2.6 million barrels a day by 2010 (cited in EIU, 2005c).

The diamond industry, which is now almost 90 years old and is concentrated mainly in the north-eastern provinces of Lunda Norte and Lunda Sul, has also seen a period of recovery and expansion following many years of wartime disruption. At one stage, in the early to mid-1990s, the government practically lost control of the entire diamond industry to UNITA and to informal sector artisanal miners (*garimpeiros*), who arrived from all over Angola and from other African countries to exploit the scattered surface (alluvial) deposits found in the Lundas' river valleys. In 1994-97, UNITA was estimated to be marketing on average about $600 million worth of diamonds annually to finance its army, making up for the loss of the support it had received from the United States and South Africa until the end of the Cold War and the demise of the apartheid regime. Even before the war ended, the government had begun to re-establish its control of key mining areas (this was one of the key factors that led to UNITA's eventual defeat) and revive the 'official' production and marketing of diamonds. The value of diamonds exported through official channels, whether originating from informal *garimpeiro* operations or from formal industrial mines, rose from $267 million in 1996 to $788 million in 2003 (IMF, 2005b).

This expansion has resulted partly from the extension of mining from alluvial deposits to underground (kimberlite) deposits, which began for the first time at Catoca in Lunda Sul in 1997. With the restoration of security permitting new exploration and large investment in mine development, kimberlite mining holds out the promise of a major increase in production over the next few years: the government has projected that diamond exports will rise above $2 billion by 2007 (EIU, 2005b).

The rapid development of the mining sector, in particular the oil industry, had raised Angola's gross domestic product to almost $20 billion by 2004 (and per capita income to $1,305). Only two other Sub-Saharan African countries have a larger GDP: South Africa and Nigeria. Oil accounts for almost half of Angola's GDP (48 per cent in 2003), with diamonds contributing a further 4 to 5 per cent. Angola no longer has the highly diversified economy it had in the late colonial period, when it was the world's fourth largest producer of coffee, produced a wide range of other cash crops and had a manufacturing sector on a par with Kenya's, oriented mainly to the processing of agricultural raw materials.

Most sectors of the economy went into steep decline during and immediately after independence, as a result of the outbreak of the war and the exodus of more than 95 per cent of the 340,000 Portuguese settlers, who had owned and managed most companies and commercial farms. The government had tried to revive production by nationalising (or informally confiscating) the abandoned companies and farms and then attempting to establish a system of centralised planning in accordance with its ideology of Marxism-Leninism, which it officially adopted in 1976. However, the continuation of the war, which had spread across most of the country by the mid-1980s, undermined efforts to rebuild the economy. The effects were particularly devastating in the rural areas, where millions of people were displaced and agricultural production declined steeply. The experiments in state ownership and centralised planning also failed, owing in part to the lack of skilled managers to run the thousands of state-owned companies and farms and to plan production and exchange. Large-scale shortages and price distortions arose, encouraging the emergence of a huge parallel market.

In 1985, at the second congress of the MPLA, the country's leaders began to take stock of these failures and a period of gradual reform began in 1987, speeding up after the MPLA's official renunciation of Marxism-Leninism in 1990 and the start of reforms intended to set up a market-based capitalist economy. However, numerous factors held up recovery: the continuation of the war, with only brief interludes of unstable cessations of hostilities, until 2002; the destruction and decay of physical infrastructure, from roads and railways to electricity installations and water supply systems; the low level of human capital (in particular low levels of schooling and literacy); an undeveloped financial sector; the absence of an independent legal system; extreme macroeconomic instability; an overvalued exchange rate; and the maintenance of numerous administrative rules and procedures that burdened the economy with red tape and provided opportunities for officials to allocate business opportunities such as contracts and licences on the basis of favouritism, denying access to others and creating oligopolistic market structures.

The end of the war and the recent surge in oil earnings have helped to overcome or reduce some of these constraints. The restoration of security has permitted the return of displaced people to the rural areas, the resumption of internal trade and the partial revival of food production. The high oil revenues and declining military expenditure have enabled the government to expand public investment in physical infrastructure and increase what had previously been pitifully low levels of expenditure on education and health.[2] The same factors have also made it possible to reduce the fiscal deficit, which for years has been the main cause of macroeconomic instability, and to draw down international reserves to stabilise the national currency, the kwanza, as a way of curbing inflation in Angola's highly import-dependent economy. The government deficit (on an accrual basis), expressed as a percentage of GDP, fell from 35 per cent in 1999 (a year of exceptionally low world oil prices) to 4 per cent in 2004, while inflation, which had peaked at 12,035 per cent in July 1996, fell below 100 per cent in 2003 and had been brought down to 31 per cent by December 2004 (IMF, 2005a and 2005b)

However, the effects of the war will take many years to overcome fully and some of the adverse institutional factors mentioned above (in particular the legal and policy environment) have not yet shown significant improvements. The cereal harvest was expected to increase by 23 per cent in 2005/2006, but this would still leave a deficit

2 According to the IMF (2005b), government expenditure on education and health rose from a mere 3.5 per cent of total government expenditure in 1999 to 11.9 per cent in 2003, while defence and security expenditure fell from 31.4 per cent to 6.4 per cent, although the latter figures may be underestimates as there has habitually been large unrecorded extra-budgetary expenditure on the military.

of 625,000 tons—in a country which once exported maize.[3] About 700,000 Angolans remain dependent on food aid, more than three years after the end of the war.[4] As for the cultivation of cash crops, this has barely begun. Coffee production, which averaged about 200,000 tons a year in the late colonial period, was only 5,000 tons in 2004. Likewise, the manufacturing sector remains a shadow of what it once was and is now limited to a few bulky products like cement, beer and soft drinks that are particularly costly to import. The manufacturing sector's share of GDP has fallen from 16 per cent in 1973 to 4 per cent in 2003.

Economic effects of the dominance of the oil sector

Angola's economy is thus a highly imbalanced one, with oil accounting not only for almost half of GDP but also for 94 per cent of exports (diamonds making up almost all the rest) and 77 per cent of government revenue in 2004 (see Figure 3). This has important economic and institutional implications. Beginning at a purely economic level, it should be noted, first, that as a highly capital intensive industry the oil sector provides relatively few jobs: only about 15,000 at the beginning of the present decade.

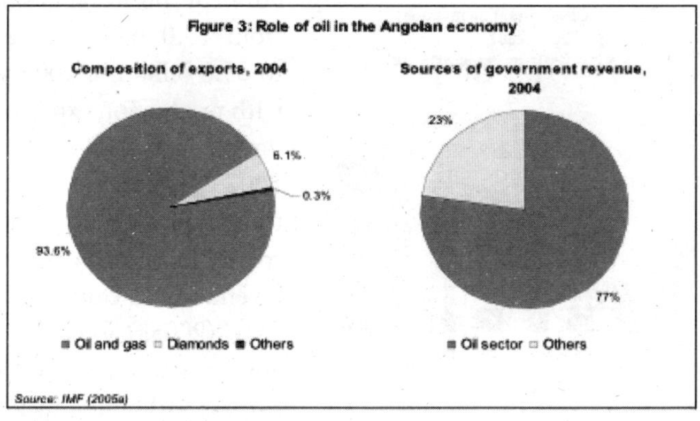

3 Data from the Famine Early Warning Systems Network (Fewsnet), cited by the EIU (2005c).

4 News24.com, 3 November 2005.

Second, it has very weak backward and forward linkages to the rest of the economy. Apart from 50,000 b/d of oil delivered to the single refinery in Luanda, all the oil is exported unrefined, although the government is hoping to attract investors for the building of a second, much larger refinery in Lobito. Likewise, while some local oil industry service companies have emerged in recent years, the vast majority of goods and services required by the industry are imported, which is why net oil exports are slightly less than half the value of gross oil exports.

The potential benefits of the oil industry for broader economic development and poverty reduction therefore lie primarily in the resources available to the state from the taxation of the industry. High tax rates are a characteristic of oil industries everywhere and Angola is no exception, although the proportion of the value of oil production accruing to the state has been declining (from 53 per cent in 2000 to 43 per cent in 2003) because of the amortisation of the large investments made in developing the new deep water fields, the higher operating costs of these fields and the lower quality of their oil (IMF, 2005b).

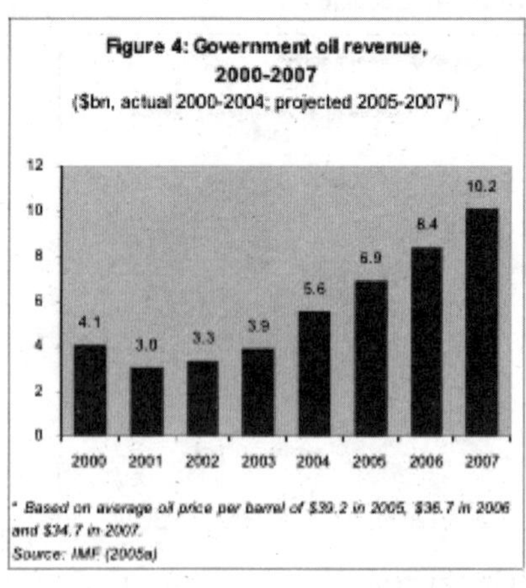

In absolute terms, government oil revenues rose from $3.0 billion in 2001 to $5.6 billion in 2004 and, with production expected to double between 2004 and 2007 and prices expected to remain high, the upward trend in government oil revenue will continue: the IMF (2005a) forecasts that government oil revenue will surpass $10 billion by 2007, as shown in Figure 4.

Since oil also contributes such a large share of GDP, the ratio of government revenue to GDP is also especially high (37 per cent in 2004), which is another characteristic of highly oil-dependent economies. By contrast, as Figure 5 shows, African countries without large oil industries generally have revenue/GDP ratios in the range of 10 to 25 per cent.

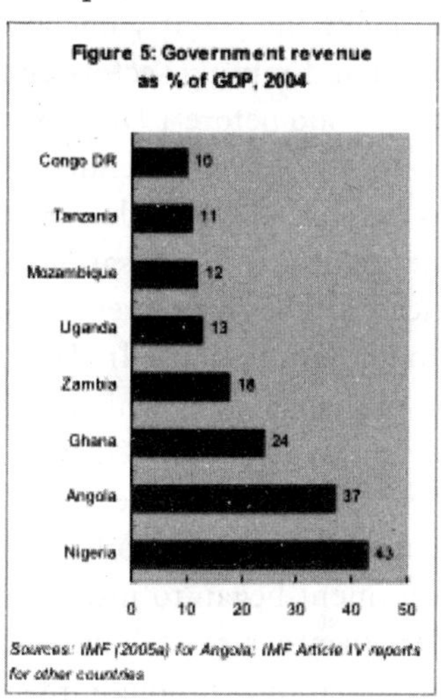

The key question therefore is whether the tax revenues from oil are well managed and are used to diversify the economy, through investment in infrastructure and human capital, contributing to employment generation and poverty reduction. One of the main problems in Angola has been the tendency for these resources to be wasted on military expenditure or transferred to the elite for consumption—or investment outside the country—although a positive recent development has been the improvement in the share of expenditure allocated to infrastructure and social services.

The sustainability of these improvements will depend in part on international oil prices. Although the highly positive scenario for government revenue given above is based on forecasts of continuing strength in the world oil market, the latter is notoriously volatile and a sudden downturn in the market could have severe consequences for a country so dependent on oil as Angola. This has happened twice in the past two decades—first in 1986, when a collapse in oil prices plunged Angola into a debt crisis for the first time, and then again in 1998/99, when prices dipped below $10 a barrel, making it difficult for Angola to service its oil-guaranteed loans, which had become virtually the only available source of external financing since the build-up of external arrears began in 1986.[5]

In addition to the risk of sudden oil price shocks, it is noteworthy that the dominance of the oil sector also results in 'Dutch disease' conditions, i.e. an appreciation of the real effective exchange rate, unless this is counteracted by macroeconomic policies. Appreciation of the domestic currency tends to make the country uncompetitive in most industries outside the oil and mining sectors and so block economic diversification. In the period before 1999, when Angola had a fixed official exchange rate, the currency tended to increase in value in real effective terms because of the high rate of inflation, which in turn was a consequence of the monetisation of the large deficits in government finances, although this tendency was temporarily counteracted by periodic devaluations. In 1999, the government introduced a flexible exchange rate, which was henceforth set by demand and supply in an inter-bank market. However, as international reserves rose, particularly after 2000, as a result of rising oil revenues and increased access to oil-guaranteed loans and credit lines, the government began to intervene heavily in the market by selling dollars in order to stabilise the nominal exchange rate and thereby curb inflation. Although inflation declined from its previously very high levels, it was still in double figures in 2003-5, largely because of the continuing fiscal deficits, although these were smaller than in the late 1990s. As a result, the kwanza strengthened considerably throughout the first half of the present decade. In short, the government's 'hard kwanza policy', as it came to be known, reinforced rather than mitigated the Dutch disease effects of high oil export earnings, making commercial agriculture and most private industry outside oil and diamonds uncompetitive.

5 The external debt totalled $9.5 billion, equivalent to 130 per cent of GDP in net present value terms, at the end of 2004. This debt included $2.4 billion in arrears (IMF, 2005a and 2005b).

Institutional effects

Even more important have been the political effects of the rise in the oil rent accruing to the state. Not only are these resources much higher in absolute terms than in all other Sub-Saharan African countries apart from Nigeria and South Africa, but as has been indicated above they are unusually high compared with the size of the economy as a whole. In short, the dominance of the oil industry in the Angolan economy and the spectacular rise in oil revenue during the present decade are concentrating unusually large resources in the state.

Although the Ministry of Finance is the government agency formally responsible for managing these resources, it is well known that in practice the presidency exerts a high degree of control over these resources through the state oil company Sonangol. This state company plays multiple roles, acting not only as the exclusive concessionaire for all oil exploration and production, but also as a partner in some oil bloc contractor groups and joint ventures, as well as a conduit for the channelling of oil company taxes to the state, an investor in various oil sector service companies as well as businesses entirely outside the oil sector (such as the Banco Africano de Investimentos and the airline Sonair), and an institution used by the presidency for raising external finance through oil-collateralised loans. The most important point here is that a large part of the taxes and other revenue (such as signature bonuses) from the oil companies is not paid directly to the Ministry of Finance, but passes through accounts held by Sonangol, which has been externally audited only once, in 2003. The most recent available information indicates that about half of government oil revenue is handled by Sonangol (IMF, 2005a). Making matters even more complex, a shroud of secrecy envelops some of the oil-guaranteed loans raised by Sonangol on behalf of the state.

Furthermore, the presidency has been able to engage in large-scale extra-budgetary operations, bypassing the formally instituted rules for managing state finances, by exploiting its direct access to the financial resources available both from oil taxes and oil-guaranteed loans. A sizeable proportion of government finances is managed off-budget: payments are made without going through the legally established procedures and expenditures are not recorded and classified correctly in the state accounts. According to IMF estimates, on average 36 per cent of government expenditure was off-budget between 1998 and 2002 and 11 per cent of expenditure could not be accounted for at all (IMF, 2003).[6]

Some of these features of the political economy of Angola are not unique, but the scale of the resources under the control of the presidency has no parallel elsewhere in Sub-Saharan Africa except Nigeria. During the war, the sheer scale of oil and diamond wealth not only raised the stakes for both the incumbent regime and the UNITA rebels, but provided huge resources (oil wealth for the government and diamonds for UNITA) for sustaining the conflict after the loss of external support at the end of the Cold War. It was the combination of rising government oil revenues and UNITA's loss of control of its main diamond mines in the north-east that finally gave the government a decisive edge, leading to outright military victory over UNITA in 2002. Even higher now, oil revenue will give the president vast resources with which to 'lubricate' the long postponed general elections, when they are eventually held, and thus crown his military victory with a political victory too.

The economic mechanisms of patrimonialism and accumulation

The methods used in the elections will almost certainly exemplify the patrimonial or clientelist mechanisms that have become the hallmark of President José Eduardo dos Santos's style of rule, particularly since the shift to a formally more 'pluralistic' political system and a market economy in the early 1990s. Oil-financed patronage has been a fundamental part of the strategy pursued by the President for the conservation of political power, making it necessary to resort to violence or repression only to deal with the least malleable of opponents, such

6 This was the discrepancy (calculated by the IMF) between the government's known expenditure (recorded and unrecorded) and known revenue and financing.

as Jonas Savimbi, who wanted to take supreme power rather than merely share in its spoils.

The patronage that has bought loyalty or acquiescence (from army officers, former rebels and politicians alike) depends largely though not entirely on the President's access to the large and rising flow of oil revenue and has contributed to the formation of a rentier class through a process akin to one of primitive capital accumulation—although it is far from certain that this will really engender a sustainable development of indigenous capitalism, since the wealth acquired is largely being dissipated through luxury consumption or invested abroad. The mechanisms through which patronage has been dispensed and accumulation has proceeded have been manifold. Many are linked to the oil or diamond sectors, either directly or through the financial resources generated by these sectors, while others concern land or business opportunities of various other types.

One of the most important mechanisms in the 1990s was the system for allocating foreign exchange, almost all of which has come from oil revenues or the loans guaranteed by oil. The granting of privileged access to subsidised foreign exchange at the official exchange rate provided opportunities for arbitrage, or 'round-tripping', between the official and parallel markets. On average, during the period from 1991 to 1998, there was a ratio of 2.9 to one between the parallel and official exchange rates, giving those selected to receive foreign exchange at the official rate what Munslow (1999: 563) described as a 'licence to make money'. Political connections were the main criterion for rationing the distribution of these golden eggs, which amounted to a massive transfer of oil-generated resources from the state to those selected to benefit. It was only the acute economic crisis triggered by the collapse of oil prices in 1998-99 that forced the government to abolish the fixed official exchange rate in May 1999 and introduce a managed float, closing off this avenue for patronage, which was probably the single most important source of private enrichment for the leading families of the regime during the first decade of capitalist restoration.

Second, the allocation of bank credit performed a rather similar, supplementary function in the 1990s, serving to enrich a small number of administratively selected individuals, who by and large were the same people who were enjoying access to foreign exchange at the official exchange rate. Since this credit was provided at negative real interest rates, administrative methods of selection were used to allocate loans to these individuals through the dominant state-owned banks. This subsidised credit, which like the subsidised foreign exchange constituted a form of quasi-fiscal resource transfer to the beneficiaries, played a complementary role as virtually all the credit was for short-term financing of import operations. Moreover, owing to the weakness of the legal system and the lack of political will to pursue defaulters, many of the loans were never serviced or repaid. Again, the economic crisis in 1998-99 forced the government to introduce reforms that raised interest rates to positive real levels and began to introduce more competition into the banking sector. One state bank, the Caixa de Crédito Agro-Pecuária e Pescas (CAP), which was heavily burdened with non-performing loans, was liquidated in 2001, but the defaulters were never forced to repay.

While these first two mechanisms for transferring resources to the politico-business elite receded in importance after 1999, other mechanisms continued and became even more important as oil revenues rose to record levels. The weakness of procurement procedures has provided opportunities for kick-backs on government contracts, while the opaqueness of public finances, resulting from the high level of extra-budgetary operations and the secrecy surrounding the oil-guaranteed loans, makes it easy to hide the diversion of state resources to private individuals and companies. By the very nature of such a situation, it is impossible to be completely sure about the total value of government revenue and financing flows or to know exactly how all the resources available to the state are used. Indeed, the independent oil diagnostic study which was carried out by the auditing company KPMG under the short-lived IMF 'staff monitored programme' in 2000-2001 (see below) failed to achieve a full reconciliation of recorded oil revenue payments in 2000 and no analysis has been done for subsequent years, while on the expenditure side a significant proportion of government expenditure is unrecorded or unclassified, as we have seen above.

Given this lack of transparency, it is widely suspected that substantial state resources have been diverted to private bank accounts. An inkling of what may have been going on was provided in the allegations first made in 2002 about financial transfers through the Swiss banking system relating to Angola's debt to Russia. In 1996, this debt which had been inherited from Soviet times and totalled about $5 billion was restructured: a large part was written off and the rest was converted into a $1.9 billion loan, which in turn was sold at an undisclosed price to a private company, Abalone Investment Ltd, involving Pierre Falcone and Arkadi Gaydamak, two international financiers of Franco-Brazilian and Israeli-Russian origin who had earlier been the main actors in the 'Angolagate' arms-for-oil scandal.[7] Although the original Russian loan had a 15-year maturity and a five-year grace period, the Angolan government raised costly short-term oil-guaranteed loans to pre-pay Abalone Investment and, by early 2002, $1.5 billion had been paid to this company (IMF, 2002). Following investigations by the Swiss judicial authorities, Falcone was charged with money laundering, 'support to a criminal organisation', 'corrupting foreign public officials' and being involved in a 'secret organisation working between Geneva, Moscow and Luanda and pursuing the aim of procuring illicit income by criminal means'. The Swiss judicial authorities alleged that Abalone Investment had been set up to 'extort financial resources, to the prejudice of the Republic of Angola and the Russian Federation' and had passed on to the Russian Finance Ministry only $161 million out of $774 million received in Angolan debt service payments between 1996

7 The Angolagate affair concerned the financing of arms deliveries to Angola in 1993 with oil-backed loans and resulted in the arrest of Falcone and Jean-Christophe Mitterrand, the son of the former French president, in France in December 2000. The charges were later dismissed on legal technicalities.

and 2000. Some of the missing funds had allegedly been found in bank accounts belonging to Falcone, Gaydamak and several Angolan government officials. These included funds totalling $40 million in accounts whose ultimate beneficiaries were 'very probably' President dos Santos and his personal ambassador, Elísio de Figueiredo.[8]

The then Interior Minister, Fernando de Piedade 'Nandó', admitted in the Angolan parliament on 5 June 2002 that government funds had been placed in private individuals' bank accounts, claiming that this was a common practice in countries facing exceptional situations, like war-torn Angola. The previous March, a report on an IMF mission to Angola revealed that the Angolan authorities had refused to provide the Fund with details of the oil-guaranteed loans raised to pay Abalone 'because it would infringe on their national sovereignty' (IMF, 2002). The case was eventually dropped and the funds frozen in Swiss accounts were unblocked in December 2004, when the Swiss Attorney-General accepted the position of the Angolan authorities that these funds could be reasonably classified as 'secret strategic funds' because of the situation of civil war (EIU, 2005a).

With the capital acquired in the early phases of accumulation, some wealthy Angolans are now ready to move on to a new form of rentier activity involving their direct participation in the oil industry. This began with the establishment of service companies that the oil operators were pressured by Sonangol to contract. The process of Angolanisation is now extending to the licensing of the consortia for oil exploration and production, following a pattern seen for some time in the Nigerian oil industry. Legislative changes in 2004 made it more attractive for smaller oil companies to enter the market and a number of indigenous Angolan oil companies have been established, among them Somoil Sociedade Petrolífera Angolana SARL and Prodoil Exploração e Produção de Hidrocarbonetos SARL. Somoil, which is 100 per cent Angolan owned and has been described by the

8 *Le Monde*, 23 May 2002. According to the Economist Intelligence Unit, $34 million was paid into a Panamanian account controlled by President dos Santos (EIU, 2005a).

US-Angola Chamber of Commerce as an initiative of the 'Angolan nomenklatura', was given a stake in three oil blocks (3/05, 3/05A and 4/05) in October 2005.[9] This is in line with an official policy to give preference to consortia including private Angolan companies, communicated the previous June to a conference in London by the head of licensing and exploration at the Ministry of Petroleum, Alfredo Rafael, and reiterated in October by the Vice President of Sonangol, Syanga Abílio, at the World Petroleum Congress in South Africa.[10]

This development, which seems to be focused initially on the smaller, more marginal onshore and shallow water blocks where there is less interest by the oil majors, mirrors what began to happen a decade earlier in the diamond industry. In a response both to the informal *garimpo* phenomenon and to the domination of the formal mining industry by large multinational companies, the government introduced a series of legislative changes in the early 1990s to permit the licensing of small-scale private mining and marketing of diamonds. The liberalisation of the marketing system, which legalised the possession and trading of rough diamonds (law no. 30/91), was followed by a mining law (law no. 1/92) and a new diamond industry law (law no. 16/94), which opened the way for the licensing of mining operations by small private Angolan companies. The government awarded more than 20 concessions involving 30 to 40 Angolan companies between 1994 and 1999.[11] By mid-2004, there were 264 national firms and 34 international companies with a total of 90 concessions (IMF, 2005b).

Although the vast majority of these concessions have not yet been put into operation (PAC, 2005), the opportunities bestowed on the

9 US-Angola Chamber of Commerce website, news item posted 21 January 2005; *Alexander's Gas and Oil Connections*, Vol. 10, No. 20, 26 October 2005; *WINNE World Investment News*, 19 October 2005.

10 *SouthScan*, London, 1 November 2005; *Alexander's Gas and Oil Connections*, 23 June 2005.

11 Among them were Antigos Combatentes, the Angola Diamond Company, Lumanhe, Esplendor, Anglo Sul, Consórcio Mineiro do Lucula, Mombo, Opala Negra and Transcoi. See Hodges, 2003: 183-96.

concession-holders are considerable. License fees are minimal or waived entirely and, in contrast to the oil industry, tax payments to the state are modest: $112 million or 14 per cent of the value of diamond sales in 2003 (IMF, 2005b). To develop mining operations, the Angolan concessionaires have usually entered into partnership arrangements with foreign mining companies with the necessary technical expertise and capital. While the latter assume all the risks, the concessionaires take a cut of the profits, acting in effect as 'sleeping partners' in what amounts to a classic example of rent-seeking behaviour.

For those able to exploit their concessions, diamond mining has become one of the main avenues for accumulation of wealth. Army generals and other senior officials are prominent in several of the companies and some of the concessions seem to have served the specific purpose of rewarding military loyalty. More generally, the non-transparent procedures for awarding the concessions and the direct involvement of the presidency in the process have become a prime example of the role of presidential patronage in resource management.

It should be noted also that, to advance the interests of the concessionaires, both Angolan and foreign, the diamond mining law (16/94) provides for the forcible relocation of local villages and a ban on all unauthorised movement in and around the concession areas. This has occasioned severe human rights abuses, as well as impoverishing much of the local population, who have lost rather than gained from the wealth in their vicinity (Marques and Falcão de Campos, 2005). In addition, to remove unwanted competition, in 2003 the government launched a massive campaign to deport foreign *garimpeiros*, Operação Brilhante, which by April 2005 had resulted in the expulsion of 256,400 foreigners from the diamond regions, sometimes under brutal conditions (PAC, 2005).

Marques and Falcão de Campos have documented how some military, police and other officials continue to mine illegally, sometimes by virtually enslaving local villagers to work in informal artisanal mines. Many officials also remain deeply involved in illicit diamond trading, despite various attempts by the government to channel the diamond trade through officially recognised marketing companies. These attempts included the establishment of a marketing monopoly, the Angola Selling Corporation (Ascorp), in 2000, and then the opening up of the market to competition from other licensed companies in 2004. While the establishment of Ascorp was clearly motivated, at least in part, by the hope that this would halt the trade in illegal diamonds of UNITA provenance, other factors seem to have driven the frequent changes in policy, legislation and regulations, among them a desire on the part of the state to capture a larger share of the profits at the expense of the miners and traders. Dietrich has highlighted the coexistence of competition and patron-client dependency in the relationship between the presidency and the elite groups with interests in diamond trading (Dietrich, 2001; Cilliers and Dietrich, 2000: 190).[12]

Finally, in this review of the mechanisms by which patronage is dispensed and wealth accumulated, mention must be made of various mechanisms that are related neither to oil nor to diamonds. One of the most well-known has been the divestiture of state assets, which began in the early 1990s after the decision to shift to a capitalist type of economy. There have been parallels here with the process by which state assets in the former USSR were acquired by former members of the Soviet *nomenklatura*. In the early 1990s, the main focus of privatisation was on small and medium sized state companies, which were specifically earmarked for transfer to Angolan rather than foreign investors. The divestiture of these companies took place without proper valuations or competitive bidding, so that they were transferred at knock-down prices to administratively selected individuals, many of them high-ranking officials or members of their families. By the

12 Following a period in the 1990s when several companies competed to purchase diamonds, including diamonds of UNITA provenance, a diamond trading monopoly was established in 2000 through Ascorp, a joint venture between a newly created state company, the Sociedade Angolana de Diamantes (SODIAM) and Israeli and Belgian companies. The monopoly was rescinded in 2003, after which three diamond marketing companies were licensed by SODIAM over the following two years.

end of 1996, a total of 202 companies had been privatised. Since then, privatisation has slowed down, partly because of complaints about the non-transparent manner in which the first stage took place but also because the remaining companies are much larger and in many cases would require foreign investment.

As part of the first wave of privatisation, hundreds of former state farms, which had been created out of the commercial farms (*fazendas*) abandoned by the departing settlers in 1975/76, were broken up and sold to high officials, army officers and their relatives, often at nominal prices and without any open process of competitive bidding. A similar process took place in the cities, where tens of thousands of state-owned villas and apartments were transferred by the State Secretariat for Housing to private owners: many were the occupants who had moved into these homes after the departure of the settlers in 1975/76, but the best properties, some of them worth hundreds of thousands or even millions of dollars as a result of the lack of investment in housing stock since independence and the influx of foreign companies into Angola, were handed over to elite families at a fraction of their true value.

In the countryside, the privatisation of the state farms took place at the expense of the small farmers who had been squatting on and tilling the land of many of these farms, most of which had been more or less moribund since the mid-1980s. By 1999, more than 2 million hectares, equivalent to half the land belonging to colonial settlers before 1975/76, had been handed over to a new class of Angolan *fazendeiros* (Pacheco, 2002). This process, which reflects a deliberate policy option in favour of large-scale commercial agriculture instead of and at the expense of development of the small farming sector, has continued since then; as a result of a new land law adopted in 2004, it threatens to encroach further on peasant agriculture, owing to the lack of legal protection for small farmers whose traditional land-use rights are derived from a communal land tenure system without individual, documented land titles.

Last but not least, the retention of a web of complex administrative procedures, rules and regulations for most business activities, in spite of the shift to a capitalist economy, has created a situation where the establishment and development of businesses depends to a large extent on connections at the highest level of the state. The extent of red tape in Angola was revealed in a worldwide survey of the investment climate by the World Bank, covering more than 170 countries, which found that it took on average 146 days to start up a business in Angola, requiring 14 separate procedures, compared with a global average of 51 days.[13] Besides discouraging investment and thus holding back economic diversification and development, the problems of red tape and the associated favouritism shown to those permitted to engage in business activities hold back competition, creating markets that are often oligopolistic in nature. Along with poor infrastructure and high transport costs, this is one of the main reasons why prices are so high in Angola. Patronage is also evident in the process by which certain well-placed individuals are nominated to the boards of foreign companies investing in Angola or are given equity stakes in joint ventures with foreign companies.[14]

Although the mechanisms described above are quite varied, and some have been more prominent in certain periods than others, they all have one thing in common. Without exception they involve the presidency's command over resources or business opportunities and the allocation or awarding of these resources and opportunities through licenses, contracts or concessions, using non-transparent methods, to the benefit of a small nexus of elite families.

Interests and capacity to resist reform

The enormous interests involved in this process of patronage and private accumulation have profoundly coloured the process of eco-

13 It also took an average of 1,011 days to enforce a contract through the courts and 335 days to register a property, respectively the fourth and sixth longest amounts of time in the world (World Bank, 2004).

14 In one well-known case, disagreements over the selection of Angolan partners led to a four-year delay of a $26 million investment by Coca-Cola, which was finally resolved in 1998 (*Africa Confidential*, 29 November 1996).

nomic 'reform' in Angola since the start of the shift from a largely state-owned economy to one based primarily on private ownership. The result has been the retention of mechanisms that permit the state—and the presidency in particular—to manipulate and distort the market.

These interests are at once material (on the part of the beneficiaries of the resources and opportunities provided) and political (on the part of the patron at the summit of the system). Among the beneficiaries has been the President's own family. Reference has been made above to the allegations of substantial transfers of public funds to accounts controlled by the President. It is also well known that the President's daughter has acquired a veritable business empire in diamond mining and trade, telecommunications and banking, by means of the administrative procedures used to bestow concessions and licences and foist partners on foreign investors.[15] The scale of these interests explains why there has been such resistance to the adoption of more transparent and rule-based procedures, whether in the management of public finances or in the awarding of business licenses, diamond concessions and land titles.

Moreover, the capacity to resist change is as substantial as the interests in maintenance of the *status quo*. Riding on a cushion of rising oil revenues, despite occasional downturns brought about by sudden falls in oil prices that have briefly offset the upward trend in production and exports, the Angolan state has by and large been able to withstand pressures for reform from the IMF and donors, unlike almost all other African states. The United States, which is the main destination of Angolan oil (47 per cent in 2003), is keen to cultivate close relations with oil-producing countries outside the Middle East and so is unlikely to put strong pressure on the Angolan government

15 Isabel dos Santos has a stake in Unitel, a mobile telecommunications company co-owned by Portugal Telecom, as well as interests in the Camatue kimberlite in Lunda Norte (through the Angolan Diamond Corporation) and the Banco Internacional de Crédito (BIC), a new bank set up in 2005. For further details, see Hodges, 2003 (pages 138-9), Cilliers and Dietrich, 2000 (pages 158-59) and EIU, 2005c.

over issues of economic governance. For many industrialised countries, a desire to protect the interests of their national oil companies is another factor encouraging a non-conflictual relationship.

The rapid economic development of Asian countries, in particular China and India, is also providing opportunities for the Angolan government to diversify its international economic relations. China, which is now the world's second largest oil importer (and in 2004 accounted for 31 per cent of the global growth in oil demand), has taken a keen interest in securing access to oil supplies in many parts of the world, including Angola, through exploration and supply agreements (Zweig and Jianhai, 2005). This resulted in China's provision of a $2 billion oil-guaranteed loan to Angola in 2004 on relatively attractive terms, followed in 2005 by the awarding of stakes in two Angolan oil blocks to the Chinese oil company Sinopec (though a joint venture called Sonangol Sinopec International) and the signing of a bilateral agreement for the supply of up to 100,000 b/d of Angolan oil to China (Malaquias, 2005, and EIU, 2005a and 2005b).

In any case, the high level of oil revenues means that the regime can usually rely on its own resources and so avoid dependence on donors. Official Development Assistance (ODA) contributes very little to Angolan government expenditure (only 4.8 per cent in 2001 and probably much less now), providing a stark contrast with the aid dependency of most African governments, many of which rely on aid for over 30 or even 40 per cent of their expenditure (see Figure 6).

Furthermore, despite the high level of oil-guaranteed borrowing on costly commercial terms, the debt burden has generally been manageable except during temporary periods of crisis resulting from transient oil price shocks. Not surprisingly, Angola is one of the very few African countries that have never had to borrow from the IMF, although it entered into two short-lived and unsuccessful periods of IMF-monitored reforms in 1995 and 2000-1, on the latter occasion as a direct result of the collapse of oil prices in 1998-9. The strong recovery in oil prices in the first half of the present decade has since allowed the Government to dispense with IMF intrusion.

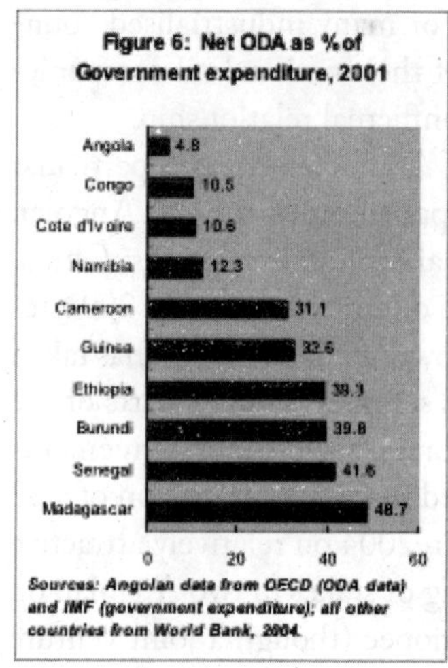

Figure 6: Net ODA as % of Government expenditure, 2001

Sources: Angolan data from OECD (ODA data) and IMF (government expenditure); all other countries from World Bank, 2004.

In conclusion, only a dramatic external shock in the form of a large unexpected fall in oil prices might make the debt burden unsustainable and force the regime to make significant concessions to the IMF. Even then, as in 1998-99, the pressures are likely only to be transitory and the government would probably seek to find ways of circumventing them by making overtures to alternative sources of financial succour, notably China, which is ready to provide assistance to secure its access to sources of energy. In short, entrenched material and political interests and the rapidly strengthening financial capacity of the state make it extremely unlikely that the Angolan regime will move forward with reforms that would decisively transform the nature of economic governance. Ultimately the driving forces for change are most likely to come from within, but that too is probably in the very long run, as oil wealth provides those in power with the means to buy off opposition for the foreseeable future.

BIBLIOGRAPHY

Cilliers, Jackie and Christian Dietrich (2000), *Angola's War Economy: The Role of Oil and Diamonds*, Pretoria Institute for Security Studies.

Dietrich, Christian (2001), 'Have African-Based Diamond Monopolies Been Effective?', *Central Africa Minerals and Arms Research Bulletin*, No. 2, 18 June.

EIU (2005a), *Country Report: Angola*, London: Economist Intelligence Unit, 1st Quarter, March.

EIU (2005b), *Country Report: Angola*, London: Economist Intelligence Unit, 2nd Quarter, June.

EIU (2005c), *Country Report: Angola*, London: Economist Intelligence Unit, 3rd Quarter, September.

Hodges, Tony (2003), *Angola: Anatomy of an Oil State*, Oxford: James Currey and Bloomington, USA: Indiana University Press.

Hodges, Tony (2004), 'The Role of Resource Management in Building Sustainable Peace', in Guss Meijer, 'From Military Peace to Social Justice? The Angolan Peace Process', *Accord*, No. 15, London: Conciliation Resources, 2004.

IMF (2002), *Angola: Staff Report for the 2002 Article IV Consultation*, Washington, DC: International Monetary Fund, March.

IMF (2003), *Angola: Staff Report for the 2003 Article IV Consultation*, Washington, DC: International Monetary Fund, July.

IMF (2005a), *Angola: Staff Report for the 2004 Article IV Consultation*, Country Report No. 05/228, Washington, DC: International Monetary Fund, July.

IMF (2005b), *Angola: Selected Issues and Statistical Appendix*, Country Report no. 05/125, Washington, DC: International Monetary Fund, April.

Marques, Rafael and Rui Falcão de Campos (2005), *Lundas—The Stones of Death*, Open Society Foundation.

Malaquias, Assis (2005), 'A China entra em África com Muito Dinheiro e sem Exigências', *Público*, Lisbon, 20 November.

Munslow, Barry (1999), 'Angola: The Politics of Unsustainable Development', *Third World Quarterly*, 20 (3): 551-68.

PAC (2005), *Diamond Industry Annual Review: Republic of Angola 2005*, Ottawa: Partnership Africa Canada.

Pacheco, Fernando (2002), *A Questão da Terra para Fins Agrícolas em Angola*, Luanda: Food and Agriculture Organisation of the United Nations.

World Bank (2004), *The Cost of Doing Business*, Washington, DC.

Zweig, David, and Bi Jianhai (2005), 'China's Global Hunt for Energy', *Foreign Affairs*, New York, 84 (5), September/October: 25-38.

6

SOCIAL NEGLECT AND THE EMERGENCE OF CIVIL SOCIETY IN ANGOLA[1]

Nuno Vidal

Introduction

Soon after independence, the Angolan political system assumed a modern patrimonial character. With a single party regime, there was a juxtaposition of state and party structures. Power was exercised by means of a mechanism for distribution of state resources operated through the appointment of key figures in the top positions. Within the state administration, jobs were the access route to state resources for personal or private benefit. Public office became a perk or a personal reward and was thus divorced from its mission to implement policies of national interest. Accordingly, the differentiation between public and private spheres vanished along with notions of common good and collective interest.[2]

1 Research for this work was financed by the Portuguese Foundation for Science and Technology and developed under the aegis of the Faculty of Economics—University of Coimbra. It is the result of consistent field research over a period of three years and of the cooperation of the author with a number of international research teams operating in Angola.

2 On the working logic of the Angolan political system see Nuno Vidal, Post-modern Patrimonialism in Africa: the Genesis and Development of the Angolan Political-economic System, 1961-1987, PhD tesis, King's College, London, 2002.

Following the 27 May 1977 attempted coup, the state security apparatus grew stronger and came under close presidential and party control, spreading fear and terror, as thousands were killed.[3] This resulted in the overlapping of the judicial, legislative and executive, with tight political control of the judiciary. Political power became concentrated in the hands of the President and administration was centralised in Luanda. The regime increased its authoritarianism and showed the first signs of elitism in the access to resources and benefits.[4]

Popular discontent and the loss of political legitimacy were partially disguised by the civil war. The conflict 'justified' hardships in living conditions and the deterioration of public services. As the conflict gained increasing ethnic overtones in the 1980s, it also allowed the regime to neglect its social obligations towards the majority of the population, which survived at the margins of the patrimonial system, without entirely losing the support of those who still identified with the great socio-political alliance at the heart of the MPLA.[5] The availability of valuable natural wealth made it possible for the regime to forego the 'exploitation' of the population for the purpose of generating the resources needed to sustain the state. Together, these characteristics rendered the system unaccountable but with no penalty for those in power, who could simply ignore the poor or *l'Afrique inutile* (to use Reno's expression).[6]

3 On the attempted coup see Nuno Vidal, *Post-modern Patrimonialism in Africa*, ch. 5.

4 See my chapter on politics in this volume.

5 On the increasing ethnic overtones of the conflict in the eighties see Christine Messiant, 'MPLA et UNITA, processus de paix et logique de guerre', *Politique Africaine*, 57 (1995), p. 44; also Christine Messiant, 'Angola, les voies de l'ethnisation et de la décomposition—I—de la guerre à la paix (1975–1991): le conflit armé, les interventions internationales et le peuple angolais', *Lusotopie*, 1 (1994) pp. 155–210; Christine Messiant, 'Angola les voies de l'ethnisation et de la décomposition—II—Transition à la démocratie ou marche à la guerre? L'épanouissement des deux 'partis armés' (Mai 1991–Septembre 1992)', *Lusotopie*, 3 (1995), pp. 181–221; also, David Birmingham, *Frontline Nationalism in Angola and Mozambique,* London: James Currey, 1992, p. 88.

6 William Reno, *Warlord Politics and African States,* London: Lynne Rienner,

During the Agostinho Neto administration (1975-79), the Angolan political and economic system clearly exhibited the characteristics of modern (neo-) patrimonialism as described by authors such as Chabal and Daloz, Médard and Bayart.[7] However, contrary to that analytical framework, Angola's neo-patrimonialism did not reach a point of coherent and operative stability: the ties of distributive interdependence between patrons and clients loosened, patrimonial networks were restricted to the top of the state apparatus and the majority of the population became increasingly more remote from the prevailing system of redistribution. Service delivery by the state progressively collapsed, especially within the social sector, and this primarily affected the bottom layers of society and the poor. The social tissue became deeply fragmented and the party's 'social compact' entered a process of terminal dereliction, shattering whatever remained of the MPLA's ambitions for the well-being of the newly independent nation-state.[8] Although this process started during Ne-

1998, p. 35.

7 Reference is made mainly to the following works: Jean-François Médard, 'The Underdeveloped State in Tropical Africa: Political Clientelism or Neo-Patrimonialism?', in C. Clapham, (ed.), *Private Patronage and Public Power,* London: Frances Pinter, 1982, pp. 162-92; Jean-François Médard, 'L'État néo-patrimonial en Afrique noire' in Jean-François Médard (ed.), *États d'Afrique noire,* Paris: Karthala, 1991, pp. 323-53; Jean-François Bayart, The State in Africa, the Politics of the Belly, London: Longman, 1989; J.-F. Bayart et al., *The Criminalization of the State in Africa,* London: James Currey, 1998; Patrick Chabal, *Power in Africa,* London: Macmillan Press, 1994; Patrick Chabal and Jean-Pascal Daloz, *Africa Works,* London: James Currey, 1999.

8 Such patrimonial dynamics occurred in Angola throughout the eighties, during the so-called Socialist administration of President Eduardo dos Santos, and is probably not much different from the ones occurring in different periods and in other mineral rich countries, such as the Democratic Republic of Congo, Liberia, Sierra Leone and Nigeria; it is not possible here to explain at length the whole dynamics involved in this form of patrimonialism; on that subject see Nuno Vidal, *Post-modern Patrimonialism in Africa*; also Nuno Vidal, 'Modern and Post-Modern Patrimonialism' in Malyn Newitt with Patrick Chabal and Norrie MacQueen (eds), *Community and the State in Lusophone Africa,* London: King's College London, 2003, pp. 1-14; also Nuno Vidal, 'The Genesis and Development of the Angolan Political and Administrative System from 1975

to's term of office, it accelerated during the Dos Santos administration in the first half of the eighties—that is, well before the end of the socialist phase of government.

A dominant patrimonial logic pervaded the social system; an authoritarian and repressive one-party regime manipulated the state media and mass organisations, all within the context of civil war. There developed a political rationality, shared and practiced at all levels of society, with an established set of rules for appropriation and distribution. People positioned themselves vertically in relation to the state structures and along preferential solidarity chains of clientelism according to an 'ethic' of neo-patrimonialism. This inhibited the appearance of an alternative social logic based upon notions of citizenship or class (where people place themselves horizontally in relation to the state) and therefore hampered the emergence of civil society as understood in the West.[9]

In a situation such as Angola's (and possibly elsewhere in Africa), where there is no longer any distribution of resources to the great majority of the population, public services collapse and poverty thrives. The patrimonial ethics dilutes and social fragmentation reaches very high levels. Political power becomes illegitimate since it is unaccountable to those marginalised by the system, who might then be recruited by political rivals who may or may not continue to function within a patrimonial logic.

In such situations, there is room for competing patrimonial projects, led by ambitious or unsatisfied leaders gathering those cast out by the system in an attempt to replicate the central model at the regional or local level. These might aim to overthrow the current elites in power and take their place but without questioning the inner logic of the whole system. On the other hand, within a context of deep social fragmentation as well as poverty and despair, there might be some opportunity to fill part of the social void with

to the Present', in Steve Kyle (org.), *Intersections between Social Sciences,* Cornell NY: Institute for African Development of Cornell University, 2004', pp. 1-16.

9 See Patrick Chabal and Jean-Pascal Daloz, *Africa Works,* ch. 2.

small counter-projects. Transnational networks linking national and foreign actors with a radically different social perspective in relation to patrimonialism, some national and international NGOs, International Governmental Organisations IGOs, church organisations, etc., are able to recruit those marginalised by the system in order to seek to develop 'civil society', denounce patrimonialism and promote democratic notions of citizenship and human rights.

In the late eighties and early nineties, the transition to a multiparty system and a market economy brought into the country a large number of such international organisations. Transnational networks gathered together expatriate activists, local communities and a marginalised Angolan intellectual elite, including some middle and high level cadres. Joining forces, they began to work with the people most in need of basic social support and progressively took over an ever increasing portfolio of state responsibilities in social sectors such as education, health, basic sanitation, housing, assistance for Internal Displaced Persons (IDPs) and rural development. Accordingly, the government was able to relax further its already minimal care of the millions of people affected by war. These dynamics were reinforced by the new multiparty 'freedom' and 'democratic' legislative framework, fuelling the emerging Angolan civil society organisations (CSOs), which were able to grow throughout the nineties and voice growing criticism of the government despite the severe constraints imposed by the regime.

Several major financial scandals in the late nineties and the end of the civil war in 2002 changed the context within which CSOs operated. As international humanitarian aid progressively decreased, pressure was put on the government to invest in the social sector and to assume a more transparent procedure in relation to public accounts, mainly oil revenues. However, results have been limited and the Angolan government has been able largely to ignore such pressure and thus keep to the same policies. So far the main impact has been felt at the level of the CSOs—small, dependent and fighting hard to survive within an increasingly adverse context.

This chapter discusses the reasons why the social sector collapsed in Angola, the impact of transnational networks and projects, the effects of the transition to a multiparty system, the process whereby CSOs emerged and the constraints and challenges they faced to survive. It is organised chronologically: the first part touches on the progressive neglect of the social sector during the socialist period; the second is concerned with the consequences of the transition to a multiparty system on the workings of the transnational networks and the emergence of civil society.

The social sector during the socialist period

The first signs of neglect became visible by the end of Neto's administration. In the very first few years after independence, at the height of ideological and revolutionary fervour, there was a certain commitment to the idea of devising policies and initiating programmes for the development of the social sector—including education, health, housing, social security and community services. This commitment was also nurtured by the arrival of Cuban volunteers trained in these areas (especially health and education), who made a contribution to its management and organisation.[10] However, after an initial phase during which the government showed some concern with these issues, by the end of Neto's presidency 1979 there were clear signs of contraction in social expenditure, which eventually led to the strangulation of programmes in most sectors.

Education was one of the main priorities of the new government and in the first years after independence, several measures were successfully introduced. There was a massive enrolment of children in the first four school years.[11] Significant efforts were made in adult

10 By 1977 these Cubans numbered 5,000: *Le Monde,* 9 November 1977; *Africa Contemporary Record—ACR,* 10 (1979), p. B510.

11 In 1979, the intake was 2.4 million children, four times greater than in 1973: In *Relatório do Comité Central ao I° Congresso Extraordinário do Partido, realizado em Luanda de 17 a 23 de Dezembro de 1980,* Luanda: Secretariado do Comité Central, 1980, p. 80.

education, especially for the veterans of the armed forces (FAPLA), and for workers and peasants: between 1976 and 1979 around 330,000 people were made literate.[12] Almost 759,000 illiterate adults were enrolled in 37,000 literacy classes.[13] A system of technical and professional training was set up along with higher education.[14]

However, between 1979 and 1981, the number of primary school children remained exactly the same[15] and the number of literate people grew by only 9,000[16] an insignificant number when compared with the previous 330,000 rise and the illiteracy rate of 80 per cent at the time of independence. Of the two thousand university students enrolled in 1980 it was later known that only 180 had finished their courses, and the number of literacy enrolments dropped in the following years from the previous 759,000 to just 100,000.[17] These were clear signs of regression in the education sector, a tendency that would be strongly confirmed in the ensuing five years.[18]

Within the health sector, assistance was given by foreign doctors (the number of Cuban doctors increased by 16.5 per cent between 1977 and 1980).[19] The government set up under its own auspices 1,260 health units, the most important of which were the Central

12 Ibid.

13 70,000 literacy teachers had been trained and 615 literacy brigades constituted, composed of 4,950 young volunteers; *ACR*, 14 (1983), p. B590.

14 The Faculty of Legal and Administrative Sciences was inaugurated, as was the Higher Institute of Educational Sciences; by 1980, there were over 2,000 university students: *Relatório do Comité Central ao I° Congresso Extraordinário*, 1980, pp. 80–1.

15 *ACR*, 13 (1982), p. B651.

16 In *ACR*, 14 (1983), p. B590.

17 *Relatório do Comité Central ao II° Congresso do Partido, realizado em Luanda de 2 a 10 de Dezembro de 1985,* Luanda: Edição do Secretariado do Comité Central, 1985, pp. 120–2.

18 Ibid.

19 *Relatório do Comité Central ao I° Congresso Extraordinário*...1980, p. 81; see also *ACR*, 13 (1982), p. B 651.

Hospitals of Luanda.[20] Several free vaccination campaigns for children were launched every year.[21] Primary health care was developed, with the creation of health centres, especially in rural and suburban areas. A project for the education of paramedical professionals was implemented.[22]

However, as with education, many problems including the contraction of funding available and the lack of financial and material resources, along with poor transport to the provinces and poor co-ordination between sectors for import and distribution of medicines,[23] all brought about a rapid reversal of the short lived successes of the health sector.[24]

Housing became one of the most severe social problems. After independence, some flats and villas were confiscated to accommodate the new rulers and others were taken over by the general mass of population already living in less desirable areas (with a clear priority given to the urban middle social strata). Despite such occupation of vacant places, there was an ever increasing demand for housing due to a number of factors such as the continuous exodus of the rural population towards the cities prompted by the war; the arrival of a growing number of foreign advisers, counsellors, technicians and

20 It comprised 8 hospitals, 16 provincial health centres, 32 municipal hospitals, 16 centres for mothers and children, 16 leprosy hospices and 6 tuberculosis sanatoria: *Relatório do Comité Central ao I° Congresso Extraordinário*...1980, p. 81.

21 For example, to mark World Health Day (7 April, 1977), 1.5 million children were vaccinated against polio; see *ACR*, 10 (1979), p. 508.

22 For example, training of nurses, midwives and other health care technicians; In *Relatório do Comité Central ao I° Congresso Extraordinário*...1980, p. 81.

23 Serious failures in medicine distribution emerged throughout the whole country, as reported in 'Principais resultados do desenvolvimento económico-social da RPA no triénio 1978-1980' in *Orientações Fundamentais para o Desenvolvimento Económico e Social para o período 1981-1985*, Luanda: Secretariado do Comité Central, 1980, p. 25.

24 See *Relatório do Comité Central ao II° Congresso*...1985, pp. 123–125; also reporting problems in the health sector by David Lamb in *Los Angeles Times*, 3 December 1978; see also *International Herald Tribune*, 6 December 1978.

military personnel (the majority of whom were Cuban[25]) and the training of new State cadres demanding to be properly housed by the state.[26]

For the lower social strata, who were flocking to the cities from rural areas, the solution was obviously to build more *muceques* (shanty towns) and these spread out of control around the cities, especially in Luanda. This started as soon as 1976/77 [27] and gathered momentum during the eighties and nineties. Among the newcomers to the capital city were the Bakongos, who returned from Zaire and numbered 200,000 as early as 1977. They set up their own *muceques* such as Palanca, Maborr or Petrangol.[28]

For the new state middle cadres and the Cubans, a few dozen low-quality blocks of flats were built (with Cuban aid) in Luanda during the late seventies and early eighties. However the state's building programme did not extend much beyond those few buildings in Luanda and in any event it soon ceased. It was the informal sector that filled the gap and the whole city of Luanda turned to unofficial (and anarchic) construction,[29] whereby thousands of annexes were built in the yards and gardens of houses or even on the flat roofs of blocks of flats.

In terms of social provisions, several national projects were discussed and began to be implemented under the pressure of workers and neighbourhood commissions as well as youth committees and

25 The number of Cuban military was not made official but in 1978 was estimated at 19,000; *ACR*, vol. 11 (1980), p. B493. As already mentioned, as early as 1977 the number of Cuban civilians in Angola under co-operation agreements (economic, scientific, cultural, technical and so on) was 5,000; *Le Monde*, 9 November 1977; also *ACR*, 10 (1979), p. B510.

26 Nuno Vidal, *Post-modern Patrimonialism in Africa.*

27 *ACR*, 15 (1984), p. B597; I am obviously talking about the enlargement and construction of new *muceques*, because, as is known, *muceques* have existed since the colonial period.

28 See M. R. Bhagavan, *Angola's Political Economy 1975–85*, Motala: Swedish International Development Authority, 1986, p. 24.

29 In 'Principais resultados do desenvolvimento económico-social da RPA no triénio 1978-1980', p. 25.

mass organisations. These included nurseries for children of working women; socio-economic help for former guerrillas and widows and orphans of the guerrilla veterans; homes for elderly and handicapped persons; refugee camps for people fleeing the war.[30] In 1977 around 50,000 Namibian refugees, targeted by South Africa, were transferred from the South to the North, where new camps were set up to house them. In the northeast provinces (Lunda South and Lunda North), camps were set up for around 18,000 refugees from Shaba (in Zaire) and several other initiatives of this kind were taken to support hundreds of thousands of displaced Angolans.[31]

However, as early as the end of 1977 and early 1978, the funds to support such initiatives decreased and the first signs of neglect became evident.[32] By the 1980 party congress, future commitments to such programmes were reduced to a mere declaration of intent and remained without any concrete plans.[33] As an alternative, and especially because of the acute pressure of refugees and internally displaced people, the Angolan government increased its demands for international support from organisations such as the UN system (UNHCR, UNICEF, WHO, FAO, WFP), the League of Red Cross Societies and Northern European countries like Sweden and Norway.[34] These were the first signs of a tendency which grew stronger in 1979.[35] Significant humanitarian aid to Angola began during this period (1977-78), when the first signs of collapse in the

30 See 'Principais resultados do desenvolvimento económico-social da RPA no triénio 1978-1980'.

31 See *UNHCR publication*, 5 (October 1977), p. 2; also *ACR*, 14 (1983), p. B590.

32 Nuno Vidal, *Post-modern Patrimonialism in Africa.*

33 See *Relatório do Comité Central ao Iº Congresso Extraordinário,* 1980, pp. 93-4.

34 In *UNHCR publication*, 5 October 1977, p. 2; The UNHCR built up a sum of $1.2 million into its 1977 emergency programme and a further 4.1 million for 1978 to finance the relief phase. A programme of longer-term assistance was to follow; ibid. p. 2.

35 In *ACR*, 14, (1983), p. B590.

social sector became apparent. Such aid increased markedly during the first five years of the 1980s.

In the field of community services, in parallel with the main responsibilities of the provincial commissariats (currently the provincial governments), several tasks were given to ODP (People's Defence Organisation) groups. Apart from their role as paramilitary forces, these groups were to offer social provisions in their respective provinces, municipalities, neighbourhoods or villages—such as carrying out maintenance and repairs on schools, hospitals and various other public buildings; and cleaning and sanitation. During the first two years after independence, there were regular government appeals for voluntary civic work on specific days of the month to clean the cities. These activities were quite successful.[36] Nevertheless, as early as 1978, all these activities became neglected not only in the provinces but even in the capital city. By then, Luanda was reported to have fallen 'into a tatty and dirty state of disrepair', with rubbish and rubble in the ill–repaired streets, with chronic and progressively acute lack of water, electricity, basic sanitation, drains and refuse collection.[37]

In sum and taken as a whole, the analysis of the social sector during Neto's administration reveals an initial concern and some effective policy commitments, but even before his death (September 1979), the first signs of political failure in these sectors had started to appear. The key question is why?

The standard answer is that this was due to the war effort, which required large imports of goods and equipment (and that was in part the official argument used[38]). However, if such increased expenditure must be acknowledged, it cannot be taken as the main reason for that sudden collapse, and this for three reasons. First, that period also co-

36 Nuno Vidal, *Post-modern Patrimonialism in Africa.* p. 231-232.

37 Reported by David Lamb to the *Los Angeles Times* 3 December 1978, also in the same vein is a report in the *The Sunday Telegraph.* 25 June 1978.

38 On the use of the war argument to justify the non-achievement of several socio-economic goals during the three year period of 1977-1980 see See *Relatório do Comité Central ao I° Congresso Extraordinário.* 1980. p. 83.

incided with an increase in Angolan oil production and the dramatic rise in the price of oil (from $12 per barrel in 1974 to $28 in 1979),[39] representing an average income of $1 billion/year between 1975 and 1980.[40] Second, arms expenditure remained relatively constant in the late 1970s (around $500 million per year) and only increased significantly in the early eighties.[41] Finally, those services did not depend exclusively on the state but relied also significantly on voluntary work and the community commitments of the general population. Thus, a different explanation must be found.[42]

From the government's perspective, the decline in social policies seems to be related to the appearance of a phenomenon whereby the ruling elites became progressively more 'comfortable' with neglecting the general population. In the first instance, they began to feel quite secure in economic terms, with a huge oil rent that did not depend on the productive efforts of the general population. Secondly, they also felt politically secure because, on the one hand, the population had no votes to express their political disaffection with a tightly controlled party, which was able to rely on a feared political police and judicial system. On the other, insofar as UNITA was militarily active, the government could always count on support generated by the fear of that enemy, which represented a threat against the great Creole/M'Bundu alliance at the heart of the MPLA.[43]

39 In *Shell Bulletin SBS*. 1986.

40 Tony Hodges, *Angola from Afro-Stalinism to Petro-Diamond Capitalism*. London: James Currey, 2001. p. 2.

41 In Thomas Collelo, ed., *Angola, A Country Study*, Washington DC: Federal Research Division, 1991, p. 234.

42 Even approaching the war impact in more general terms, at the level of the whole economy and from a strictly economic point of view, the war *per se* cannot explain the decline in production as explained by a Portuguese economist: see Manuel Ennes Ferreira, *A Indústria em tempo de Guerra (Angola, 1975–91)*, Lisbon: Edições Cosmos/IDN, 1999.

43 Nuno Vidal, *Post-modern Patrimonialism in Africa* op. cit., pp. 224-6; on this subject see also Christine Messiant, 'Angola, les voies de l'ethnisation et de la décomposition—I—de la guerre à la paix (1975–1991): le conflit armé, les interventions internationales et le peuple angolais', in *Lusotopie*, 1, 1994 pp.

From the perspective of those supposed to participate in voluntary work, the reasons for the lack of community commitment seemed also to be twofold. First, it was related to the post-27 May 1977 repression that was mainly directed against the revolutionary and ideologically fervent generation of the youth committees (usually involved with and committed to social policies). This also undermined the independent activity of workers and neighbourhood committees, trade unions and mass organisations (initially linked to the youth committees in terms of social initiatives).[44] Secondly, the decline in social service appeared to be related to the general disillusionment that came from the realisation that Angola's wealth, previously exploited by the Portuguese,[45] was not to be shared by all. Moreover, growing economic austerity forced most to resort to informal activities in order to compensate for the loss of the purchasing power of their salaries.

As Zenha Rela states:

> [The 27th May] marks the end of any 'état de grâce' that the politicians might have used to mobilise the people. It was the crude awakening from the state of euphoria in which people lived until then, the consciousness

---

155–210, especially 169; also Christine Messiant, 'MPLA et UNITA, processus de paix et logique de guerre', *Politique Africaine*, 57 (1995) p.46 ; Christine Messiant, 'Angola: entre guerre et paix', in Roland Marchal and Christine Messiant, *Les chemins de la guerre et la paix: fins de conflit en Afrique orientale et australe*, Paris: Karthala, 1997, p. 169; also Linda Heywood, *Contested Power in Angola, 1840's to the Present,* New York: University of Rochester Press, 2000, p. 152.

44 It is not possible to explain here the sociological and political phenomenon of the youth committees and the impact of the 27 May attempted coup, for a deeper analysis see Jean-Michel Mabeko-Tali, *Dissidências e poder de Estado: o MPLA perante si próprio (1962-1974),* 2 Volumes, Luanda: Editorial N'Zila, 2001; also Nuno Vidal, *Post-modern Patrimonialism in Africa*, Chap. 5.

45 On this issue see for instance, Iko Carreira, *O Pensamento estratégico de Agostinho Neto*. Lisboa: Dom Quixote, 1996, p. 148. Also supporting the same argument of a different conception of independence among the lower ranks of society, essentially based upon expectations of material benefits is Daniel Chipenda in a public interview to the National Radio of Angola, programme *Foi há vinte anos*, 17 June 1995.

of daily difficulties and a *transformation of attitude: the solution of problems which was until then considered a collective action [...] became each individual's problem*, because people had to solve their own problems; if underhand 'schemes' were the only way to solve these problems, then everyone tried to be involved in one[46] [my italics].

Therefore, there were clear signs of a weak commitment to public welfare. The palpable result was a progressive decline in social services during the period 1977-79. Consequently, not only did the existing living conditions deteriorate for most of the people (in terms of education, health services, housing, social support and community services) but their future prospects were also jeopardised (diminishing, for instance, their children's chances of socio-professional and economic advancement or even their life expectancy). In the medium and even longer term, such decline meant increasing economic and social fragility for the bottom layers of society (the majority of the population) most in need of social support.

The dos Santos administration and the collapse of the social sector

During the socialist phase of the dos Santos Presidency (1979-1987),[47] the social sector was increasingly neglected, which reinforced the tendency that had begun to be noticeable by the end of Neto's administration. As was clearly recognised by the Central Committee (CC) report to the 1985 Congress, social provisions had worsened between 1980 and 1985. Education had clearly declined from the early independence successes:

46 José Manuel Zenha Rela, *Angola entre o presente e o futuro,* Lisboa: Escher, Agropromotora, 1992, p. 53.

47 Although officially sanctioned only in 1990 (MPLA's IIIrd congress), the change to a market economy and to a multiparty system was already discernible by 1987 (*see below*)—as has been recognised by other authors as well; see Christine Messiant, 'À propos des "transitions démocratiques", notes comparatives et préalables à l'analyse du cas Angolais', *Africana Studia*, 2 (2000), p. 61–95; also in the same sense is Tony Hodges, *Angola from Afro-Stalinism to Petro-Diamond Capitalism*, London: James Currey, 2001.

In spite of the efforts made, there was a drop in the education system. The literacy programmes that were so successful during the first years of independence also show signs of regression.[48]

Health care services were also failing rapidly:

The sharp deterioration during the first phase of the five-year period was expressed through the negative evolution of available indicators, including access to health services and increased morbidity from the main contagious diseases.[49]

The state housing sector was stagnant and unable to face demand:

It is a fact that without constructing new houses and finishing the building work that has already been started, it will not be possible to solve the problems of housing. On the other hand, State housing has not been regularly maintained and has even deteriorated somewhat, which again adds to the acuity of the problem.[50]

Despite substantial international aid, the State sector was unable to fund, or even implement, government social policies:

In terms of support to the displaced population and the integration of returnees there have been difficulties in bringing the guidelines to fruition [...]. In spite of the high levels of international aid, the resources given were insufficient.[51]

As for community services the report simply admitted that:

48 In *Relatório do Comité Central ao II° Congresso* ...op. cit...1985, p. 121. According to Mohanty, 'From 1980-85, in primary education there was a decrease in the number of pupils (10 per cent annually) and teachers (14 per cent annually) on average'; in Susama Mohanty, *Political Development and Ethnic Identity in Africa, a study of Angola since 1960* (London: Sangam Books, 1992), p. 209. Education accounted for 2 per cent of the country's total foreign exchange expenditure during 1980-85; ibid. p. 209.

49 *Relatório do Comité Central ao II° Congresso*, 1985, p.123. 'Health, like education, accounted for 2 per cent of the country's total foreign exchange expenditure during 1980-85'; in Mohanty, *Political Development* p. 209.

50 In *Relatório do Comité Central ao II° Congresso* ...op. cit...1985, p. 128.

51 Ibid. p. 125.

During the past five years, the services were not given the necessary means to function.[52]

This general deterioration of the social sector (at a time of greater want due to a worsening of socio-economic conditions and the intensification of the war) had the most immediate and dramatic effect upon the lower social strata, not only in rural areas (where an estimated 500,000 to 700,000 Internal Displaced Persons, or IDPs, were in critical need of social assistance[53]) but also in the urban areas, where there was a desperate need for clean drinking water[54] and street cleaning, and where public sanitation systems had collapsed.[55] Diseases such as yellow fever and cholera made a frightening reappearance. In 1985, cholera was responsible for the death of 4,000 people in the city of Luanda alone[56] and one out of every three children died.[57]

52 Ibid. p. 128.

53 According to the UN in 1985, 'More than 500,000 people are estimated to be in critical need of assistance, mainly in the Northern, Central and Southern provinces. [...] Many displaced people are in dire need of clothing, blankets and shelter; *Africa Emergency—UN Office for Emergency Operations in Africa* (June 1985). Under the clarifying title 'Les stigmates d'un effondrement', Jean-Claude Pomonti reported that 'Le comité international de la Croix Rouge, qui dispose d'antennes locales, estime la situation 'très grave'. Sur les hauts plateaux [...] se trouveraient la majorité des 467.000 'personnes deplacées' selon les calculs officiels angolais. En fait, d'autres sources font état, pour l'ensemble du territoire, de 700.000 refugiés de l'intérieur, soit un habitant sur dix'; In *Le Monde,* 28 January 1981.

54 Article by Jean-Claude Pomonti under the title 'Les stigmates d'un effondrement', *Le Monde* 28 January 1981; the same problem of the lack of water is reported by Quentin Peel in the *Financial Times,* 14 September, 1981.

55 Article by Jean-Claude Pomonti, in *Le Monde*, 28 January 1981; also stressing the grubby and run-down condition of Luanda is the report of Michael Holman in *Financial Times* 21 June 1982. Referring to 1982, a description of these problems can also be found in Pepetela, *Geração da Utopia* (Lisboa: Dom Quixote, 1992), pp. 212-213, 234, 236-237.

56 According to Western aid workers 'it was a miracle that not more people died'; article by Paul Betts in the *Financial Times,* 21 September 1987.

57 In *Africa Emergency—UN Office for Emergency Operations in Africa* (June 1985).

The main official argument used to justify such a collapse was the difficult financial situation resulting from the increased war effort:

> The activities in the social sector over the past five years have reflected the general difficulties caused by the military situation and by financial and economic matters, which were affected by the limitations on budget, foreign currency and investment. [58]

Indeed, arms expenditure doubled in 1980 (increasing to more than $1 billion[59]) and in 1983 it was estimated that Angola spent 50% of its foreign exchange earnings on defence.[60] However, such an explanation cannot be taken at face value because the report itself denied such argumentation when, despite the chaotic situation in that area, it clearly set as the main objective for future social policy a reduction in spending, with the following argument:

> Some measures have been taken and others are under way aimed at diminishing the dependence of these sectors on the State's general budget, so that those who benefit from them can realise the true value of some of the services that the State provides for them. [61]

In other words, the government's neglect of the social sector (mostly affecting the poor) was to become the norm, independently of any possible later increases in State revenues—thus clearly breaking any future linkage between State revenues and social policy. So, the obvious question is why?

From the rulers' perspective the answer here provided is related to the trend already noticeable during Neto's presidency: the social strata most affected by social neglect had decreasing economic and political relevance. Economically, the ruling elites were more autonomous than ever in relation to the productive effort of the masses. Politically, there were virtually no formal mechanisms through which the population might express their political disaffection with the

58 In *Relatório do Comité Central ao IIº Congresso* 1985, p. 120.

59 Until then they had remained stable (around $500 million per year in late 1970s); Thomas Collelo, ed., *Angola,* p. 234.

60 In *ACR,* vol. 15 (1984), p. B594.

61 In *Relatório do Comité Central ao IIº Congresso*, 1985, p. 120.

government given single party dominance in an authoritarian and repressive regime. Moreover, the regime could still count on some political support from large parts of the population because of the fear of UNITA.

On the other hand, because the collapse of the social sector had already become obvious by the end of Neto's presidency, there were a number of international donors willing to fund social initiatives in order to save people from starvation. Therefore, the government intensified its requests for international aid during the first five years of the 1980s, having received a very positive answer from several countries and organisations—namely the UNDP, UNHCR, UNICEF, FAO, WFP, UNESCO, ILO, and WHO as well as from co-operation and development agencies in Northern and Western countries,[62] the EEC, and the International Red Cross (which had been helping to feed thousands of people in the most affected provinces since 1981).[63]

Accordingly, the government's future strategy for social policy began to rest on foreign aid, as clearly and officially outlined in that same December 1985 Central Committee report:

> Resorting to international co-operation to complement the resources available internally and to accelerate the pace of national reconstruction and of social and economic development is an objective necessity.[64]

As a consequence of the new policy and despite the major recovery in oil revenues (which nearly doubled in 1987),[65] the emergency aid

62 Ibid. p. 140. In June 1982, the UN Food and Agriculture Organisation (FAO) announced that it was giving $21m to Angola; *Rádio Nacional de Angola* (June 6, 1982), cited in *SWB*—Summary of World Broadcasts, 8 June 1982; Three years later, on 15 January 1985, the same organisation announced that Angola expected to commercially import about two-thirds of its 1984-1985 food deficit and had succeeded in securing food aid pledges for most (71.000t) of the 83.000t balance; cited in *ACR*, vol. 17 (1986), p. B621.

63 In M.R. Bhagavan, *Angola's*. p. 20.

64 *Relatório do Comité Central ao II° Congresso,* 1985, p. 146.

65 Angola's annual oil revenues almost doubled, from previous $1.1 billion in 1986 to $2 billion in 1987; in Tony Hodges, *Angola from Afro-Stalinism*. p. 2.

requested by the government increased from $96.1m in 1985[66] to $116m in 1987.[67] It was becoming increasingly clear that social sector expenditure was not directly linked to the availability of internal resources.

The social sector during the transition to multi party politics

With the end of socialism in the late eighties, with the transition to a multiparty system (1990), the peace agreement (Bicesse, 1991) and the preparation for the first general elections, a new political situation emerged.

A constitutional amendment in 1991 (law 12/91) approved the basic principles of a multiparty democracy, defining Angola as a democratic State based on the rule of law. Other complementary legislation was approved, including laws on the right to assembly and demonstration (law 16/91), freedom of association (law 14/91), freedom of the press (law 25/91), the right to strike (law 23/91) and independent radio broadcasting (law 16/92). Preparing itself for the first elections and facing strong international and domestic pressure, the MPLA had to allow some real openness, to become more tolerant and flexible.

Up to 1991, the absence of independent CSOs meant that the Church was the isolated voice defending human rights. But the new legal and political context opened a space for the emergence of a myriad organisations within civil society, along with opposition political parties, private media, independent trade unions and professional unions and NGOs—several of which were concerned with social and humanitarian problems such as the deterioration of social services, increasing poverty and the deplorable living conditions of the majority of the population.

International organisations arrived *en masse* (from IGOs to NGOs, churches, charitable institutions, solidarity assistance, etc.). It was

66 In *Africa Emergency—UN Office for Emergency Operations in Africa* (June 1985).

67 Reported by Paul Betts to the *Financial Times*, 14 and 21 September 1987.

time to think about reconstruction and development. Money flew in along with development activists, ideas, projects and strategies, which had in common a shared belief that the centralised, authoritarian, top-down socialist model along with so-called democratic centralism was outdated and had clearly failed. It was felt that it should be replaced by a more encompassing and inclusive development approach, centred on the people's needs and the recognition of democratic values and principles such as citizenship and the universality of human rights.

Cooperation between national and international activists supporting Angolan civil society organisations—CSOs[68]

An important degree of cooperation emerged between the newcomers (IGOs, International NGOs, the donor community) and all those internally committed to the emergence of CSOs. This 'alliance' was beneficial to both. The newcomers needed local expertise and competence to help them with their projects' design, implementation and development. The local organisations needed foreign partners, whose aid (financial, institutional and for capacity building) was vital in their struggle for survival in a society controlled in all sectors by an authoritarian party/State.[69]

The labour market thus created offered an alternative opportunity to underpaid middle and high level cadres within the state administration (technical cadres, academics, intellectuals, public servants, etc.), who had been professionally frustrated, politically silenced and

68 Unable to enter into the specific historical development of Angolan CSOs and having dealt with the media in my chapter on politics in this volume, I will focus on national NGOs and related forms of association such as Church organisations and solidarity assistance that clearly dominate the civil society arena insofar as social sector is concerned. For a detailed study on the Angolan CSOs *parcours* see 'Country profile Angola' in *An Assessment of Human Rights Defender Initiatives in Southern Africa*, a report of the Netherlands Institute of Southern Africa—NiZA by Ahmed Motala, Nuno Vidal, Piers Pigou and Venitia Govender, Amsterdam: NiZA, June 2005, p. 47-62.

69 See my chapter on politics in this volume.

socially repressed by an authoritarian regime, which kept them economically dependent and politically subdued. Under the cover of the new multiparty dispensation, they were able to find jobs in national and international NGOs. Picking up on issues raised by donors, some of those who had been silenced after the Nito Alves coup started to voice genuine criticism against regime abuses, the miserable living conditions of the majority of the population, the neglect of the social sector. They began advocating the respect of human rights.

Although the government initially tried to influence some of the national NGOs (infiltrating and controlling a number of them, such as the Angolan Action for Development, AAD), it soon became clear that it was not possible to control each and every new organization. The number of NGOs increased steadily, eventually requiring a Forum for Coordination—FONGA (*Forum das ONGs Angolanas*—Forum of Angolan NGOs). The same happened with international NGOs, which came under the umbrella of CONGA (*Comité das Organizações Não Governamentais em Angola*—Committee of NGOs in Angola). Progressively, an Angolan civil society began to emerge. At first, the government did not seem to pay much attention to the dynamics arising from the relationship between internal and external social activism. This was due to three main reasons.

First, the new development perspective (more encompassing and inclusive) was related to development programmes that were supposed to be relegated to a secondary level in face of the priority given to emergency humanitarian intervention as soon as the war resumed in October 1992 (after UNITA rejected the outcome of the polls). Second, the Angolan government was mainly concerned with the supervision not only of the amount of aid coming in but also of its distribution inside the country—that is, the definition of priority projects and geographical areas of intervention (favouring the areas controlled by the government to the detriment of those in the hands of UNITA). Third, insofar as the war resumed right after the elections and there was consequently a need for a reinvestment in armament, the government became even more dependent on international aid to guarantee food deliveries and shore up social provisions.

By the early nineties, focus was directed to the setting up of mechanisms for the coordination and management of the international organisations' activities—both in the provinces (through provincial governments) and in Luanda (through the Ministry of Social Assistance and Reintegration (MINARS) as well as the Technical Unit for Coordination of Humanitarian Aid (UTCAH)—initially under the supervision of the Council of Ministers and after that of MINARS.[70] Insofar as the donor community preferred to channel aid through the UN and international or national NGOs rather than providing bilateral aid directly to the government, those controlling mechanisms were extremely important. The Angolan administration sought to keep some control on, and derive political advantage from, the significant resources coming into the country. The myriad development projects concerned with social sector issues (housing, health, education, rural development, capacity building and so on) were often overtly used by the government for its own benefit.[71]

70 Now also articulated with the Ministry of Planning; not to be confused with UN UCAH (Humanitarian Assistance Co-ordination Unit, of the United Nations), later replaced by the UN OCHA (UN Organization for the Coordination of Humanitarian Affairs) and recently substituted by the UN Transitional Coordination Unit.

71 While studying several of those projects in the province of Malange in 1995, I had the opportunity to experience such procedures. There used to be a weekly meeting between the provincial government and all NGOs and IGOs working in the province and the main issues under discussion (besides security issues) were two: first, the government wanted to know exactly who was getting what (amounts of aid coming into the province every week); second, which organisations would assume specific social services and works that the government was interested in providing. The vice-governor would read a list of works (for example, schools in need of rehabilitation, health centres to be supplied with material) and the organisations were supposed to pick up the ones that best suited them (some kind of a work distribution); see See Nuno Vidal, Strategies of participatory development: the Project Kuíje 91 in Malange/ Angola, Lisbon: ISCTE, Instituto Superior de Ciências do Trabalho e da Empresa, 1997, Master's dissertation.

Throughout the nineties, the State's failure to deliver social services to the poorest sections of the population prompted national and international NGOs together with Church organisations to provide healthcare, education, food, sanitation, and support to IDPs in provinces all over the country. Emergency humanitarian aid was rarely considered in isolation and was in many cases linked to small CSO development projects (WFP 'food for work' and micro agricultural projects in the outskirts of cities, where the population flocked to escape the war). These organisations were slowly trying to disseminate a more inclusive and 'democratic' way of functioning, supporting a number of other local projects, helping with capacity-building and stressing the need to respect and enforce human rights.[72] The engagement of donors and other developmental partners with CSOs also helped to create a wide range of small community-based organisations (CBOs), which also provided basic social services.[73]

This led to a situation in which the State was responsible for very little expenditure in these areas and where the role of international cooperation became critical. And this despite the astonishing growth in annual oil revenues throughout the period—$2 billions in 1987, $3.5 billions in 1990, $5.1 billions in 1996 and $7 billions in 2000.[74]

Civil society in Angola emerged out of this transition having benefited greatly from the involvement and support of foreign organisations and from the dynamics of transnational networks. However, if this involvement was essential to the creation of CSOs, it also came to represent one of its major weaknesses—that is, serious dependency on foreign expertise, technical support and funding.[75]

---

72 See Nuno Vidal, *Strategies of Participatory Development.*

73 See *Engaging Civil Society Organisations in Conflict-Affected and Fragile States,* World Bank Report n.32538-GLB Washington: The International Bank for Reconstruction and Development/The World Bank, 28 June 2005.

74 In Tony Hodges, *Angola from Afro-Stalinism*, p. 2.

75 There are obviously a few exceptions to this general rule, see "Country profile Angola" in *An Assessment,* p. 47-62.

Insofar as there was no private sector independent from the party and State,[76] there was no alternative for CSOs but to depend on external funding. Even so, it was still difficult to survive without any form of 'cooperation' with the State. The biggest Angolan NGO—ADRA (*Acção para o Desenvolvimento Rural e Ambiente*—Action for Rural Development and Environment)—had to find ways and means of pursuing 'constructive engagement' with State organisations whilst at the same time diversifying its external funding as much as possible.[77]

The fragmentation of CSOs, which failed to engage in sound endogenous and sustainable capacity building, arose from two structural factors. First, there was limited, disjointed, short-term and project-by-project driven involvement of donors and international organisations. Second, there was competition for funds between CSOs and preferential allocation from each donor or group of donors to their 'favourite' national partners (according to their own criteria). The same can be said about the cyclically changing development priorities of donors, usually moving from one fashionable area to the other without taking into consideration the specificity of each country and the dynamics already in place. The capacity-building deficit was much more serious for those smaller national organisations that never managed to go beyond the status of being sub-contracted by international NGOs to implement or co-implement small parts of bigger projects.[78]

76 The privatisation process in the early nineties mainly benefited the nomenklatura, see Manuel Ennes Ferreira, 'La reconversion économique de la nomenklature pétrolière', in *Politique Africaine*, 57 (1995), pp. 11–26; also Renato Aguilar, 'Angola's private sector : rents distribution and oligarchy', in Karl Wohlmuth, Achim Gutowski, Tobias Knedlick, Mareike Meyn & Sunita Pitamber, *African Development Perspectives*, Germany: Lit Verlag, 2003; Renato Aguilar, *Angola: getting off the hook*, a report for Sida, Gothenburg: Gothenburg University, 2005, especially p. 13-18; see also my chapter on politics in this volume.

77 See 'Country profile Angola' in *An Assessment*, p. 52.

78 See Nuno Vidal, *Angola: Preconditions for Elections*, a report for the Netherlands Institute for Southern Africa—NiZA (Amsterdam: NiZA, 2006);

Such shortcomings and fragilities became all the more visible when external funding began to decrease at the end of the 1990s and the beginning of the 2000s, at a time when the domestic context was becoming increasingly adverse.

Government-friendly CSOs and the donors' change of attitude

Being the main providers of social services, those national and international organisations gained increasing legitimacy by defending human rights. They publicised and documented serious abuses and violations. They criticised and pressured government institutions, demanding a change of attitude.[79] The Angolan private media and the international press began echoing these criticisms and demands. Opposition political parties sometimes joined in, though they rarely had as much leeway as the CSOs in this respect.

At times, such a posture made CSOs politically inconvenient to the regime, which took every opportunity to restrict the social or civic space they enjoyed. Although that space did contract on several occasions, especially when the war escalated, there was still some room for manoeuvring, especially because the party and the presidency soon came to understand that CSOs were of central concern for the donor community as well as pivotal protagonists within the contemporary developmental discourse.

Nevertheless, the party and the presidency also understood that something had to be done, considering the increasing criticism voiced by these organisations against the lack of government involvement in a severely disrupted social sector. Another major problem for the regime was the fact that the institution and person of the President was now (internally and externally) associated with poor governmental performance, which dos Santos had always tried to avoid.[80]

also 'Country profile Angola' in *An Assessment*, p. 47-62.

79 See "Country profile Angola" in *An Assessment* p. 47-62.

80 Even though the President has been the effective head of government since he came to power in 1979, he has always made an effort to distinguish the Presidency from the government, rejecting governmental responsibilities,

In order to tackle these issues, the regime created 'government friendly' CSOs, comprising organisations such as the President's Foundation (Eduardo dos Santos Foundation—FESA[81]—established in 1996) and the Lwini Social Solidarity Fund (set up by the first lady, Ana Paula dos Santos). Both organisations sought to improve the political image of the President, providing services that were supposed to be delivered by the State by using social bonus funds from oil and other international companies. These 'parallel' CSOs had easier access to national and provincial governments, official State permits and to the public and private sectors of the economy—both clearly dominated by the party in power. The strategy of a parallel civil society has continued to this day, with an increasing number of organisations set up or, in some cases co-opted, by top officials.[82]

Because independent CSOs were seen as a threat to the regime, they became ever more dependent on outside donors. Nevertheless, more and more external actors began to question this dependence. Some of the organisations that had worked for years in the country became progres-

especially after the nomination of the so-called Government of Unity and National Reconciliation (GURN) in 1994 (comprising most of the parliamentary political parties, but completely dominated by the MPLA); also see my chapter on politics in this volume.

81 On FESA and the regime investment on Civil Society see Christine Messiant, 'La Fondation Eduardo dos Santos (FESA): autour de l'investissement de la société civile par le pouvoir angolais', in *Politique Africaine*, 73 (1999), p. 82–101.

82 AJAPRZ (*Associação de Jovens Angolanos Provenientes da Zâmbia*), *Criança Futuro* (under the supervision of the former State security chief, Miala), *Acção Solidária* e *Amigos do Rangel*, among a few others, are clear examples of such organisations. They basically serve the government and presidential need to have a cooperative 'civil society' that can be politically manipulated within the general patrimonial working logic: providing an extra source of well remunerated jobs that can be distributed among new or old clients and dependants; supplying selected social services as required by the president or the party according to specific political objectives and needs; participating in politically sensitive processes (*e.g.* law approval) without contesting it and therefore satisfying the international demand for taking into account 'civil society' opinion.; see 'Country profile Angola' in *An Assessment*, p. 47-62; also Christine Messiant's chapter in this volume.

sively disenchanted with their true role in Angola, which was taking over the social responsibilities of the state. In a shocking public announcement, Jean Marc Perrain, chief executive of Médecins Sans Frontières Angola, expressed what had become clear to everybody:

It is not understandable how a country as rich as Angola, producing and selling oil and diamonds, with an estimated annual oil revenue of $7 billion per year, can invest so little in areas such as health. In our view, it is not normal that a humanitarian association such as MSF should provide absolutely everything that is required for the running of a hospital, be it in Kahala or in Kuíto. This does seem to be quite illogical. It would appear logical to us that complementary assistance would be given to the Ministry of Health because of the difficult situation in the country at present.[83]

This statement came out at a time when the Angolan government was already facing the 1999 'Mitterand, Falcone and Gaidamak scandal', the Global Witness Report and other reports exposing the mismanagement of oil revenues and endemic corruption within the Angolan political system, along with a long list of illegal activities uncovered by the media.[84]

83 Statement made by Jean Marc Perrin in Angola, on 9 November 2000, broadcast on Channel 2 of the *Rádio Televisão Portuguesa* news programme 'Jornal de África' 11 November 2000; see also *Diário de Notícias*, 12 November 2000; *Público* 27 April 2000. Such a statement was made at the presentation of the Médecins Sans Frontières Report *Angola: as aparências de 'normalização' escondem graves cenas de guerra*. Luanda: MSF, 9 November 2000.

84 For an in-depth approach on the scandals of gun-running, diamond trafficking and money-laundering involving Jean-Christophe Mitterrand (son of François Mitterrand), Jacques Attali (former president of the EBRD, European Bank for Reconstruction and Development), Pierre Falcone (arms dealer and main supplier of arms to Luanda) and Arkadi Gaidamak (arms and diamonds merchant, holder of the former Angolan debt to the USSR), with multiple ramifications (including Sonangol), see *O Independente* 23 July 1999; also *Público,* 5 and 6 December 1999, 14 January 2000, 11 April 2000; also *Expresso,* 16 December 2000, 8 September 2001; also the reports by Global Witness that names several members of the presidential clique involved in networks of arms dealing, missing accounts from oil income to the State and so on: 'A Crude Awakening: the role of the oil and banking industries in Angola's civil war and the plunder of the state assets', a report by *Global Witness,* December 1999; also 'All the Presidents' men', a report by *Global Witness*, March 2002: also 'A Rough Trade: the role of Companies and Governments in the Angolan Conflict', a report by *Global Witness*, December 1998. Editions at [www.oneworld.org/

This, at the time when the national budget allocated excessively small amounts to the social sector.[85]

With the end of the civil war, which followed the death of Jonas Savimbi (February 2002) and the signature of the Luena peace memorandum (April 2002), many hoped for a rapid change in social policy—expecting major State investment in those areas since an estimated three quarters of the country's 14 million people lived on less than a dollar a day and some 2 million were in danger of starvation[86]. International organisations working in the field such as CARE International or MSF virtually accused the government of criminal neglect towards its own population.[87] The much exhausted war argument could no longer be used to justify the lack of investment in those areas. Moreover, oil production increased and provided the government with an average income of $5 billion a year.[88]

In consequence, humanitarian aid decreased substantially[89] and the much awaited international donor conference kept being adjourned because it was conditioned on an agreement between the government and the IMF, which was supposed to set some principles of

globalwitness/]; also John McMillan, *The Main Institution in The Country is Corruption: Creating Transparency in Angola*, Stanford: Center on Democracy, Development and the Rule of Law, Stanford Institute of International Studies, February, 2005.

85 Angolan National Budgets: in 2001—education, 5.06 per cent; health, 5.03 per cent; social security, 3.95 per cent; housing and community services, 3.77 per cent; in 2002—education, 5.19 per cent; health, 4.57 per cent; social security, 3.36 per cent; housing and community services, 2.14 per cent. Angolan State budgets available at [www.minfin.gv.ao/].

86 *The Guardian,* 7 February 2003.

87 *Voice of América News Online*, 11 June 2002; *The Guardian*, 7 February 2003.

88 From 2000 to 2003 Angola received an average of $5 billion a year; see article 'Angola should be able to finance its own post war rebuilding' by Michael Dynes in *Times online*, 24 February 2003; Angola is currently producing 1.3 million barrels a day and is greatly benefiting from the steady increases in international oil prices over these two last years.

89 See *Human Rights Watch World Report 2006*, New York: HRW & Seven Stories Press, 2006, p. 74-79.

accountability and transparency in public accounts.[90] Humanitarian assistance was halted in several regions (mainly in the centre-north) that were no longer considered in need of such support.

In order to push the Angolan government to become more directly involved with local communities and their needs in the new peace context, the UNOCHA (United Nations Office for the Coordination of Humanitarian Affairs) was replaced by the UN Transitional Coordination Unit (dependent on the UNDP), which was supposed to pass on the responsibility for coordination to government institutions such as the UTCAH and the Ministry of Assistance and Social Reintegration (MINARS).

This new dispensation was supposed to put some pressure on the Angolan government to assume more responsibility for the provision of social services. However, contrary to any reasonable expectation, that did not happen. The decrease in humanitarian aid mainly affected development projects implemented by international and national NGOs or CBOs that indirectly benefited from that aid, leaving the government's attitude unchanged as the national budgets of the following years make plain.[91] Resorting to new and more favourable

90 For a summary of the relationship between the Angolan government and the IMF see 'Some transparency, no accountability, the use of oil revenue in Angola and its impact on human rights', a report by Human Rights Watch, January 2004, vol. 16, no. 1; this report also exposes the oil revenue and expenditure discrepancies in government accounts.

91 Angolan national budgets: in 2003—education, 6.24 per cent; health, 5.82 per cent; social security, 1.47 per cent; housing and community services, 1.57 per cent; in 2004—education, 10.47 per cent; health, 5.69 per cent (of which 2.40 per cent were for management services); social security, 4.30 per cent; housing and community services, 3.07 per cent; in 2005—education, 7.14 per cent; health, 4.97 per cent (1.93 per cent for management); social security, 6.47 per cent; housing and community services, 4.13 per cent. It is also worth noting that a significant part of these amounts was spent on salaries and management activities. The relative increase in education spending in 2003 is deceptive: more than a half of the 6.4 per cent allocated to education was spent on salaries and management (3.27 per cent); in 2004, of the 10.47 per cent, allocated to education, 8.10 per cent was spent on salaries and management and the same happened in 2005, with management alone absorbing 3.43 per cent of a total of 7.14 per cent. Angola is far below the 16.7 per cent SADC countries average of

oil-backed loans (such as the one from China), the party drew up economic development plans with heavy investment in infrastructure and technology transfer[92] without paying proper attention to more immediate social problems such as the extreme poverty affecting most of the population, the disruption of health and education systems and the poor index of human development in Angola, which remains one of the world's poorest countries.[93] Moreover, it now became clear that the mechanisms of embezzlement entrenched during the war could be redirected towards profiteering from the country's reconstruction efforts.[94]

As for the transfer of institutional responsibilities from the UN Transitional Coordination Unit to the government's UTCAH and MINARS, once again the results were different from those expected. According to many interviewees, the government became convinced that with such a transfer of responsibilities it would finally be able to tighten the grip on NGO resources and impose a more effective control on their activities in the field. Accordingly, government

national budget expenditures with education; Angolan State budgets available at [www.minfin.gv.ao/]. According to the World Bank in 2004 by function: health an education expenditures as a percentage of GDP in Angola (less than 2 per cent for health and less than 5 per cent for education) were (with the exception of Equatorial Guinea) amongst the lowest in the African context, "such composition of public spending is far below the country's needs in terms of infrastructure reconstruction and provision of essential services to the population and seems to reflect political choices still concerned with the prevalence of a wartime budget; in World Bank report n. 29036-AO, *Angola public expenditure, management and financial accountability*, 16 February 2005, p. i, also p. 5-6.

92 See my chapter on politics in this same volume.

93 Ranked at position 160 out of 177 of the UN Human Development Index and remaining one of world's poorest countries; see *Human Development Report*, New York: United Nations Development Programme, 2005, p. 125, p. 222.

94 See *Time for Transparency, Coming Clean on Oil, Mining and Gas Revenues*, a report from Global Witness, March 2004, p. 35. It is worth remembering that, according to the IMF between 1997 and 2001, $8.45 billion of public funds remain unaccounted for (representing an average of 23 per cent of GDP), Ibid. It is also noteworthy that Angola was ranked 133 out of the 145 most corrupt countries in the world by Transparency International (145 being the most corrupt), in [www.transparencyinternational.com].

institutions have been less concerned with effective coordination of humanitarian assistance than with the control of NGO funds and equipment. A new NGO registration programme began in 2005 and is being progressively extended to integrate all national and international NGOs. The registration procedure and the requirements of regular report, specifying all activities, projects, funds, equipment, personnel, socio-economic impact, etc. gives the Ministry of Justice virtually total discretion. The approval or rejection of registration applications now depend, as the UTCAH director clearly stated, on his body's favourable opinion and on the level of project partnership established with government organisations.[95]

In the end, the donors' change of attitude had no impact whatsoever on government social policy. On the contrary, it added more constraints to the work of CSOs and affected negatively the conditions of the poor. Without external funding, CSOs can hardly survive and most of them have to manage a rather complex balance between the donors' agendas, some form of cooperation with State organisations and the needs of the communities they are supposed to serve.

Because Angola is a major oil producer, it can exert leverage upon the international community.[96] An illustration of this fact is that previous accusations made by international organisations of the government's neglect of its own people and the lack of governmental

95 *Working meeting of UTCAH with national and international NGOs* (Luanda: Catholic University of Angola auditorium, 29 November 2005); agenda: (…) 3—Presentation of national and international NGOs activities in the first semester of 2005; 4—Directory of NGOs, information bulletin to be created, research on case studies, draft of the specific reports that must be presented by NGOs throughout the year; 5. Legalization of NGOs (…), Access to public funds.

96 See *More Than Humanitarianism: A Strategic Approach Towards Africa*, a report of an independent task force sponsored by the US Council on Foreign Relations, New York: Council on Foreign Relations, 2005, especially pp. 32-3, 49-50; also Renato Aguilar, *Angola: Getting off* especially p. 13-18; Arlindo Miranda, *Angola 2003/2004, Waiting for Elections*, a report for the Christian Michelsen Institute, 2004; also Patrick Chabal, 'Preface' in Nuno Vidal, & Justino Pinto de Andrade, *O processo de transição para o multipartidarismo em Angola* (Luanda and Lisbon: Firmamento, 2006), pp. xxvii-xxxviii.

transparency or political accountability stopped when the international strategic importance of Angola changed—that is, when oil prices reached record heights, competition to secure future oil supplies increased worldwide and the government was able to strike new economic partnerships with Asian governments showing no concern whatsoever for human rights.[97] The same can be said of the so-called 'Angolagate' Falcone episode of September/October 2004, in which the French government drew back on its intentions as soon as the Angolan government retaliated by delaying the recognition of the French ambassador and refusing to renew Total's oil contract on block 3/80.[98] Equally, the World Bank, the IMF and the West gradually dropped their campaign for transparency, accountability and human rights in the face of the new international and economic importance of Angola.[99]

Angolan CSOs also face increasing difficulties when they confront the government about access to external funding. Organizations such as SOS Habitat (standing for the rights of communities forcedly evicted by the State as a result of new urban development plans in Luanda)[100] have extreme trouble in accessing external funding. According

97 See my chapter on politics in this same volume; also *More than humanitarianism*, especially pp. 32-33, 49-50; also Renato Aguilar, *Angola: Getting off*, especially p. 2, 13-18; also John Reed, 'Angola o capitalismo dos petrodiamantes' in *Courrier Internacional*, 25 November 2005, n. 34, p. 22-23; also Global Witness Press Release: *Western Banks to Give Huge New Loan to Angola in Further Blow to Transparency*, 23 September 2005.

98 On the Falcone-Angola-gate affair see my chapter on politics in this volume; also, *Financial Times London*, 6 August 2004; *World Markets Analysis* (September 08, 2004); *International Oil Daily*, 26 October 2004; *Voice Of America-VOA*, 1 November 2004; *ANGOP*, 2 November 2004.

99 See *More Than Humanitarianism*, especially p. 32-33, 49-50; also *Human Rights Watch World Report 2006*, p. 74-79; Renato Aguilar, *Angola: Getting Off*, especially p. 2, 13-18; also John Reed, 'Angola o capitalismo dos petrodiamantes' in *Courrier Internacional* 25 November 2005, n. 34, p. 22-3.

100 See Amnesty International, *Mass Forced Evictions in Luanda—A Call for a Human Rights-Based Housing Policy* (2003); also Amnesty International, *Angola: Forced Evictions/Use of Excessive Force*, AI reference: AFR 12/001/2006, 25 January 2006, AFR 12/005/2005, 2 December 2005; URL: http://web.amnesty.org

to its main representative, Luís Araújo, some donors refuse to fund the organisation directly and even when they use an intermediary—such as international NGOs—they usually request secrecy.

Despite all the above mentioned constraints, it must nevertheless be acknowledged that some Angolan CSOs have been at the forefront of the most significant initiatives in the defence of human rights (civil, political and economic). They have been much more active in that area than the political parties in parliament (recent examples include the land law, the HIV law, the struggle for the rights of forcibly evicted communities, improvements in the judicial system, better conditions for detainees and the media law).[101]

Conclusion

Angolan CSOs were conditioned from the start by two main factors: an adverse domestic context and external dependency. From colonial days to the present, Angolans have almost permanently been under authoritarian rule. A lack of democratic traditions hampered the emergence of CSOs, which only came into being with the implementation of a multiparty system in 1991 and mainly during the short periods of peace in 1991-92 (Bicesse agreement), 1994-98 (Lusaka protocol) and from 2002 onwards (Luena peace memorandum). The transition to a multiparty system, the 1991 legal reforms and the electoral process opened a space for civil society, but the MPLA still dominates the State and controls all social, political and economic levers, thus imposing continuous constraint on CSOs. The regime sees non-cooperative CSOs as a threat and is reluctant to accede to their demands.

---

101 See 'Country profile Angola' in *An Assessment,* p. 47-62; Hina Jilani, *Promotion and Protection of Human Rights Defenders*, 21 February 2005, Report submitted by the Special Representative of the Secretary General on the situation of the Human Rights Defenders Mission to Angola (21 February 2005). Comerford, G. Michael, *O Rosto Pacífico de Angola,* Luanda: published by author, 2005, especially ch. 4.

At the same time, the short-term and project-by-project driven involvement of donors and international organisations, the internal competition for external funds and the preferential relationships with selected national partners have contributed to the fragmenting of Angolan CSOs. Furthermore, their agendas are primarily determined by donors and foreign partners rather than by the needs of the communities in which they work. Born out of an extremely tight relationship with Western international organisations, Angolan CSOs are now facing a major challenge: reduced external support forces them to rely more and more on their own capacities at a time when the domestic context remains unfavourable.

According to a number of civil society activists, the institutionalisation of a multiparty political system could be an opportunity for a major step forward in the assertiveness of Angolan CSOs[102]—but only if they get appropriate international support. The MPLA needs to legitimise its power through internationally recognised free and fair elections and that might be the right opportunity for the international community and Angolan CSOs to put pressure for more openness. If international support was important in 1992, it is now vital—since the MPLA has reinforced its control over the state apparatus (in the face of a weak political opposition) and tightened its grip over civil society in general.[103]

It is worth remembering that CSOs and opposition parties were all excluded from the Luena cease-fire memorandum of April 2002 (solely negotiated and signed between the two contenders)—just as they had been from the Bicesse peace agreement of 1991 and the Lusaka protocol of 1994. Since it has won the war, the government has felt free to impose more constraints on civil society, hampering the involvement of Churches and NGOs in politically sensitive is-

102 On the challenges faced by Angola in its development towards democracy and the role that needs to be played by CSOs and human rights defenders in the next electoral process, see, Hina Jilani, *Promotion and Protection,* op. cit.

103 See Nuno Vidal, *Angola: Preconditions*; Nuno Vidal, 'Multipartidarismo em Angola' in Nuno Vidal and Justino Pinto de Andrade, *O processo de transição,* p. 11-57; also my chapter on politics in this volume.

sues such as the question of Cabinda.[104] It approved a new NGO bill in 2002, prohibiting NGOs from any political and partisan activities (Art. 21 b). And it is up to the government and to the judicial system controlled by the government to assess the political nature of NGOs activities.

The majority of civil society activists think that internal leverage pushing for more openness can only be effective with the strong co-operation of external partners. However, in contrast to the situation in 1992, this external partner is not so much the so-called 'international community' as a whole as those International CSOs committed to the respect of human rights and democratisation. There seems to be general disappointment with IGOs and the donor community, which have failed to increase pressure on the regime with regard to cases such as the so-called 'Angolagate' case, and with the World Bank and IMF reluctance to press for more for transparency and accountability.

Several of my interviewees insisted that the initiative for external leverage now rests with those International CSOs that have efficient and global lobbying power, networking and advocacy capacity. Only they can mobilise international public opinion on the question of the Angolan political transition process. They see the need for linking internal and international activists sharing the same principles on civil, political and human rights.[105]

One of the most recent examples is the first national electoral network led by Angolan CSOs (the Angolan Civil Society National

104 The role of the Catholic Church together with Open Society was extremely important to denounce and stop serious human rights abuses in Cabinda, taking place in 2002 and 2003 in consequence of major counterinsurgency operations of the Angolan Armed forces against the Front for the Liberation of the Enclave of Cabinda (FLEC-FAC); see reports on the human rights situation in Cabinda by M'Palabanda—Associação Cívica, 1st report, *Terror em Cabinda* (2002), also 2nd report, *Cabinda um ano de dor* (2003) and 3rd report, *Cabinda o reino da impunidade* (2004); also Amnesty International, *Arbitrary Detention/Fear for Safety/Fear of Torture/Incommunicado Detention* (AI, 133 December 2002).

105 The feasibility of such is discussed at the end of my chapter on politics in this volume.

Electoral Platform or PLATA), created on 18 November 2005—at a time when the MPLA had already appointed more than a thousand members to integrate the Electoral Executive Commissions (the body responsible for the registration process in each province, municipality and commune). Still in its very initial stages, this initiative is trying to link previous projects and bring together the dispersed experience of existing independent provincial electoral networks. The project's main objective is to coordinate, revive and/or create provincial electoral networks in order to promote the participation of civil society in the electoral process. Yet, the task is obviously difficult, having to catch up on a process already in motion and controlled by the MPLA in the so-called Informal Group on Elections, coordinated by the Ministry of Territorial Administration.

As stressed by one of PLATA's leaders, given the importance of churches in Angola the project could greatly benefit from the support, experience and national structures of COIEPA (*Comité Inter Eclesial para a Paz em Angola*),which is one of the very few surviving Angolan networking CSOs still significantly funded by foreign donors.[106] However, as one more proof of the difficulty Angolan CSOs have in developing long-term sustained and effective network projects, the three different ecclesiastical congregations forming COIEPA have failed to reach agreement on a joint initiative regarding the electoral process, each one of them having its own agenda and (domestic and foreign) partners.

106 COIEPA is an ecumenical organisation created in 2000 and linking at Catholic and Protestant Churches. It is an alliance of CEAST (Catholic Conference of Bishops from São Tomé and Angola), CICA (Council of Christian Churches of Angola) and AEA (Angolan Evangelical Alliance—also an umbrella for Protestant Churches on par with CICA). Together with other CSOs, COIEPA had a significant role during the last stage of the conflict in favour of a peace settlement. On COIEPA's trajectory and the peace movement see Michael G. Comerford, *O Rosto Pacífico*; also Christine Messiant, 'Les églises et la derniére guerre en Angola (1998-2002). Les voies difficiles de l'engagement pour un pays juste', in *Le fait Missionaire—War, Peace and Religion,* n°13, October 2003, p. 75-117.

INDEX

Abalone Investment Ltd.,189-90,
Abílio, Syanga, 191
ADRA, 163, 223
Advisory Forums, 168, 169
Africa, colonial rule in 72-3; elections in 14-15; GDP ratios, 183; gold and silver mines in 25, 26; multi-party politics in 15-17, 93, 99; nationalism in 73-4; oil states 8, 13; one party states in 9, 93; and IMF 10; and slave trade 28-30
Afro-communism, 93
Afro-Portuguese, 19, 21, 23, 24-8, 29, 31-2, 33-7, 38, 41, 46, 58, 65; decline of 58, 73, 87; radicals, 52, 73
agriculture, 59, 109, 130, 138, 179, 180, 184, 194; *see also* coffee
aid, 10, 141, 181, 198, 204, 209-10, 217, 220, 221, 222, 227-8; dependency, 197
AJAPRAZ, 163
aldeamentos, 80, 83
Algeria, 73
Alvalade agreement, 161-2
Alves, Nito, 7, 11; coup 96, 128, 129, 154, 201, 212, 220
Alvor Accord, 86-7
Ambaca, 34, 35
Ambriz, 33
Ambuila, battle of, 27
ANC, 164
Andrade, Mário de, 73
Angola, 18th century 29; 1961 uprisings in 71, 77-8, 82, 86; administration of 34, 45, 128, 136-7, 149, 165; armed forces 12-13, 82, 105-6, 111, 130, 133, 135, 155; Atlantic economy 19; budgets, 109, 152, 155, 166, 180, 227, 228-9; bureaucracy in 3,7,58-9; captaincy 26; constitutional revision, 119, 160-2, 163-4, 167; decentralisation, 164-71; democracy 1, 9, 10, 15-16, 18, 71, 72, 93-4, 98-100, 108, 118, 120-1, 158; during Republic 53-6; economy 61-3, 79, 127, 179-80, 187-8; elections, 99-101, 115, 118-9, 120, 122, 124-5, 138, 158; exploration of 37; geography of 19-21; historiography of 3; independence, 86-7, 94; liberalisation of the economy, 95, 101, 198, 138, 141, 159, 179; local government in 165-7, 170; multiparty system 120, 138-43, 204, 218; nationalist politics in 73-7, 78, 84-5, 93; neo-patrimonialism, 126-7, 203-4; oil revenues 13-14, 127; opposition parties, 143, 150-2, 155, 157, 161, 172;

pacification of 43-4; political system, 94-7, 107-8, 109, 112, 113, 117, 121, 128, 133-5, 136-7; Portuguese emigration to 33,51,52, 65-6; post-independence constitution, 95; privatisation, 108, 149, 179, 193-4; public finances, 188-9' railways in 47-9; and Scramble for Africa 39-40, 43; socialism in 205; trade with Portugal 49; wars in 26; wars of independence 3, 77-81; *see also* civil society, GDP, judicial system, presidency
Angolan Action for Development (AAD), 220
Angola Selling Corporation (Ascorp), 193
Araújo, Luís, 232
Araújo, Raúl, 153
army, 12-13, 82, 105-6, 111, 130, 133, 135
Arnot, Frederick, 31, 32, 36
assimilados, 52-3, 55, 65, 73-4
Atlantic economy, 19, 22, 27, 31, 47-8; *see also* slave trade
Autarchies, 166-7
Azores, 70

Bailundu war, 41-2, 43
Banco Africano de Investimentos, 185
banks, 185, 188
Baptist mission, 51; in Kongo, 42, 70
Bakongo, 43, 74-5, 155; in Luanda, 208
bark cloth, 22
Belgian Congo, 60, 69, 70, 74, 77, 86; *see also* Zaire
Belgium, 56, 72, 77, 78; *see also* Leopold
Bengo river, 20
Benguela, 26, 28, 29, 32, 34, 35, 39, 50, 65; province, 166, 168, 169
Benguela railway, 48-9, 57, 80
Berlin Conference, 38-9, 40, 41, 43, 50; conventional basin of Congo, 38-9, 49
Bicesse agreement, 93, 99, 100, 138, 140, 143, 218, 232, 233
Bié/Bihé, kingdom of, 31, 35; province, 145, 168
Birmingham, David, 62, 83-4
Bismarck, Otto von, 39
Boers, 39, 44, 49, 51
Boma, 39
Botelho Moniz coup, 78
Brazil, 25, 26, 27, 28, 33, 34, 156; independence of, 34; slave trade to 29, 30
Bridgland, Fred, 84
Britain, 50; bilateral treaties, 38-9; secret treaties with Germany, 40, 43, 48; ultimatum to Portugal 40
British, traders 32,
BSA Company, 48
Bush, president George W., 162

Cabinda, 20, 30, 39, 63, 82, 106, 112, 161, 165, 166, 167; oil in, 176
Cabral, Ámilcar, 75
Caetano, Marcello, 85
Caixa de Crédito Agro-Pecuária e Pescas (CAP), 188
Cameron, Vernon Lovett, 37-8
candonga, 96, 98
Cão, Diogo, 22-3
Cape Verde Islands, 75
caravans, 31, 34-5, 41, 42, 49, 52
Carrier service, 35, 44, 49

Carta constitucional, 55
Catholic church, 70-1, 85, 194, 195, 112; radio station, 112, 148, 153; *see also* missions
cattle, 20, 21
Catumbela, 33
Cela, 65
Chabal, Patrick, 202
China, 8, 154, 177, 197, 198; loans to Angola, 146, 197, 229
Chokwe, 31
Chongoroi, 155
Christianity, 27, 36, 42, 66, 68, 69-71; conversion of Kongo to, 23; *see also* missions
churches, 104, 105, 113, 118, 139, 143, 204, 218, 222, 233-4, 235; *see also* missions
civil society, 96, 103, 104, 113, 114, 115, 118, 124-5, 139, 143, 155, 162-3, 157-8, 159, 203-4, 211-12; *see also* CSOs
civil wars, 1, 2, 4, 9, 36, 64, 78-9, 80. 87, 98-9, 138, 190, 203, 204, 210; first civil war, 6-7; post-1992 conflict, 95, 100, 101, 103 124, 140; final phase, 104-5, 106, 142, 143, 186, 227
civilizados, 67-9, 71, 73, 76; *see also assimilados*
clientelism, 24, 25, 34, 95-7, 98, 100, 104, 107, 109, 114, 115, 120, 125, 127, 155-6, 193, 203
coffee, 32, 49, 59, 61-2, 64, 80, 81, 176, 179, 181
COIEPA, 163
Cold War, 4, 6, 9, 79, 98, 178, 186
Colonial Act, 57
colonatos, 65
Conakry, 73
Concordat, 70
CONCP, 7
Congo-Brazzaville, 75, 82, 103
Congo Free State, 38-9, 43; *see also* Belgian Congo
Conselho da República, 118
Constitutional Commission, 118
Contra costa, 29, 40, 48
convicts, 34, 50
copper; Copper Belt, 64; mines, 22; trade, 22, 26
corruption, 96, 97-8, 104, 110, 115, 196
Cortes, 71
cori beads, 22
Cotonang, 60
cotton, 49, 59-60, 77, 176
Coutinho, Admiral Rosa, 87
Creoles; elite, 4, 11, 35, 73, 127, 187, 195, 211, 216; in Luanda 2, 4-5, 6, 11, 64, 76; in West Africa, 23
Cruz, Viriato da, 73, 82
CSOs, 143, 156, 158, 159, 172, 173, 204-5, 218, 219-20, 222-5, 230, 231, 232-3, 234-5; *see also* civil society
Cuba; 74; intervention in Angola 6, 87, 98, 138, 205, 208; doctors from, 206
Currie Institute, 66

Dande river, 20
Davidson, Basil, 84
debt, 184, 185, 189-90, 197
Delagoa Bay, 38
Delgado, Humberto, 72
Dembos, 44
demobilisation, 111, 156
Development Plans, 61, 65;
Diallo, Issa, 103
Diamang, 56, 57

diamonds, in Angola, 56, 63, 76-7, 80, 105, 107, 167, 172, 175, 178, 181, 184, 186, 187, 192-4, 196; company licensing, 191-2; expulsion of *garimpeiros*, 192; finance UNITA, 142; in South Africa, 48, 85
Dias, Jill, 35
Dias, Paulo, 26
Dutch, attack on Luanda, 27; trade, 30, 32

East African slave trade, 30
Eastern Bloc, 60-1, 82
education, 66-9, 78, 104, 118-19, 128, 130, 179, 180, 204, 205-6, 207, 213, 221, 222, 229
elections, 9, 10-11, 122, 125, 139,144, 147, 158, 162-4, 172-3, 186, 218; 1992 in Angola, 1, 7, 100, 111, , 124, 138, 140, 143, 144, 146, 149, 158, 220
employment, 181
ethnicity, 24, 76, 83, 127, 201
European Union/EEC, 85, 160; aid from, 217; and PARs 168-9, 170
exchange rate, 96, 184, 187, 188
exports, 61-2; oil, 176, 177, 181-2

FAA/FAPLA, 105-6, 111, 130, 141, 206; *see also* Angola, armed forces
Falcone case, 154, 160, 189-90, 226, 231, 234
firearms, 30, 41, 54
Figueiredo, Elísio, 190
First World War, 19, 40, 44, 55
fishing, 64
Fontes Pereira, José de, 52
foreign exchange, 61; allocation, 187
France, 30, 38, 53, 72, 73, 154; colonial policy of 72-3; partition of Congo basin, 38-9; Portuguese emigration to, 81; and Mapa Cor de Rosa, 40; and Falcone affair, 231; Frelimo, 7, 16, 75, 78, 82, 83, 84, 85
Frelimo, 7, 16, 75, 78, 82, 83, 84, 85
French, capital in Diamang, 56; traders, 30, 32;
FNLA, 75, 82, 84, 87; after 1992, 160, 161; *see also* Roberto, UPA
Fundo do Apoio Social (FAS), 164, 165, 167-71

Gabon, 13
Galvão, Henrique, 58, 60, 64, 77
Gato, general, 161, 162
Gaydamak, Arkadi, 189-90, 226
Gbadolite talks, 98
GDP, 178-9, 180, 181, 183
German South West Africa, 40, 44, 48; *see also* Namibia
Germany, 38-9, 44-5, 48, 50; 1898 treaty with Britain 40, 43, 48; and Mapa Cor de Rosa, 40; Portuguese emigration to 81; travellers in Angola 37
Ghana, 73
GONGOS, 114, 115; *see also* NGOs
GRAE, 75, 82, 84
Grêmio do Milho Colonial, 59
Grêmios, 72
Guinea Bissau, 4, 40, 75, 76-7, 78, 86; slave trade, 28
Gulf Oil, 63

GURN, 102-3, 104-5, 111, 116-8, 141, 152
health, 104, 128, 180, 204, 205, 206-7, 213, 214, 215, 221, 222, 226, 229
Herero, 21
High Commissioners, 55, 57; *see also* Norton de Matos
HIV law, 232
Holy Ghost Fathers, 37, 45
housing, 204, 205, 207-8, 213, 214, 221, 231
Huambo, 49, 51, 65, 84, 166, 167, 168; MPLA membership in 145
Huila plateau, 21, 33, 39, 44, 48, 51
Huila province, 166, 168, 169; MPLA membership in 145
hydroelectric power, 61

ideology, 76, 83, 96, 120-1, 205; *see also* Marxism
IDPs, 204, 215, 222
IGOs, 204, 218, 219, 234
Imbangala, 29; *see also* Jaga
IMF, 10, 40, 107, 149, 154, 160, 177, 182, 186, 196, 197, 198, 227, 231, 234; staff monitored programme, 188,
India, 8, 37, 154, 197
Indian Ocean, 22, 30
indígenato, 47, 53, 80
indirect rule, 41, 43
industry, 62-3, 138, 179, 181,
inflation, 180, 184
interest rates, 188
iron ore mining, 80, 175
ivory trade, 31

Jaga, 27
Japan, 25
Jehovah's Witnesses, 70
Jellala rapids, 22
Jesuits, 25
Jews, 25
judicial system in Angola, 101, 110, 129, 131, 135, 148, 153-4, 172
Junta de Exportação dos Cereis, 59

Kalahari, 39
Kasai river, 20, 31
Kasanje, 28, 32, 36; 1961 insurrection in, 62, 75, 77
Katanga, 48, 57; Katangese gendarmes, 79
Kazembe, 29
Kazengo, 32
Kenya, 73, 179; Mau Mau, 74, 78
Khoi, 22
Kibokolo, 70
Kikongo language, 20, 69, 74
Kimbangu, Simon, 70, 74
Kimbundu language, 21, 33, 34, 36-7
Kisama, 22
Kongo kingdom, 20, 21, 22-4, 25, 26, 27, 30, 31, 33, 42, 74; 1913 war in, 43
Kongo region, 36, 42, 69; partition of, 39
KPMG, 188-9
Kuando Kubango province, 145
Kunene river, 21, 39, 61
Kwango river, 20, 39, 44
Kwanyama, 44
Kwanza currency, 180, 184
Kwanza river, 20, 21, 26, 31, 61, 176

labour; in coffee regions, 62; contract, 46, 54, 63-4, 80; laws 46, 53-4; service, 32, 35-6, 45
Land law, 109-110, 147, 165, 194, 232
land privatisation, 194
Lara, Lúcio, 73, 139-40, 144
Liga Angolana, 71
Liga Nacional Angolana, 72
Leopold, king of the Belgians, 38-9, 48
Leopoldville, 74, 75, 82
Lisbon, 71; African students in 73, 74, 84
Lisbon Geographical Society, 38, 39
Literacy, 179, 206; in Kongo kingdom, 23
Loango, 28, 30
Lobito, 49, 65, 146, 182
loans, 146, 185, 189, 197, 229
Lourenço, João, 139
Luanda, 3, 5, 22, 24, 26, 27, 29, 32, 33, 35, 36, 39, 41, 47, 48, 63, 71, 72, 73, 87, 142, 148, 151, 153, 155, 201, 210, 231; 1961 insurrection, 74, 75, 77, 86; captured by Dutch, 27; creole community, 2, 3, 4, 5, 34, 64; health in, 215; hospitals in 207; province, 166; MPLA membership in, 145; refinery in, 182; *Senado da Câmara*, 28;
Lubango, 71
Luena memorandum, 124, 143, 156, 227, 232, 233
Lunda, 29, 39, 44; kingdom 20, 22, 31; province, 56, 161, 165, 166, 167, 178, 209
Lusaka Accord, 102-3, 104, 106, 113, 114, 139, 141-2, 143, 156, 160, 161, 232, 233
Lusotropicalism, 81
Luwemba, 155
Lwini Social Solidarity Fund, 225

Madagascar, 73
Madeira, settlers from 45, 51
maize, 24, 59, 181
Malanje province, 60, 77
Maoism, 85
Mariano, António, 77
Marxism, 73-4, 82, 93, 95, 126, 131, 138, 172, 179
Matamba, 28, 36
Mau Mau, 74, 78
Mavinga, 155
Mbali, 33
Mbundu, 24, 26, 36-7, 64, 75, 76, 211; *see also* Kimbundu language
Médecins sans Frontières, 226
Methodists, 51
Middle East oil, 8, 196
Miller, Joseph, 24, 29
military budget, 216
MINARS, 221, 228
Ministry of Finance, 185
Misericórdia, 28
missionaries, 41, 43, 45, 46, 51, 69; catholic, 37, 42, 45, 67-8; protestant, 37, 42, 51, 66-9, 77-8, 85; *see also,* Catholic Church
Mobutu, general Seke, 82
Moçamedes, 33, 39, 48, 50, 71; railway, 48
Mocidade Portuguesa, 72
Moco, Marcolino, 141
Mondlane, Eduardo, 84

Movimento das Forças Armadas (MFA), 86-7
Mozambique, 4, 7, 15, 29, 40, 45, 57, 61, 64, 75, 76-7, 86, 165, 166; cotton growing in, 60; elections in, 164; wars of independence in, 78, 80
Mpinda, 23
MPLA, vii, 5, 12, 37, 40, 71, 75-6, 94, 111-112, 114, 115, 129, 131, 143, 202; 1992 elections, 140; Central Committee, 133, 134, 140, 144,145, 215-17; controls National Assembly, 109, 116; and constitutional revisions, 161-2; and elections, 10-11, 12, 16, 18, 100-103, 119, 122, 144, 145, 163, 167, 233, 235; Extraordinary Congress, 139; Fifth Party Congress, 116, 144, 146; foundation of, 73-4, 75; Fourth Party Congress, 139, 142-3; funding, 151; ideology of, 74, 76, 82, 83, 84, 96, 120-1; membership, 129-30, 132, 139, 144-5, party structure, 95-6, 134, 139, 145; rivalry with UNITA 85; Second Party Congress, 132, 139, 179; Stalinist tendency, 3, 84; Third Party Congress, 138, 213-14; and wars of independence, 78, 81, 82-4, 85, 87
muceques, 167, 208
Munslow, Barry, 187
Mwata Yamvo, 29; *see also* Lunda

Namibia, 21, 39, 40, 44, 146; independence of, 6, 98, 138; refugees from, 209
Nascimento, Lopo do, 139-40
National Assembly, 101, 103, 109, 110, 111, 115, 116, 118, 144, 148, 150, 157, 160, 162
National Electoral Commission, 119, 147, 156,173
NATO, 80
Ndongo, 24
Négritude, 73
Neto, Agostinho, 12, 82, 84, 85, 127, 128, 130, 157, 202, 205, 210, 216
Neto, Alberto Correia, 156
New State, 56-66, 71-2, 73; economic policy of, 57, 59; and wars of independence, 78, 85; *see also* Salazar
Ngangela people, 22
Ngola, 24
NGOs, 104, 110, 113, 139, 141, 161, 168-9, 204, 218, 219, 220, 222-3, 227, 228, 229, 233-4; official, 113, 114; *see also* GONGOs
Niger river, 38
Nigeria, 13, 73, 135, 175, 177, 178, 185
Non-aligned countries, 74
Norton de Matos, José de, 53-4, 55-6, 66, 71
Nova Lisboa, *see* Huambo
Novo Redondo, 33
Nyaneka people, 21, 33
Nyerere, Julius, 75
nzimbu shells, 22, 24

OAU, 75, 79, 86
ODP, 210
Oil, vii, 2, 63, 80, 85, 96, 108, 175, 193; and economy, 181-4; management of industry, 185; oil-rich countries, 1, 3, 7-8, 13;

origin and development, 176-7; and patrimonialism, 186; production figures, 176-7; refining, 146, 182; world demand for, 108, 154, 177, 180, 183, 197
Oil companies; Angolan, 190-1
Oil revenues, 8-9, 10, 13-14, 76-7, 97, 99, 107, 127, 133, 135, 141, 142, 146, 156, 167, 172, 175, 177, 178, 180, 182-3, 188, 196, 104, 217, 222, 226, 227
Okavango, 21
Operadores de Referência Municipal (ORM), 168-9
Organisation for Civil Defence, 155
Ovambo, 21
Ovimbundu, 21, 29, 66, 67, 75, 76, 77, 84; Bailundu War, 41-2, 43; identity, 42, 66-7

PAC, 74
PAIGC, 75, 82, 83, 85
Paiva Couceiro, Henrique de, 44, 50-1
PAJOCA, 151
palm oil trade, 31, 42, 59
Papacy, 39, 65-6; Kongo correspondence with, 24, 27
Paris; Afrcan students in, 73
Partido Communista Angolana, 72
patrimonialism, 9, 11-12, 116, 125-7, 146, 156, 172-3, 175, 186-8, 201-2
PDP-ANA, 151, 155
People's Assembly, 132
Perrain, Jean Marc, 226
Petrangol, 63
PIDE, 71, 72
Piedade, Fernando Dias da, 150, 190
Pinto de Andrade, Joaquim, 71
Pinto de Andrade, Manuel, 73
PLATA, 235
population, 35, 51, 64; exodus to city, 207-8; white, 51, 65-6
Portugal, vii, 25, 34, 72, 100, 212; 1974 Revolution, 81, 86-7; abolition of the slave trade, 30; Black Legend, 38; Caetano regime, 85; colonial policy, 47, 49, 52, 53-6; Development Plans, 61; empire in Africa, 3-4; and Scramble for Africa, 38-40, 43
Portuguese; army, 77-9, 85, 86-7; contacts with Kongo, 22-3, 24, 25; Crown monopoly, 23, 25; culture, 4; education policy, 67-8; emigration to Angola, 33, 51; exodus from Angola 179, 194; language, 4, 67-8; navigators, 22; settlement, 3, 50-1, 52, 55, 65; traders in Angola, 24-5, 32
Portuguese Communist Party, 73
presidency, 8-9, 10, 11-12, 97, 102, 104-8, 110, 111, 114, 116, 118, 127, 128, 131, 132, 133-5, 139, 141, 147-9, 150, 157, 162, 172, 185, 195-6, 201, 224; *see also* Santos
press; Afro-Portuguese, 52; after independence, 104, 106, 109, 112, 142, 148, 153
Prime minister, office of, 128, 141, 142, 150, 161, 162
Príncipe; sleeping sickness in 47
Prodoil Exploração e Produção de Hidrocarbonetos, 190
Programa de Apoio à Reabilitação (PAR), 165, 167-71
Programa de Saneamento Económico e Financeiro (SEF), 138

PRS, 160, 161
Pungo Ndongo, 34

Race relations, 3
Radio Eclésia, 112, 148, 153
Rafael, Alfredo, 191
railways, 38, 146, 179; Benguela, 48-9, 57, 80; Malanje, 48-9; Moçamedes, 48
Real Companhia de Caminho de Ferro através de África, 48
refugees, 204, 209, 215
Reis, Alves, 56
Rela, José Manuel Zenha, 212-3
Republic, 37, 40, 53-6, 57, 64, 67, 71, 73
Roberto, Holden, 75, 82, 84, 85
rubber trade, 31, 42, 43
Russia; debt to 189-90; *see also* Falcone, Gaydamak, Switzerland, USSR

Salazar, António de Oliveira, 40, 56-8, 65, 78, 80, 85; *see also* New State
Salt trade, 22, 26
Samakuva, Isaias, 153, 162
San, 22
Santa Maria, 77
Santos, Ana Paula dos, 225
Santos, Eduardo dos, 5, 8, 11, 12, 14, 73, 97, 101-2, 104, 105, 107-8, 111, 118, 127, 131, 133-5, 139, 142-3, 162-3, 164, 165-6, 186, 203, 213-4, 224; continuation of mandate, 148-9; and Falcone affair, 190; Foundation (FESA) 104, 114, 225; *see also* presidency
Santos, Marcellino dos, 85
São Salvador, 23, 27, 39, 42; *see also* Kongo
São Tomé, 245, 25, 30, 34, 46; labour scandal, 46-7
Savimbi, Jonas, 7, 84, 106, 117, 124, 142, 187; and 1992 election 140, 161; death of 143, 227
Scandinavian aid, 209
Second World War, 61, 65, 72
Selvagem, Carlos, *see* Galvão
Silva Porto, 31, 32
Silva Teles, F.X. da, 51-2
Silver mines, in Angola, 25, 26
Sinopec, 197
slave trade, 22, 26-7, 28-30, 32, 46, 55; end of, 30-33; internal, 30-1, 37-8, 41, 42, 50;
slavery, 24, 25, 35, 42; in 20th century, 46, 54-5; abolition in Angola, 45; slave numbers, 28
sobas, 35, 36, 58-9
Somoil Sociedade Petrolífera Angolana, 1901
Sonair, 185
Sonangol, 8, 14, 185, 191, 197
South Africa, 54, 74, 80, 146, 164, 178, 185, 191; capital, 56; collaboration with UNITA, 85; intervention in Angola, 87, 133; labour recruitment, 57; peace negotiations with, 138; war in Namibia, 209
South Korea, 154
South West Africa, *see* Namibia
Southern Rhodesia, 54, 58, 80, 81
Spanish America, 25
Spínola, António de, 86
spirit cults, 22, 36; in Kongo, 23, 69
State farms, 194
steam navigation, 37

Suez Canal, 37
sugar, 49, 176
Switzerland, 189, 190; banks, 189

Tanzania, 75
taxation, 60-1
textiles, 49; production, 62
tobacco trade, 28
Toko, Simon, 70, 74
trade, long distance, 22, 23, 24
transport, 49, 63; ox wagon, 44; *see also* railways
Transvaal, 39; railway to 38
Tribunal de Contas, 110

Uíge province, 155
Ultimatum of 1890, 40
Umbundu language, 66
UN, 9, 79, 100, 101, 103, 115, 140; agencies, 209, 217, 228, 229; sanctions against UNITA, 105
UNDP, 164-5, 170
Union Minière, 48
UNITA, vii, 1, 5, 7, 9, 10, 75-6, 81, 87, 94, 98, 100, 105, 113, 138, 142, 167, 211; and 1992 elections, 10, 101-2, 140-1; constitutional proposals, 161; defeat of, 104, 106, 116, 143, 186; and diamonds, 105, 142, 186, 193; final phase of war, 105; foundation of, 84-5; and GURN, 103-4, 111, 116,-17, 141; and Lusaka Accord, 102-3; soldiers, 111, 156
UNITA-Renovada, 105, 142, 153
UPA, 75-6, 78, 84; *see also* FNLA
UPNA, 75
USA, 37, 47, 49, 80. 98, 100, 138, 159, 162; loans to Angola, 146; oil needs, 8, 196; recognises MPLA, 6, 101, 141; slave trade to 30; supports FNLA, 76
US-Angola Chamber of Commerce, 191
USSR, 74, 100, 159, 189, 193; intervention in Angola, 6, 87, 138; support for MPLA, 76
UTCAH, 221, 228, 229, 230

Van Dunem, França, 142
Victor, M'Fulupinga Landu, 155
Vili, 28, 30
Voz d'Angola clamando no Deserto, 52

wax trade, 31
Weber, Max, 94
Wheeler, Douglas, 50, 72
White Fathers, 37
Williams, Robert, 48
Williams, Rosa, 51
wine trade, 49, 52
witchcraft, 83, 85
WNLA, 57
women, 95, 209; importance of 35, 51-2
World Bank, 10, 40, 169, 195, 231, 234; *see also* IMF
World Petroleum congress, 191

Zaire province, 155
Zaire river, 20, 22, 23, 25, 27, 28, 31, 33, 42, 43; partition of basin, 38-9
Zaire State, 77, 79, 67, 208, 209; support for UPA/FNLA, 75, 82, 103; *see also* Belgian Congo
Zambia, 75, 79-80, 85
Zimbabwe, 115